THE REVISED CANADIAN CONSTITUTION

POLITICS AS LAW

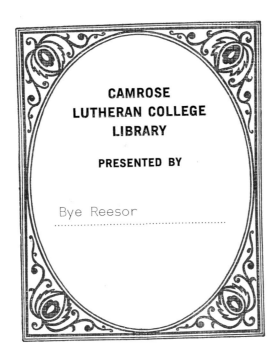

SERIES LIST

McGraw-Hill Ryerson Series in Canadian Politics
General Editor — Paul W. Fox

POLITICS: Canada, 5th Ed. Paul W. Fox

CANADIAN FOREIGN POLICY, D. C. Thomson & R. F. Swanson

THE CONSTITUTIONAL PROCESS IN CANADA, 2nd Edition
R. I. Cheffins & R. N. Tucker

POLITICAL PARTIES AND IDEOLOGIES IN CANADA, 2nd. Edition
W. Christian & C. Campbell

PRESSURE GROUP BEHAVIOUR IN CANADIAN POLITICS,
A. Paul Pross

POLITICAL PARTIES IN CANADA,
C. Winn & J. C. McMenemy

GOVERNMENT IN CANADA, T. A. Hockin

CANADIAN POLITICS: AN INTRODUCTION TO SYSTEMATIC ANALYSIS
J. Jenson & B. W. Tomlin

LOCAL GOVERNMENT IN CANADA, 2nd Edition
C. R. Tindal & S. Nobes Tindal

PUBLIC POLICY AND PROVINCIAL POLITICS
M. Chandler and W. Chandler

POLITICAL CHOICE IN CANADA (Abridged Edition)
Harold D. Clarke, Jane Jenson, Lawrence LeDuc, Jon H. Pammett

CANADIAN FOREIGN POLICY: Contemporary Issues and Themes
Michael Tucker

POLITICS AND THE MEDIA IN CANADA
Arthur Siegel

CANADA IN QUESTION: Federalism in the Eighties 3rd Edition
D. V. Smiley

THE L-SHAPED PARTY: The Liberal Party of Canada 1958–1980
Joseph Wearing

WOMEN AND POLITICS IN CANADA
Janine Brodie

THE REVISED CANADIAN CONSTITUTION: Politics as Law
R. Cheffins and P. Johnson

Forthcoming

GOVERNMENT IN CANADA 2nd Edition
T. A. Hockin

CANADA'S JUDICIAL SYSTEM
Peter H. Russell

CANADIAN PARLIAMENTARY SYSTEM
Paul G. Thomas

CANADIAN FOREIGN POLICY 2nd Edition
Michael J. Tucker

FEDERAL CONDITION IN CANADA
D. V. Smiley

THE REVISED CANADIAN CONSTITUTION
POLITICS AS LAW

RONALD I. CHEFFINS, Q.C.
B.A., LL.B. (Brit. Col.), LL.M. (Yale).

PATRICIA A. JOHNSON
B.A., LL.B. (U. Vic), LL.M. (Brit. Col.).

McGraw-Hill Ryerson Limited

Toronto   Montreal   New York   Auckland   Bogotá
Cairo   Guatemala   Hamburg   Johannesburg   Lisbon
London   Madrid   Mexico   New Delhi   Panama   Paris
San Juan   São Paulo   Singapore   Sydney   Tokyo

THE REVISED CANADIAN CONSTITUTION:
POLITICS AS LAW

ISBN 0-07-548842-6

1 2 3 4 5 6 7 8 9 0   D   5 4 3 2 1 0 9 8 7 6

Printed and bound in Canada by John Deyell Company

Cover and book design by Dave Hader

Canadian Cataloguing in Publication Data

Cheffins, Ronald I.
  The revised Canadian Constitution

(McGraw-Hill series in Canadian politics)
Includes index.
ISBN 0-07-548842-6

1. Canada — Constitutional law.   2. Canada — Constitutional law — Amendments.
3. Canada. Constitution Act, 1982.   I. Johnson, Patricia A.   II. Title.
III. Series.

KE4219.C48   1986   342.71'03   C85-090879-5

TABLE OF CONTENTS

LIST OF ABBREVIATIONS USED IN
THE REFERENCES

A.C.	Appeal Cases
Alta. L. Rev.	Alberta Law Review
Can. B. Rev.	Canadian Bar Review
Can. Hist. Rev.	Canadian Historical Review
Can. J. Econ. Poli. Sci.	Canadian Journal of Economics and Political Science
Can. J. Poli. Sci.	Canadian Journal of Political Science
Can. Pub. Admin.	Canadian Public Administration
Can. Public Policy	Canadian Public Policy
Can. Tax. Fdn.	Canadian Tax Foundation
Can.-U.S. L.J.	Canada-United States Law Journal
C.R.	Criminal Reports
Dalhousie L.J.	Dalhousie Law Journal
D.L.R.	Dominion Law Reports
L. and Contemp. Prob.	Law and Contemporary Problems
Man. C.A.	Manitoba Court of Appeal
Nfld. C.A.	Newfoundland Court of Appeal
O.R.	Ontario Reports
Osgoode Hall L.J.	Osgoode Hall Law Journal
P.C.	Judicial Committee of the Privy Council
Q.B.D.	Queen's Bench Division (U.K.)
Q.B. Div.	Queen's Bench Division (Ont.)
Que. C.A.	Quebec Court of Appeal
R.S.B.C.	Revised Statutes of British Columbia
R.S.C.	Revised Statutes of Canada
S.C.C.	Supreme Court of Canada
S.C.R.	Supreme Court Reports
Stats. Alta.	Statutes of Alberta
Stats. Can.	Statutes of Canada
Stats. Que.	Statutes of Quebec
Stats. Sask.	Statutes of Saskatchewan
Supreme Court L.R.	Supreme Court Law Review
U.B.C.L. Rev.	University of British Columbia Law Review
U. Mich. J.L. Ref.	University of Michigan Journal of Law Reform
U.S.	United States Supreme Court Reports
W.W.R.	Western Weekly Reports

British statutes enacted prior to 1982 are cited by regnal year: for examaple, a reference to "7 Edw. VII" is a reference to the seventh year of the reign of King Edward VII.

FOREWORD

Ronald Cheffins and Patricia Johnson have written an excellent book. *The Revised Canadian Constitution: Politics as Law* is not only "a reasonably brief and succinct overview of the Canadian constitution," as the authors modestly state in their Preface, but it is also a trenchant and provocative critique of several major aspects of the new Constitution Act of 1982. The result is a book which students, laymen, and experts can all benefit from reading and thoroughly enjoy.

In their review of our "new" constitution the authors dig deeply and explain at just the right length how our present constitution has grown out of its roots in the British parliamentary tradition, the royal prerogative, Dicey's rule of law, conventions, judicial decisions, and the body of British and Canadian legislation which made up the previous "old" Canadian constitution.

One of the authors' most valuable contributions is to go back to the pre-Confederation period in Canadian history and trace the evolution of important political practices, such as the development of responsible government, which were carried over into the new dominion of Canada when it was created by the passage of the British North America Act in 1867. The authors continue their historical survey by noting the highlights in the transition from our "old" constitution of 1867 to our "new" constitution of 1982, paying particular attention to the steps which led to the latter's final adoption. Taken altogether, this part of the book, though brief, is a highly informative and admirable account of the growth of the Canadian constitution.

Having examined its inheritance, the authors then dissect the body of the Constitution Act of 1982. They devote individual chapters to the amending formula, executive authority, legislative authority, judicial authority, the division of powers, and the Charter of Rights and Freedoms. They explore each topic carefully and clearly and in sufficient detail to satisfy an aspiring student without overwhelming a general reader. Even an expert can profit from these precise analyses which are supported by extensive references to relevant literature.

The virtues of this book do not end, however, with mere explanations. The authors give it an edge by expressing their own opinions about recent constitutional developments. Their views not only add zest to the book but they raise important points for reflection.

The authors' first point is that the "new" constitution of 1982 is not new. It is, of course, simply an addition to and an embellishment upon all the constitutional legislation, royal prerogatives, orders, conventions, practices, traditions, and judicial decisions which have preceded it, as noted earlier in this Foreword. The B.N.A. Act itself and seventeen other United Kingdom statutes and four U.K. orders in council are incorporated within the new constitution and renamed, the B.N.A. Act, for instance, becoming the Constitution Act, 1867. While this point is obvious to any knowledgeable student of the constitution, it is still worth making since there has been so much misleading talk in the media and elsewhere about Canada having received a brand "new" constitution in 1982.

The second point the authors make is even less generally recognized although it undoubtedly will prove to be more important. The Constitution Act of 1982 makes our constitution much more rigid than it has been in the past. Some clauses will now require the unanimous consent of Ottawa and all ten provincial governments before amendment is possible while most of the remaining sections will be amendable only with the approval of Parliament and at least seven of the legislatures of provinces having not less than fifty per cent of the combined populations of the provinces. As Cheffins and Johnson note, these provisions are so restrictive that Canadians may find it exceedingly difficult in future to make the constitutional changes they desire.

Chapter 7 goes to the heart of the authors' complaint about the new constitution. They deeply regret that the process of constitutional revision did not include some attempt to redress the growing imbalance between the powers of the executive and the legislature. Noting what no one will deny — that the powers of the cabinet and the prime minister in particular have been mounting at the expense of Parliament — they deplore the fact that no effort was made to curb ministerial authority and strengthen the legislature against the executive. As they remark, "Surely in the review of Canada's constitutional structure nothing calls out more for reform than the excessive dominance of the system by the cabinet." Yet nothing was done to remedy the disparity, and since it was not, it is hard to disagree with their conclusion that the real losers in the recent revision of the constitution were Parliament and the provincial legislatures. Despite the *non obstante* clauses in the constitution and the special consideration given to Quebec, the authors conclude gloomily that the doctrine of legislative supremacy, which supposedly has been a cardinal feature of our system of government since we inherited it from Britain, has been eclipsed by the new constitution.

This view is all the more persuasive since, as the authors point out, the effect of the Constitution Act is to make the judiciary as well as the executive superior to the legislature. The courts have always had the ability to interpret our constitution, of course, but prior to 1982 the impact of their decisions was felt in the main in the distribution of powers between the federal and provincial governments. Now, however, the new Constitution Act gives the judiciary enormous opportunities to impose its judgements upon legislative acts. The power arises from the inclusion of the Charter of Rights and Freedoms in the constitution. Since it is part of the supreme law of the land, the Charter can be used to test the validity of other legislation. If a statute offends the Charter, the act can be struck down. The decision is made by the judiciary according to its own interpretation of the words in the Charter, and since the words describe numerous individual rights and liberties which have yet to be defined, the judges have been given a standing invitation to flesh out our constitution. What is more, when the pronouncements come from the Supreme Court, they are final. If a legislature disagrees with the judges' opinion, there is precious little that the parliamentarians — or the public for that matter — can do about it.

The Charter even goes as far as giving judges the right to remedy wrongs at their own discretion. Section 24(1) declares that "anyone whose rights or freedoms, as guaranteed by this Charter, have been infringed or denied may apply to a court of competent jurisdiction to obtain such remedy as the court considers appropriate and just in the circumstances." Now that is genuine power! Authority to make decisions limited only by personal discretion is a privilege that legislative supremacists or even monarchs might envy. Yet it now rests with the courts. It is no wonder that the authors conclude that "the real winner of the events of 1982 were the courts."

They might have remarked also that the Constitution of 1982 reversed a historical trend. The ancient Israelites moved from rule by judges to rule by kings which by the passage of centuries was transformed into parliamentary sovereignty. Now we seem to be moving in the opposite direction, from parliamentary supremacy back to judicial supremacy.

Whether the change is good or bad remains to be seen. However, a democrat cannot help but feel uneasy about the transfer of final authority in government from the elected representatives of the people to an appointed body of officials. It is also disturbing that so few members of the Canadian public seem to be aware of the monumental shift which has occurred in our system of government. One of the great benefits of Cheffins' and Johnson's book is that it brings this change to the attention of readers.

We can be grateful to the authors also for devoting a chapter of their book to a provocative discussion of the Charter. Though they are quick to acknowledge that their analysis is brief and limited, they raise a number of important issues. They point out, for instance, that there are many significant complexities and conundrums to be sorted out in the Charter. To take one, does the Charter apply only to matters under federal or provincial jurisdiction or do relations between private persons also come under the Charter? To take another, what different meanings will judges in different courts give to a specific right and how long will it take to get a definitive final and uniform judgement from the Supreme Court of Canada? Is it desirable to have uniform interpretations of some rights across the country when variations in accord with particular regional, ethnic, religious, or gender considerations might be closer to natural justice?

The authors become most impassioned and opinionated when they note the extent to which the inclusion of the Charter in our constitution moves Canada away from its traditional Tory strain and closer to Lockean Liberalism. They believe that the Charter makes us less like Britain which still adheres to parliamentary supremacy and more like the United States which has a Bill of Rights and a Supreme Court to give final interpretations. Indeed, they assert, we have gone farther than the United States because our Charter is much looser and more sweeping than the Bill of Rights and our judges will therefore have greater scope for interpretation.

It is on this polemic note that Cheffins and Johnson conclude their work. They fear that the Charter is a "centralizing, legalizing, and Americanizing" force within Canada and that in company with the other elements in the new Constitution of 1982 that they have criticized it will lead to a very different country from the one that we have known. They go so far as wondering whether the rewriting of our constitution was not a mistake, an error which we will live to regret.

This is, to say the least, a sobering speculation. It is a view, however, with which many readers will be inclined to agree. Even those who reject it will have to admit that the authors' outspoken opinions make a good book even better.

Ronald Cheffins completed his work on the book while he was still a Professor of Law at the University of Victoria, during which time he served as a part-time Commissioner and Vice Chairman of the British Columbia Law Reform Commission and was awarded a Q.C. He was appointed a Judge of Appeal on the British Columbia Court of Appeal on December 5, 1985. Patricia Johnson is a member of the Bar of British Columbia who practises with Crease and Company in Victoria. She is also a part-time Lecturer in the Faculty of Law at the University of Victoria.

Erindale College
University of Toronto
December 15, 1985.

Paul W. Fox
General Editor

PREFACE

This book attempts to provide a reasonably brief and succinct overview of the Canadian constitution. It was inspired by the constitutional deal of 1982, between the federal and provincial governments (excluding Quebec), which led to the passage by the United Kingdom Parliament of the Canada Act and its accompanying schedule, namely the Constitution Act, 1982. Though the developments of 1982 were significant, they definitely did not amount to a new Canadian Constitution as claimed by the federal government or as chronicled by the media. As the text of this work points out, the basic institutions of Canadian government remain as they were prior to 1982. The claim of "patriation" is only partly true in that we achieved in 1982 a signing-off by the United Kingdom Parliament with respect to further action applying to Canada. However, the Canada Act and the Constitution Act, 1982 are themselves instruments of the United Kingdom Parliament. The Schedule to the Constitution Act, 1982 lists thirteen other United Kingdom statutes and four United Kingdom Orders in Council which are still applicable to Canada and are entrenched by the amending formula. Thus, amendments to the Constitution will largely, though not exclusively, involve the use of a Canadian amending formula to amend British statutes.

Though this book does stress the changes of 1982, it basically attempts to integrate those changes into an overview of the Canadian Constitution. The chapter on pre-Confederation Canada was felt necessary, because the most important principle of the Canadian Constitution, namely responsible government, was developed prior to 1867. This basic element of the system was largely overlooked in the process of constitutional review.

The events of 1982 were important however, especially in enlarging the role of the judiciary. No attempt will be made to expand on this point here as it is a theme which is found throughout the book, particularly in chapters 10 and 11. As the authors point out, this is one more step in the direction of the United States in terms of Canada's political culture.

The authors would like to thank the Research Committee of the University of Victoria for financial assistance. The Social Science and Humanities Research Council provided a leave fellowship for one of the authors, thus greatly facilitating the completion of the manuscript. We would like to thank Mr. Paul Ceyssens for his bibliographic work on the Charter of Rights. Mrs. Barbara Judson worked tirelessly in typing all drafts of the manuscript. Her unending patience, efficiency and endurance were essential in the completion of this work. Paul Fox was, as usual, a source of valuable advice and warm encouragement. Mr. Joerg Klauck waited patiently for the final manuscript, but he had moved on to other responsibilities when we finally placed it in the competent hands of Brian Henderson. Our appreciation to both these gentlemen is very great.

In essence, we hope that this work clarifies the significance of the constitutional enactments of 1982, and provides the reader with a basic understanding of the fundamentals of the Canadian Constitution.

Victoria, B.C.
September, 1985

THE NATURE OF CONSTITUTIONS AND CONSTITUTIONALISM

In recent years, the Canadian Constitution has been the subject of considerable debate, scrutiny and important change. It is not correct to say, however, as members of the media often have, that Canada has a new constitution. That this statement is incorrect in every respect will be illustrated throughout this work.

The 1982 Revisions

In 1982 the United Kingdom Parliament made important changes in the Canadian Constitution, but the changes fell far short of a complete revision of the Constitution which might have resulted in a totally new format. The essence of that legislation, namely, the Constitution Act, 1982[1] provided for a domestic amending process,[2] a Charter of Rights,[3] an additional subsection with respect to the existing division of powers,[4] a provision that there be a conference on the rights of the aboriginal peoples of Canada,[5] and provisions with respect to equalization and regional disparities.[6] The Act, however, did not in any substantial way change the content of the many British statutes relating to Canada which have been enacted since 1867.

As an example of this limited change, the British North America Act, 1867,[7] which formed the basis of Canada's constitutional structure, was altered only in relatively minor ways: its name was changed,[8] and subsection 91(1), the subsection of the Act dealing with amendment, was repealed,[9] as was subsection 92(1) dealing with provincial constitutions.[10] It should be noted, however, that section 20 which was also repealed,[11] and subsection 92(1), were incorporated into the Constitution Act, 1982[12] and thus no substantial change has been made in the content of these sections. Therefore, the only real change in what was formerly known as the British North America Act, 1867 was the repeal of subsection 91(1) which, as will be explained later, dealt with those classes of subjects still reserved for the United Kingdom Parliament.

Similarly, if one looks through the whole series of British statutes and orders in council relating to Canada, one finds that in almost every respect the only change made is in name. In most instances the change is from "British North

America Act" to "Constitution Act." For example, the British North America Act, 1915 is now referred to as the Constitution Act, 1915.[13] Presumably the reason for the change in name is to remove the word "British" from the statutes so as to eradicate as much as possible any underlining of Canada's historical relationship and ties with Great Britain.

The Schedule to the Constitution Act, 1982 should be referred to for an overview of these changes. This schedule includes the British statutes and orders in council relevant to Canada in Column I, and in Column II indicates the sections of those thirty legal documents that have been amended or repealed. Column III indicates the new names of the documents. The only statute other than the British North America Act, 1867 which has been amended in any substantial respect is the Statute of Westminster.[14] Section 4 and subsection 7(1) of the latter still contemplated British statutory authority with respect to Canada.

The other major change effected in 1982, in addition to the adoption of a domestic amending process and a Charter of Rights, was the passage by the British parliament of the Canada Act.[15] This Act is important in that it provides that henceforth "[N]o Act of the Parliament of the United Kingdom passed after the *Constitution Act, 1982* comes into force shall extend to Canada as part of its law."[16] This statute is, in effect, a "signing-off" and merely provides that no British statutes passed after the Constitution Act, 1982 shall have force or effect in Canada. It is interesting and important to note, however, that the Constitution Act, 1982 and the majority of the preceding thirty statutes and orders in council listed in the Schedule remain statutes or orders in council of either the United Kingdom Parliament or the Privy Council of the United Kingdom, respectively.

The use of the word "patriation" has created a great deal of confusion in that many Canadians probably assume that our basic constitutional documents are now similar in legal status to the Constitution of the United States. In the United States, the constitution was the result of a constitutional convention and is not the product of any legislative enactment. This is not true in Canada where the majority of our entrenched constitutional documents, ranging from the Constitution Act, 1867 down to the Constitution Act, 1982, are and presumably will always remain, statutes of the United Kingdom Parliament. What has changed, however, is that these statutes, though British in their legal origin, can no longer be amended by the United Kingdom Parliament. As a result of the amending formula contained in the Constitution Act, 1982, these British statutes can now be amended only by a Canadian process as outlined in that Act.[17] Thus our situation is more similar to that of Australia than to that of the United States in that our basic constitutional law is composed of British statutes amendable by a wholly domestic Canadian process. Later in this work the domestic process will be described and critically analyzed. Similarly, there will be a detailed examination of most of the important British statutes described in the opening words of this book, with an analysis of their significance and impact on Canada's political and legal functioning.

However, before looking in detail at the provisions of the Canadian Constitution, we will turn to an examination of the functions of a constitution generally, and an analysis of how these functions are fulfilled by our constitutional structure.

The Nature and Functions of a Constitution

A constitution must first provide for the creation of the basic organs and institutions of public authority. Second, it must define the powers possessed by each of the public institutions and in some respects define the relationships between these various institutions. Third, a constitution must provide for the processes by which law is created, and at the same time provide for the limitations on the power exercised by the officials of public institutions. Thus a constitution assigns legal responsibility, defines the limits of authority, and establishes the processes which must be followed before this authority can be exercised. Furthermore, a constitutional document must provide for a method of change, both of political leadership and of the basic constitutional framework, the latter by way of amendment to the constitution.

In Canada it is necessary to look at a whole series of statutes and other legal documents to ascertain how, at least to some extent, power is allocated in the Canadian system. However, as will be demonstrated later, many of the rules with respect to the functioning of authority in a constitutional system are not defined in authoritative legal documents but rather are the result of consensus among the actors in a political and constitutional system. It must always be remembered that the legal rules of the constitution are inextricably linked with the informal functioning of the political process. It is impossible to detach the legal rules of the constitutional game from the political process which gives the entire polity vitality and life. It must also be remembered that quite often the legal rules are very misleading when examined without reference to the historical and political context of the country.[18] Thus throughout this work there will be a repeated effort to illustrate constitutional rules in the light of the political setting in which they exist.

A further important concept of constitutionalism is that which is usually referred to as the rule of law. This concept is that legitimate actors in the political system have only such authority as is vested in them by law, and that any attempt to move beyond the peripheries of this authority is illegal, or to use the constitutional term, *ultra vires*. This particular notion is especially underlined in Canada by the fact that ours is a federal system, which means that the basic state authority is divided between the central government on the one hand and the provincial governments on the other. The allocation of power is provided for in relevant sections of the Constitution Act, 1867, but these terms are often vague and imprecise and accordingly lead to considerable conflict between the levels of government. There is a tendency for each level of government to attempt to expand its authority and to push into the areas assigned to the other level of government. It is in this context that we see the development of the idea of the judiciary as a referee, adjudicating questions as to the appropriate demarcation of authority between the central government and its provincial counterparts.

Particularly, however, since the passage of the Charter of Rights, a new limitation has been imposed on the authority of governmental institutions. Once again it is the responsibility of the judiciary to determine when governments or their agents overstep the boundaries of legitimate authority. A good deal of power is thus put in the hands of the judiciary in defining the proper limits of governmental power. Inevitably, this involves the courts in drawing lines beyond which various government agencies and other political actors cannot go. This was illustrated in the case of *Roncarelli* v. *Duplessis*,[19] in which Premier Duplessis of Quebec had instructed the Quebec Liquor Commissioner to cancel the liquor licence of Mr. Frank Roncarelli, who operated a restaurant in the city of Montreal. The Supreme Court of Canada held that Mr. Duplessis, even though premier of the province and attorney general of Quebec, had no legal authority to give instructions to any public servant with respect to whether Mr. Roncarelli should or should not possess a liquor licence. The court said that the sheer fact of holding the offices of premier and attorney general does not give an official any authority above and beyond that vested by law in those offices. Accordingly, Mr. Duplessis was ordered by the Supreme Court of Canada to pay to Mr. Roncarelli over $50,000 in damages for his unlawful actions.

This case serves admirably to illustrate how the Constitution imposes limits on office holders with respect to functions they are not authorized by law to perform. Until recently, however, most of the decisions, as outlined earlier, tended to centre on the appropriate jurisdictions of federal and provincial governments. In future not only will the courts continue to play this major role, but they will also be increasingly called upon to determine whether a government has overstepped the barriers created by the Charter of Rights which was enacted as part of the Constitution Act, 1982. In this respect we see a substantial push in the direction of the American system, and accordingly, a heightened role for the judiciary. Whether our judiciary will become as active as the American judiciary is, of course, impossible to predict. Most of our judges have been trained in a tradition which accords considerable deference to legislative dominance. But even with a judiciary conditioned to legislative dominance there is no doubt that judges will still inevitably be pushed to apply the Charter quite frequently to strike down either the activity of governmental authorities or the actual provisions of statutes. This, of course, is the most important impact arising from the legal actions of 1982, namely, the drafting of the Charter of Rights and the resultant increased role for the judiciary in our constitutional system.

As mentioned above, until 1982 the chief area in which the courts have had to function as referee, has been in the determination of the jurisdictional lines between the authority vested in the federal parliament and the authority vested in the provincial legislatures, a necessary feature of a federal state. Federalism is a system which in its purest sense vests power in at least two levels of government by virtue of the country's basic constitutional law. This means that certain areas of authority are assigned to the central government while other areas are given to the regional governments, and that neither government can interfere with the jurisdiction of the other. K. C. Wheare developed the theoretical concept that in a pure federal system the different levels of government have independent power, each free from dominance and control by the other level of government.[20]

There is little doubt that Canada meets, in a practical sense, the test devised by Wheare in that certain features of the Constitution which allow for a high degree of federal intervention in the provincial sphere have now fallen into disuse. In particular, the power of the lieutenant governor, an appointee of the central government, to refuse to give assent[21] to a bill or to reserve it[22] for the attention of the central government is no longer employed. Similarly, the power of the central government to disallow provincial legislation[23] has not been utilized since 1942. In addition, the authority of the central parliament to pass remedial legislation in the area of education, as provided for by section 93 of the Constitution Act, 1867, has never been used although the possibility of its utilization arose at one point in the context of the Manitoba School Crisis of 1917. Thus Canada probably represents one of the purest examples of a truly functioning federal system.

The Constitution Act, 1867 is the starting point for determining the jurisdictional limits of the federal parliament and the provincial legislatures. A number of sections deal with this division of powers including sections 91, 92, 93, 94, 95, 101, 117 and 132. Although this material will not be dealt with in any detail at this point, it should be noted that sections 91 and 92 of the 1867 statute constitute the most important legal provisions for assigning legislative authority. Of these two sections, however, only a few subsections have provided the basis for most of the power of the respective legislatures and consequently have formed the basis of most of the political and legal debate about jurisdictional lines. The struggles have been particularly intense in economic matters, centring around control of commercial activity and regulation of the economy. In recent years, cases dealing with natural resources have been highly significant and have cast the courts in a central role in determining who has control over the ownership and regulation of natural resources. In one case, so bitter were the feelings of the Saskatchewan government after the decision in the case of *Canadian Industrial Gas and Oil Ltd.* v. *Government of Saskatchewan*[24] that section 92 of the Constitution Act, 1867 was amended in 1982 to deal with some of the results of that case, particularly the power of the province to impose indirect taxes on certain aspects of natural resource production.[25] Thus, a federal system produces a host of legal and fiscal questions which are of vital concern to governments and private citizens as well as constitutional lawyers.

This discussion leads to a central theme of this book: that talk of a new constitution is very misleading because, except for the just mentioned addition to section 92 on natural resources, the remainder of the provisions with respect to the division of powers in the 1867 statute remain unaltered. We thus have the same division of powers, at least in pure legal theory, that we had in 1867. Naturally the courts have played a major role in determining through judicial decisions the exact meanings of the words of sections 91 and 92 of the Constitution

Act, 1867, but the compromise of 1982 did not change the language of the original statute.

Another important area not reformed by the Constitution Act, 1982 is that of the basic institutions of Canadian government at both the federal and provincial levels. In fact, the result of that Act is the freezing of the existing institutional structure of Canada. We now see that the Supreme Court of Canada, by and large, can no longer be changed by the Parliament of Canada alone.[26] We also see that the monarchy has been entrenched.[27] This, in our view, has the effect of entrenching the cabinet system of government because that system is so tightly linked with the office of the queen and her representatives. This point will be dealt with in considerable detail later in this work. Similarly, aspects of the legislative system have now been entrenched and cannot be changed without the use of a fairly rigid amending formula.[28] One of the tragedies of the compromise of 1982 is that the functioning of the parliamentary system — and its increasing tendency to fall under executive dominance — has not been reviewed and revised. These facts reinforce our objection to the suggestion that Canada has a "new" constitution. It is our view that we have failed to draft a new constitution with respect to the area in which it is most needed, namely, the functioning and interrelationship between executive government in Canada and the legislative process.

Furthermore, in the process of constitutional review which led to the passage of the Constitution Act, 1982, no serious examination of the legislative process was carried out. The electoral system as practised in this country should have been reviewed in considerable depth in order to deal with the problems created by one party having dominance in one province, while another party has dominance in a totally different region of the country. The Pepin-Robarts Committee set up by the federal government asked very serious questions about electoral reform.[29] These questions were not addressed by the government of Canada when it placed before the House of Commons its unilateral proposals for revision to the Canadian Constitution. We are left with an unfortunate situation as a result of the Constitution Act, 1982: certain aspects of the electoral system[30] are subject to change only as a result of the utilization of the cumbersome amendment formula provided for in that Act. This is further evidence that Canada does not have a new constitution but merely an addition to the existing model. The fundamental operation of the basic institutions of Canadian government at both the federal and provincial levels has been left intact, often, in our view, to the detriment of the functioning of the Canadian polity.

The Political Impetus Leading to the Passage of the Constitution Act, 1982

We will examine later in some detail the history of events leading up to the passage of the Constitution Act, 1982 but it would be remiss in this chapter not to touch upon and introduce briefly the political impetus which led to its enactment. The finding of a domestic amending formula had been a concern of Canadian politicians since 1927 and, in fact, six attempts to achieve patriation were made prior to the events of 1982. These attempts seemed to lack a sense of urgency until the very serious drives of 1964 and 1971 brought the federal government and the provincial governments close to agreement on a domestic amending formula. In both 1964 and 1971 patriation failed because Quebec objected to the proposed formulas. On both occasions Quebec took the view that it wanted other concessions in terms of a widening of provincial jurisdiction over various matters, particularly in cultural and economic fields, before it would agree to an amending formula. In those instances the federal government was not prepared to go ahead without the agreement of the government of Quebec. We see here at least some recognition of the "compact theory" that basic federal-provincial relations are not to be altered without the agreement of the federal and provincial governments.

After the failure of 1971 a period of time elapsed before the dramatic events of 1981 and 1982 occurred. The election of the Parti Quebecois separatist government in 1976, and its referendum on the question of sovereignty-association of Quebec with the rest of Canada in 1980, opened the way for Prime Minister Pierre Trudeau to take unilateral action on the Constitution. The then leader of the Liberal party in Quebec, Claude Ryan, had argued against any form of Quebec separation with a plea that he would fight for the renegotiation of the Canadian constitutional structure. He, in fact, issued what came to be known as the "Beige Paper" outlining dramatic revisions to the Canadian constitutional system. It was particularly noteworthy that the essential theses of this paper were the widening of Quebec's economic and political jurisdiction, and the greater participation of provincial representatives in the context of federal institutions. This potential promise of a constitutional new deal for Quebec was very helpful to those who opposed the sovereignty-association proposal in the Quebec government's referendum question.

Using the opening presented by the defeat of the Levesque government's referendum, Trudeau unilaterally introduced into the federal House of Commons a resolution involving "patriation" of the Constitution and passage of a charter of rights. His argument was that the Quebec referendum had been defeated on the promise of constitutional change and that, therefore, he was taking this opportunity to put forward changes for ultimate enactment by the British parliament. Most of the provinces were both shocked and outraged by this dramatic departure from the previous constitutional practice and began a series of steps, leading ultimately to a major decision of the Supreme Court of Canada,[31] opposing the unilateral action of the prime minister. Claude Ryan, who had led the fight against the Quebec separatists' referendum, was incensed by the actions of the federal government and vociferously expressed his opposition to the federal proposals. Trudeau, recognizing the opportunity to place his stamp on Canadian history and at the same time divert attention from Canada's rapidly deteriorating economic situation, decided to push ahead at all costs. After a number of political and legal skirmishes, nine of the provinces and the federal government ultimately agreed on a compromise package to forward to the parliament of Great Britain for its enactment as the Constitution Act, 1982.

The major concession by the federal government was the acceptance of the provincial proposals with respect to an amendment formula. The federal proposal in this area, which had been based on the Victoria solution of 1971, was entirely jettisoned. The question of native rights was put off, to be dealt with at a conference to be held within one year. Then, as previously mentioned, an amendment was made to section 92 of the British North America Act, giving the provinces greater control over natural resources and their taxation. Trudeau was able to keep the Charter of Rights and Freedoms within the resolution to be forwarded to London. The provinces, however, did obtain the concession that either the federal or provincial legislatures could enact a statute which would operate without some portions of the Charter of Rights being applicable to it.[32]

Certainly one strong factor in the push by Trudeau for the Charter of Rights and Freedoms was the question of language rights. It had been one of his long-time commitments to dramatically increase French-Canadian participation in all levels of federal government activity. Similarly, he was concerned about guaranteeing French language and educational rights at the provincial level in the English-speaking provinces. This objective is achieved in a very clear way in the context of the Constitution Act, 1982. Thus bilingualism is now, by and large, solidly entrenched in the Canadian federal governmental context.

One of the chief motivating factors — both political and legal — in including the rest of the Charter of Rights and Freedoms, was the American experience. In the United States the courts had used the Bill of Rights as an important tool in diminishing states' rights. It obviously occurred to the central planners that the Charter of Rights would impact much more substantially on provincial jurisdiction than on federal jurisdiction. Thus it was anticipated that the courts would begin to make important decisions that were previously in the hands of the provincial legislatures.

The prime minister's advisors were also not unaware of the fact that in the United States, constitutional law courses centre on the interpretation of the Bill of Rights, rather than on the division of powers between federal and regional legislatures. Thus it was envisaged that true to our usual practice of imitating the United States, Canadian law teachers would more and more teach the Canadian Constitution from an American perspective of focussing on entrenched rights rather than from the traditional Canadian approach of focussing on the division of power and the evolution of Canada's political and conventional heritage.

There are others who argue that when Trudeau briefly resigned as leader after the defeat of the Liberal government at the polls in 1979, he was concerned that writers of his political obituary concentrated almost exclusively on his proclamation of the War Measures Act and the resultant infringement on civil liberties. It has been argued that he wanted to rewrite his place in history so as to be identified with the Charter of Rights rather than with the repression of the War Measures Act.

Another line of argument is that Trudeau is a rationalist, which means that he has a Cartesian or Utopian view of what the world should be, and considers that a constitution and legislation should mould the human condition to meet this idealistic model. Trudeau supporters would argue that the Charter of Rights is part of the legal technique for modelling humanity along the lines of an ultimate rationalist view for the betterment of mankind. It is somewhat difficult to accept this line of argument in view of Trudeau's conduct at the time of the proclamation of the War Measures Act and his general treatment of persons who did not share a viewpoint similar to his own. It is, in our view, much more likely that while with respect to language rights he was genuinely motivated towards extending French language rights throughout Canada, with respect to other aspects of the Charter, the realist argument that a charter is a homogenizing influence was probably the most important reason for his inclusion of them. This is consistent with Trudeau's ongoing hostility towards provincial rights, seeing them as an obstruction to the achievement of his goal of a Canada in which the central government is overwhelmingly dominant.

The Relationship between Law and Politics

In 1969 one of the authors of this book wrote

> [l]aw, in my view, is that part of the overall process of political decision-making which has achieved somewhat more technical, more obvious and more clearly defined ground rules than other aspects of politics. It is still, however, an integral subdivision of the overall political process. The student of politics, law and legal philosophy is concerned, among other things, with the question of allocation of all types of resources, and with questions of the relationships between individual citizens and between the citizen and the state, as well as the relationships between states. The study of the legal and political process in any nation is a study of how decisions are made, who makes them, what the decisions are, how they influence subsequent events, and how alternative decisions might have led to different results.[33]

The authors see no reason to alter their views with respect to the relationship between law and politics. In fact, the Charter of Rights, and its inevitable interpretation and application by the judiciary, is bound to place the courts much more in the forefront of the political process. In addition to having to determine legality based on the dividing lines of the federal system, they will now have to add another perspective of consideration, namely, whether the legislation also violates the Charter of Rights. True, commentators can argue that this is purely a legal process to be determined by legal reasoning. The difficulty, however, is that the Charter of Rights is couched in very general terms, including such phrases as "freedom of expression," which leave the judiciary considerable latitude in defining the restraints to be placed on a legislature with respect to the limitation of freedom of expression.

It is impossible to predict how far we will move down the American road; one can only pause and reflect on the Supreme Court decision in *Roe* v. *Wade*.[34]

In that case state laws prohibiting abortion during the first three months of pregnancy were struck down as unconstitutional, as being in violation of the Fourteenth Amendment of the United States Constitution. The Fourteenth Amendment provides that it is unconstitutional for a state to "deny to any person within its jurisdiction the equal protection of the laws." Who could have possibly envisaged that these very general words would involve the court in the forefront of policy making with respect to the legality of abortion?

This point has been raised simply to illustrate how the rather general rules of entrenched rights can lead the courts into very unusual directions. It is, of course, fairly well known that in the United States the courts have ended up virtually administering the rules relating to busing in order to provide for racial integration in the public schools, and have laid down rules with respect to the functioning of penal institutions. They have even ordered electoral redistribution of state upper houses on the ground that they violate the equal protection clause of the Constitution. This is not to imply that the Canadian courts will automatically follow the American route, because the inherent tradition of parliamentary supremacy will, for some time, remain embedded in our legal consciousness. However, as stated earlier, it seems inevitable that the courts will be drawn into an ever increasing number of political disputes because of the passage of the Charter of Rights.

As a result we can expect the Canadian public will become more sensitized to the judiciary being a participant in the political process. Even when acting as a referee in determining legislative boundaries between the central and provincial governments, the Supreme Court is finding it more difficult to avoid being identified with political issues. The Charter of Rights has, and will, further politicize the judiciary in the conception of the public. It will also involve directing more matters to the judiciary for final determination and away from the elected representatives. Many may approve of this direction, especially lawyers and law professors to whom will now accrue the potential heritage of the United States with its excessively lawyer-dominated society. Certainly this may have been one of the objectives of Prime Minister Trudeau and his advisors when drafting the Charter of Rights. They have through that medium been able to take issues out of the political arena and transpose them into legal forms.

The result of these manoeuvres has been to turn many political matters into legal issues. Thus we see a transposition in the direction of turning political solutions into legal ones; we have moved clearly and inexorably in the American direction of politics as law.

---

[1] Canada Act, 1982, c.11, Schedule B (U.K).

[2] Constitution Act, 1982, c.11, Schedule B, Part V (U.K.).

[3] Constitution Act, 1982, c.11, Schedule B, Part I (U.K).

[4] Section 92A added by Constitution Act, 1982, c.11, Schedule B, s.50 (U.K.).

[5] Constitution Act, 1982, c.11, Schedule B, Part IV (U.K.).

[6] Constitution Act, 1982, c.11, Schedule B, Part III (U.K.).

[7] British North America Act, 1867, 30–31 Vict., c.3 (U.K.).

[8] To Constitution Act, 1867, see Constitution Act, 1982, c.11, Schedule B, Schedule, Item 1(1) (U.K.).

[9] Constitution Act, 1982, c.11, Schedule B, Schedule, Item 1(3) (U.K.).

[10] Constitution Act, 1982, c.11, Schedule B, Schedule, Item 1(4) (U.K.).

[11] Constitution Act, 1982, c.11, Schedule B, Schedule, Item 1(2) (U.K.). Section 20 dealt with the requirement that there be a session of parliament at least once a year.

[12] Constitution Act, 1982, c.11, Schedule B, s.5 and s.45, respectively (U.K.).

[13] See Constitution Act, 1982, c.11, Schedule B, Schedule, Item 15 (U.K.).

[14] Statute of Westminster, 1931, 22 Geo. V, c.4 (U.K.).

[15] Canada Act, 1982, c.11 (U.K.).

[16] Ibid., s.2.

[17] Constitution Act, 1982, c.11, Schedule B, Part V (U.K.).

[18] See *Reference re Amendment of the Constititution of Canada*, [1981] 1 S.C.R. 753, 849–910.

[19] [1959] S.C.R. 121.

[20] K. C. Wheare, *Federal Government*. London: Oxford University Press, 4th ed., 1963.

[21] Constitution Act, 1867, 30–31 Vict., c.3, s.55, s.90 (U.K.).

[22] Ibid.

[23] Constitution Act, 1867, 30–31 Vict., c.3, s.56, s.90 (U.K.).

[24] [1978] 2 S.C.R. 545.

[25] Section 92A added by Constitution Act, 1982, c.11, Schedule B, s.50 (U.K.).

[26] Constitution Act, 1982, c.11, Schedule B, ss.41–42 (U.K.).

[27] Constitution Act, 1982, c.11, Schedule B, s.41(a) (U.K.).

[28] Constitution Act, 1982, c.11, Schedule B, ss.41–42 (U.K.).

[29] Task Force on Canadian Unity, *A Future Together: Observations and Recommendations*. Ottawa: Minister of Supply and Services Canada, 1979.

[30] Constitution Act, 1982, c.11, Schedule B, ss.41–42 (U.K.).

[31] *Reference Re Amendment of the Constitution of Canada*, [1981] 1 S.C.R. 753.

[32] Constitution Act, 1982, c.11, Schedule B, s.33 (U.K.).

[33] R. I. Cheffins, *The Constitutional Process in Canada*. Toronto: McGraw-Hill, 1969, p.3.

[34] (1973) 410 U.S. 113.

SOURCES OF THE CONSTITUTION

The fundamental questions which any student of the constitution must grapple with and understand are where the rules of the constitution are to be found, and which jurisdiction has the authoritative power to lay them down. We will find, however, that there are some limitations on this approach because, with respect to some aspects of the constitution, the appropriate rules are not likely to be a factor in the judicial process. In this regard one thinks particularly of conventions of the constitution which are of overwhelming importance in an overall study of the constitution, but which do not, except in the most extraordinary circumstances, play a role in the judicial process. Before, however, moving to the non-binding, or non-authoritative sources of the constitution, it is appropriate to begin looking systematically at where one finds the law of the constitution. In this context we are referring to those rules that the court, in a constitutional case, will find to be authoritative with respect to the question before the court.

Legislation

The logical first source of Canadian constitutional law is legislation. The term "legislation" is a generic one covering not only statutes but also, where appropriate, rules passed by bodies to whom authority has been delegated by parliamentary enactment. This latter aspect of delegation is of overwhelming importance in the area of administrative law but does not play a major role as a fundamental source of Canadian constitutional law.

The first important legislative source is, of course, statutes of the United Kingdom Parliament. Since the constitutional events of 1982 we are able, by looking at the Schedule to the Constitution Act, 1982, to see the British statutes which have contemporary application in Canada. The Schedule shows that there are thirteen British statutes (in addition to the Canada Act, 1982) which are still relevant in an analysis of the sources of Canadian constitutional law. Undoubtedly the two most important of these statutes are the British North America Act, 1867, now renamed the Constitution Act, 1867, and the Constitution Act, 1982 (Schedule B of the Canada Act 1982). In between there are twelve other statutes of varying importance but all still relevant and applicable in the context of Canadian constitutional law. They include important amendments to the division of powers, including the British North America Act, 1940[1] which vested authority with respect to unemployment insurance within the jurisdiction of the federal parliament, and amendments to the British North America Act, 1867 which dealt with old age pensions, namely British North America Act, 1964.[2] If one analyzes the situation chronologically, one naturally finds that the first listed British statute is what is now referred to as the Constitution Act, 1867. This was the British statute which brought together three British colonies, namely the Province of Canada, Nova Scotia and New Brunswick to form the Canadian nation. The intricacies of this Act will not be examined at the present time. However, it should be noted that the Act divided the Province of Canada into two component parts named Ontario and Quebec. The remainder of the contents of this statute will be examined in greater detail later in this work.

A continuing examination of the Schedule to the Constitution Act, 1982 brings us to the next important British statute, namely the British North America Act, 1871[3] now called the Constitution Act, 1871. This statute deals with the authority of the federal parliament to create new provinces out of territories which are part of Canada, but which are not part of any province. The statute was originally passed in order to retroactively remove any doubt about the legality of the federal Manitoba Act[4] which had created that province. A number of critics of the government of the day felt that, since there was no specific authority in the British North America Act, 1867 to create new provinces, there was severe doubt as to the legality of federal parliamentary action. The Constitution Act, 1871 removed this doubt and also vested in the federal parliament the right to create additional new provinces. The federal parliament used this authority on two occasions in 1905 to pass respectively the Alberta Act[5] and the Saskatchewan Act,[6] thereby creating two new provinces as part of the Canadian nation. The Constitution Act, 1871, however, did have the important rider that once the federal parliament had created a province, it could not later amend the province-creating statute to either abolish the province or to change its jurisdiction.

The Parliament of Canada Act, 1875[7] merely amended the provisions of section 18 of the Constitution Act, 1867 to allow the Parliament of Canada to increase the privileges and immunities enjoyed by the Senate and the House of Commons.

The British North America Act, 1886,[8] now called the Constitution Act, 1886, dealt with the problem of representation in parliament of Canadian territories.It has enabled the Parliament of Canada to make provisions with respect to representation in the Senate and House of Commons from those parts of Canada which, though territories of Canada, are not included as part of any province. This, of course, has enabled the Parliament of Canada to provide for parliamentary representation for the Yukon and the Northwest Territories.

The Canada (Ontario Boundary) Act,1889[9] is, as its name suggests, a statute dealing with a final definition of the westerly, northerly and easterly boundaries of the province of Ontario. The British North America Act, 1907,[10] now called the Constitution Act, 1907, dealt with payments to the provinces by the federal parliament. It is of very limited interest for the purposes of this book.

The British North America Act, 1915,[11] now called the Constitution Act, 1915, increased the number of members of the Canadian Senate from 72 to 96 and provided that each of the four western provinces was to be represented by six senators.

The British North America Act, 1930,[12] now called the Constitution Act, 1930, placed the western provinces in the same position with respect to jurisdiction over natural resources as that enjoyed by the eastern provinces under Section 109 of the Constitution Act, 1867.

The next statute of interest is one of great importance in the constitutional history of Canada, namely the Statute of Westminster, 1931.[13] It is pleasant to report that the name of this document has not been changed as a result of the constitutional developments of 1982. This statute went a long way towards providing for Canadian autonomy both legally and in terms of political reality. It allowed Canada to pass statutes having extra-territorial effect and, even more significantly, abolished the doctrine of repugnancy except with respect to the British North America Act, 1867 and its amendments. In a few words, the doctrine of repugnancy was the concept that any Canadian statute which clashed with a British statute specifically applicable to Canada was null and void. This proposition in its latest form was contained in the Colonial Laws Validity Act of 1865.[14]

Although the Statute of Westminster abolished the doctrine of repugnancy generally, it was retained with respect to the British North America Acts, for purposes of preserving the federal system. By definition, a genuine federal system cannot exist if the federal parliament can unilaterally change or alter in any way the structure and jurisdiction of the regional units. Thus, British parliamentary authority over the British North America Acts was retained in order to underline the fact that supremacy of the constitution remained with the United Kingdom Parliament rather than with the Parliament of Canada. As we shall later see, two key amendments are made to the Statute of Westminster which combine with other changes in the Constitution Act, 1982 to remove the legality of United Kingdom parliamentary action with respect to Canada.

In 1940, responding to a constitutional decision of the courts which struck down a federal attempt at passing unemployment insurance legislation,[15] the government of Canada, with the consent of the provinces, requested that the United Kingdom Parliament pass the British North America Act, 1940,[16] vesting in the federal parliament jurisdiction over unemployment insurance. Naturally this is one of the British statutes still applicable to Canada and it is accordingly listed in the Schedule to the Constitution Act of 1982, as the Constitution Act, 1940.

The next British statute of contemporary relevance is the British North America Act, 1949,[17] now referred to as the Newfoundland Act. This was the statute which made Newfoundland a part of Canada. The Act, however, is very skeletal in nature, and must be read in conjunction with the Schedule to both it and to an ordinary federal statute, namely the Terms of Union of Newfoundland with Canada Act.[18]

In 1960 the British parliament passed the British North America Act, 1960,[19] now known as the Constitution Act, 1960, providing for the retirement of federally appointed judges at the age of 75.

As mentioned earlier, in 1964 the British North America Act, 1867 was amended to give concurrent jurisdiction to the federal parliament and provincial legislatures to make laws in relation to old age pensions and supplementary benefits.[20] In the event of a disparity between the terms of the federal and provincial enactments, however, the provincial legislation will prevail.

The final British statute relevant to Canada is, of course, the Canada Act, 1982[21] and Schedule B to that Act, namely the Constitution Act, 1982. The Canada Act, 1982 was the statute which provided in section 2, that "No Act of the Parliament of the United Kingdom passed after the *Constitution Act, 1982* comes into force shall extend to Canada as part of its law." This "signing-off" provision is, in essence, the only relevant portion of the Canada Act. The other important provisions with respect to 1982 are all contained in the Constitution Act, 1982 which will be analyzed in depth later in this work.

A further examination of the Schedule to the Constitution Act, 1982 reveals that three significant British orders in council are relevant sources of Canadian constitutional law. Acting under section 146 of the Constitution Act, 1867, the British Privy Council admitted to Canada in 1870 Rupert's Land and the North-Western Territory.[22] Then in 1871 and 1873 respectively, British Columbia and Prince Edward Island were admitted by British order in council,[23] the Privy Council again acting under the terms of section 146 of the Constitution Act, 1867. The terms of entry for these units constitute parts of the constitutional law of Canada which cannot be changed except by using the new amending formula contained in the Constitution Act, 1982.

Newfoundland could also have been admitted pursuant to the terms of section 146. However, by 1949 it was probably deemed inappropriate to take such an important step via the relatively back-door route of an order in council. Instead, by the British North America Act, 1949,[24] the United Kingdom Parliament admitted Newfoundland to the nation of Canada. This Act is very brief and its terms are very general. The essence of the arrangements between Canada and Newfoundland is contained in the schedule to the Act. These terms of union are very extensive dealing with provincial constitutional matters, representation in the federal parliament, fisheries, education, patents and trade marks, and a great many detailed provisions with respect to the financial terms of entry. In addition, extensive provisions are included with respect to public services, works and property. Of special note is section 37 which deals with jurisdiction over natural resources, a matter of ever-increasing concern and debate with respect to federal-provincial jurisdiction. The terms of union deal with a number of other important matters but, perhaps on a lighter note, also allow margarine to be manufactured and sold in Newfoundland after the entry of the province into confederation. This provision, of course, was included because of restrictions on the sale and manufacture of that product in other parts of the country.

The next statutory source of Canadian constitutional law is, of course, Canadian statutes. In this regard a distinction must be drawn between Canadian statutes which are entrenched and those which remain ordinary statutes of the Parliament of Canada. There are many important Canadian statutes which can be amended or repealed in the ordinary way, namely by the bill passing through the House of Commons and the Senate, and then receiving Royal Assent by the governor general. These statutes are considered to be within the scope of the Canadian constitutional system because they deal with important institutions and processes with respect to the general framework of Canadian government. These would include statutes such as the Senate and House of Commons Act,[25] the Speaker of the Senate Act,[26] the Speaker of the House of Commons Act,[27], the Canada Elections Act,[28] the Official Secrets Act,[29]the War Measures Act[30] and the Canadian Bill of Rights.[31]All of these are significant and important in relation to the constitution. However, all of them are purely within federal jurisdiction and all of them can be passed, amended and repealed by ordinary federal legislative action.

Prior to the events of 1982 there were three federal statutes which, though passed by the federal parliament, could not be changed by that parliament. These statutes were the Manitoba Act of 1870,[32] the Alberta Act of 1905[33] and the Saskatchewan Act of 1905.[34] The Manitoba Act of 1870, it will be remembered, was passed to create a new province out of part of Rupert's Land and the North-Western Territory. Except for section 146 which allows for the admission of certain colonies and territories under British order in council, there was no provision in the British North America Act, 1867 for the creation of new provinces. Shortly after the passage of the Manitoba Act, 1870 many people raised questions about the legality of the federal parliament's action. Accordingly, at the request of Canada, the British parliament passed the British North America Act, 1871[35] which retroactively validated the federal parliament's enactment creating Manitoba. Section 6 of the British North America Act, 1871, however, provided that the federal parliament could not alter the provisions of the Manitoba Act except with respect to boundaries with the agreement of the legislature of the province. This automatically had the effect of entrenching the Manitoba Act, meaning that the power to amend it would now pass from the federal parliament to that of the United Kingdom should major changes be desired. It was, of course, possible for the provincial legislature to render spent portions of the Manitoba Act using the power to alter its own constitution under subsection 92(1) of the British North America Act, 1867.

Similarly, in 1905, acting under the authority of the British North America Act, 1871, which allowed the federal parliament to create provinces out of territories that were part of Canada but not part of any province, Ottawa created the provinces of Saskatchewan and Alberta. But, once again, though the federal parliament created these provinces it was bound by the provisions of section 6 of British North America Act, 1871, which did not allow it to amend its own statutes. It should be noted that all three of the foregoing statutes are included in the Schedule to the Constitution Act, 1982, and accordingly can now be amended only by following the new amending process.

The last four Canadian statutes mentioned in the Schedule should also be noted. In each case they are ordinary acts of the Canadian parliament, but since the passage of the Constitution Act, 1982, are now subject to the terms of the amending formula by reason of their inclusion in the Schedule. These four statutes are the British North America Act, 1965,[36] which provided for retirement from the Senate at age seventy-five; the British North America Act, 1974,[37] which amended section 51 of the British North America Act, 1867, and dealt with representation in the House of Commons; the British North America Act, 1975,[38] which gave one member of parliament to the Yukon and two members of parliament to the Northwest Territories; and the British North America Act (No. 2), 1975,[39] which increased the number of senators to 104 by providing for one senator from the Yukon and one senator from the Northwest Territories. All of these Canadian statutes were passed pursuant to subsection 91(1) of the British North America Act, 1867, which allowed the amendment of the Constitution of Canada with the exception of six categories of subjects. The four amendments were deemed to be alterations to the Constitution of Canada not invading the six categories of subjects reserved to the United Kingdom Parliament. Now, of course, subsection 91(1) has been repealed and totally replaced by the Constitution Act, 1982. The effect of this is to remove the aforementioned four statutes from unilateral federal control and to now make them amendable only by the use of the new amending formula.

There are other Canadian statutes which, when passed prior to 1982, were amendable and subject to repeal by ordinary federal parliamentary action, but which now may be entrenched by virtue of the Constitution Act, 1982 although not included in the Schedule. In particular, and without going into detail at the present time, these might include acts such as the Supreme Court Act,[40] the Royal Style and Titles Act,[41] the Oaths of Allegiance Act[42] and the Governor General's Act.[43] All of these matters relating to the Supreme Court and the Crown are in some ways covered in sections 41 and 42 of the Constitution Act, 1982. For example, the offices of the queen, the governor general and the lieutenant governor can be changed only by following a process which requires the agreement of all eleven legislative chambers in Canada, ten provincial and one federal. It is possible to assume that any statute relating to the office of the queen cannot be amended except through the process set forth in section 41. Similarly both sections 41 and 42 deal with "the composition of the Supreme Court of Canada" and "subject to paragraph 41(d), the Supreme Court of Canada" respectively. Are we therefore to assume that the Supreme Court Act, an ordinary act of the Parliament of Canada, is now amendable only by use of the amending process? These complex points have only been touched on briefly here. However, the authors will examine them in considerably more detail when they look at the terms and effect of the amending process laid down in the Constitution Act, 1982, in chapter 5.[44]

Another important source of Canadian constitutional law is provincial statutes. Formerly under subsection 92(1) of the British North America Act, 1867, and now under section 45 of the Constitution Act, 1982, the legislature of each province "may exclusively make laws amending the constitution of the province." As will be discussed in more detail in the chapter on the amending process, this appears to give the provinces considerably more flexibility than is in fact the case. As will be pointed out later, this is due to the fact that the entrenchment of the office of lieutenant governor as provided for in paragraph 41(a) freezes the provincial constitutional model much more solidly than might be expected. Nevertheless, as a result of subsection 92(1), prior to 1982, and now as a result of section 45, each province has a number of important statutes which are vital to Canada's constitutional functioning. For example, it is quite typical for most provinces to have an Executive Council Act and a Legislative Assembly Act. British Columbia deals with the usual matters raised in these statutes, in one enactment entitled the Constitution Act.[45] In essence, however, all of the provinces have legislation relating to the executive council of the province and the legislative assembly. The statutes vary somewhat in content, yet are important sources of Canadian constitutional law.

In addition, every province has an Election Act which prescribes the processes and procedures with respect to elections. All of the provinces have legislation dealing with the ability of the lieutenant governor in council of the province to refer questions of law to the courts of the province for an opinion as to legality. Every province acting under the authority of subsection 92(14) of the Constitution Act, 1867 has statutes providing for the creation of provincial courts. Other statutes provide for the rules and regulations relating to access to the courts in both ordinary civil law actions and with relation to judicial control of administrative activities. All of these statutes, though essentially procedural, are vital in the functioning of constitutional government. Similarly, all provinces now have provisions with respect to suits against the provincial Crown, an important principle for the average citizen, since for many years the Crown at various levels of government could not be sued without its consent. It must be remembered that all of these statutes are merely ordinary statutes of the legislatures of the provinces and can be amended by the ordinary legislative processes.

It should be noted also that all provinces have statutes dealing with human rights, particularly with respect to discrimination based on race, colour and religion among other things.Different names are used for these statutes but the usual name is the Human Rights Act. Some provinces, for example, Alberta and Saskatchewan, have in addition Bills of Rights.These statutes tend to cover the additional political rights such as freedom of speech, religion and assembly. They tend to be relatively recent in origin and are often overlooked by constitutional scholars. Nevertheless, in any overview of the Canadian constitutional sytem, they must still be counted as sources.

The Royal Prerogative

The second authoritative source of law is the royal prerogative. This source of law is the subject of very considerable misunderstanding on the part of almost everyone, not excluding politicians. Many bureaucrats and politicians like to harbour the notion that acting under the royal prerogative, the cabinet, whether it be federal or provincial, has some inherent power in some way tied mysteriously to the royal prerogative. This is, of course, totally untrue and was laid to rest legally by the *Reference re Anti-Inflation Act* case.[46] This case states clearly that the lieutenant governor in council has only such power as is vested in him by statute, no more and no less.

In a later chapter the royal prerogative will be dealt with in considerable detail. However, at this point it is sufficient to say that it is the residue of legal power residing in the Crown and passing through the Crown to the Crown's representatives, which in Canada are the governor general of Canada and the lieutenant governors of the provinces. These prerogative powers are to a considerable extent outlined in the Letters Patent of 1947, which both creates the office of governor general and vests in the governor general important powers of the Crown. Among the powers vested in the Crown's representatives in Canada by the royal prerogative are the powers to appoint the prime minister (or premier at the provincial level) and ministers and also to dismiss them. Similarly, the power of dissolving the elected chamber and thereby beginning the process of a general election is a prerogative power vested in the Crown's representatives. At the federal level, the governor general has the authority to appoint ambassadors and sign treaties. The declaration of war is also a prerogative power of the Crown. Though these powers are defined by the courts, their authority rests in historical recognition of the Crown and its prerogative legal rights. Since the Constitution Act, 1982 entrenches the monarchy and the offices of governor general and lieutenant governor, any change in these powers would now require the use of the amending formula, and, in particular, the approval of the ten provincial legislatures and the Senate and House of Commons of Canada.

Judicial Decisions

The third binding source of constitutional law is decisions of the courts. The vast majority of these decisions involve the interpretation of key sections of the basic constitutional documents. Up until 1982 an overwhelming number of these decisions involved the interpretation of the words of sections 91 and 92 of the British North America Act, 1867, allocating power between the provincial and federal legislatures. In addition there are important common law decisions not involving the interpretation of constitutional statutes, especially in the area of civil liberties. A notable example is the case of *Roncarelli* v. *Duplessis*[47] discussed earlier, which established that no official has authority to act unless empowered by statute. In that case the plaintiff Roncarelli sued under the terms of the

Quebec civil law for the wrongful actions of Premier Duplessis and was accordingly awarded damages. Decisions of the Supreme Court of Canada are of course binding on lower courts and thus form an essential part of the Constitution of Canada. With the passage of the Charter of Rights judicial decisions will play an increasing role as sources of Canadian constitutional law.

Conventions

There are important principles of the constitution referred to as conventions which guide political actors in how they function but which are not enforceable by the courts. These are what Dicey[48] labelled "conventions of the constitution." They are not contained in any written document but instead are generally accepted traditions or principles of how participants in the process should function at particular times. The Supreme Court of Canada addressed the question of their enforceability in the decision *Reference Re Amendment of the Constitution of Canada*.[49] The court pointed out that "in contradistinction to the laws of the constitution, they are not enforced by the courts."[50] They went on to say that conventions, unlike judge-made rules, are neither created by the courts nor enforceable by the courts. They stressed the fact, however, that "some conventions may be more important than some laws."[51] They drew the equation "constitutional conventions plus constitutional law equal the total constitution of the country."[52] In their analysis of conventions the court held that they come within the meaning of the word "constitution" which is part of the preamble of the British North America Act, 1867. The preamble provides that Canada shall have a "Constitution, similar in Principle to that of the United Kingdom." In this regard the court was referring to the fact that principles of responsible government as devised in Great Britain and Canada prior to 1867 were a fundamental part of our constitutional functioning. Later in this work more detail will be given with respect to the development of the principles of responsible government. However, it is sufficient to say at this point that the concept's fundamental principle is that a cabinet remains responsible to the elected legislative body and holds office only so long as it has the confidence of that elected legislative body. Constitutional convention requires that any government losing the confidence of the House must immediately resign. This could result in the formation of an alternate government without the necessity of a general election such as happened in 1926, or more likely, it could result in the prime minister asking the governor general to dissolve the House in order that an election might take place and the political electorate express its will.

This most fundamental concept of Canadian government is nowhere mentioned in any legal document. In fact the Constitution Act, 1867 makes no mention whatsoever of the office of prime minister, the cabinet, or responsible government. As outlined above, the closest reference to this phenomenon is the phrase "a Constitution similar in principle to that of the United Kingdom." Yet this is what the court was referring to when it indicated that convention can sometimes be more important than law. Law would not require resignation of the government upon defeat. Convention, however, would, and this convention is central to insuring that the political will of the country is carried out.

Most of the conventions of the constitution tend to centre around the functioning of the monarchy or the monarch's representatives in Canada, the governor general and the lieutenant governors of the provinces. This fact is consistent with the Anglo-Canadian tradition of retaining the form and changing the substance. Thus if one looks at the Constitution Act, 1867 it appears as if the primary governing figure is the governor general in that many of the most important appointments are made by him. The power of appointment includes members of the Senate, certain members of the judiciary and members of the Privy Council. In addition to these statutory powers the governor general, by virtue of the prerogative powers of the Crown, has the authority to appoint the prime minister and members of the cabinet. Similarly the governor general has the power to dissolve the House and thus precipitate a general election. These same powers are exercised by the lieutenant governor, either by virtue of the prerogative or by virtue of statute.

Convention, of course, requires that these very important legal powers, among others, possessed by the Crown's representative, be exercised in almost all cases on the advice of the Crown's first minister. This was, for example, exhibited quite clearly in the old Province of Canada when in 1849 Lord Elgin, on the advice of his cabinet, gave royal assent to the Rebellion Losses Bill even though he was personally opposed to its content. In the *Reference Re Amendment of the Constitution of Canada* case[53] the Supreme Court, however, showed conclusively that the spirit of British positivism as represented by Austin and Dicey was going to prevail over the spirit of the living law as portrayed in the writings of Ehrlich. Only those rules emanating from persons in positions of authority were going to be enforced by the courts. Later in this work we will be looking again at conventions of the Constitution and how they impact upon the functioning of the system.

An important distinction must be drawn between conventions and usages. Conventions are generally regarded as binding, if not in law at least in spirit, on participants in the system. Usages are merely practices which have developed, usually for reasons of political expediency. For example, usages have developed with respect to the office of chief justice and the office of the speaker of the House of Commons in that they alternate between English-speaking and French-speaking persons. These usages are not regarded as necessarily binding on the actors but are merely rules of thumb that probably are wise as matters of political practice. They are, of course, much more easily broken and usually with much less serious consequences. For example, in the appointment of Bora Laskin to the office of chief justice of the Supreme Court of Canada, the usage of selecting the most senior judge as chief justice was ignored. The traditional usage would have lead to the appointment of Mr. Justice Martland, but Prime Minister Trudeau preferred to have Mr. Justice Laskin in that position. This deviation from usage occasioned comment but was not sufficient to provoke any kind of major political storm. In contrast, failure to observe the usual conventions would undoubtedly lead to very serious political repercussions. Such repercussions were, of course, evidenced by the outcries that followed the attempt by Prime Minister Trudeau to unilaterally have the British parliament amend the constitution of Canada without obtaining provincial consent.

Texts and Extraneous Material

There is occasionally other material which judges will look at to assist them in making judicial decisions. It is becoming increasingly common for judges to look at the text of authoritative works on the constitution. There was at one time a rule that the courts would never refer to an author of a book or journal article unless that author was dead. Happily this rule is now ignored and contemporary scholars are often referred to on points of practice and law.

Somewhat surprisingly, the Quebec and London resolutions which formed the background to the drafting and passage of the British North America Act, 1867 have seldom been referred to by the courts. This is odd as they often give indications as to the thinking of those formulating the original constitutional document. This policy, however, is in keeping with the general tradition of Canadian and British courts of trying to interpret statutes as far as possible by using their actual wording, rather than by perusing external sources such as parliamentary debates. It should be noted, however, that in the famous "Persons" case[54] where the question arose as to whether women could be appointed to the Senate, the Judicial Committee of the Privy Council, overruling the Supreme Court of Canada, said that the words of the Constitution must be interpreted in the light of changing circumstances. This line of thought was encapsulated in the famous phrase that the Constitution must be looked upon as a "living tree." Perhaps further evidence of this trend comes from the *Reference re Anti-Inflation Act* case[55] where the court was prepared to give consideration to a submission made by one of the parties drafted by Professor Richard Lipsey on whether, in fact, inflation was of such a nature in Canada as to amount to an emergency. The court was not prepared to accept the position reached by Professor Lipsey. Nevertheless, the judges were prepared to give it very considerable weight. As the courts become increasingly activist, especially as a result of the inclusion in the Constitution of a Charter of Rights, there will undoubtedly be a greater tendency to rely on extraneous evidence of different kinds for purposes of constitutional interpretation. Here again, these extraneous sources — whether they be parliamentary debate, pre-statute resolutions or opinions of experts — will only be of persuasive value in helping the court to determine the meaning of words and phrases in the positive law. Nevertheless, these extraneous sources could be of overwhelming importance in determining how phrases which are often vague are to be interpreted.

[1] 3-4 Geo. VI, c.36 (U.K.).

[2] 12-13 Eliz. II, c.73 (U.K.).

[3] 34-35 Vict., c.28 (U.K.).

[4] 33 Vict., c.3 (Can.).

[5] 4-5 Edw. VII, c.3 (Can.).

[6] 4-5 Edw. VII, c.42 (Can.).

[7] 38-39 Vict., c.38 (U.K.).

[8] 49-50 Vict., c.35 (U.K.).

[9] 52-53 Vict., c.28 (U.K.).

[10] 7 Edw. VII, c.11 (U.K.).

[11] 5-6 Geo. V, c.45 (U.K.).

[12] 20-21 Geo. V, c.26 (U.K.).

[13] 22 Geo. V, c.4 (U.K.).

[14] 28-29 Vict., c.63 (U.K.).

[15] *Attorney General for Canada* v. *Attorney General for Ontario*, [1937] A.C. 355 (P.C.).

[16] 3-4 Geo. VI, c.36 (U.K.).

[17] 12-13 Geo. VI, c.22 (U.K.).

[18] 13 Geo. VI, c.1 (Can.).

[19] 9 Eliz. II, c.2 (U.K.).

[20] British North America Act, 1964, 12-13 Eliz. II, c.73 (U.K.).

[21] 1982, c.11 (U.K.).

[22] Order of Her Majesty in Council admitting Rupert's Land and the North-Western Territory into the Union, dated the 23rd day of June, 1870, now called the Rupert's Land and North-Western Territory Order.

[23] Order of Her Majesty in Council admitting British Columbia into the Union, dated the 16th day of May, 1871, now called the British Columbia Terms of Union; Order of Her Majesty in Council admitting Prince Edward Island into the Union, dated the 26th day of June, 1873, now called the Prince Edward Island Terms of Union, respectively. Also included as Item 8 in the schedule is a fourth British Order in Council now referred to as the Adjacent Territories Order.

[24] 12-13 Geo. VI, c.22 (U.K.).

[25] R.S.C. 1970, c.S-8.

[26] R.S.C. 1970, c.S-14.

[27] R.S.C. 1970, c.S-13.

[28] R.S.C. 1970 (1st Supp.), c.14.

[29] R.S.C. 1970, c.O-3.

[30] R.S.C. 1970, c.W-2.

[31] Stats. Can. 1960, c.44, Part I.

[32] 33 Vict., c.3 (Can.).

[33] 4-5 Edw. VII, c.3 (Can.).

[34] 4-5 Edw. VII, c.42 (Can.).

[35] 34-35 Vict., c.28 (U.K.).

[36] 14 Eliz. II, c.4, Part I (Can.).

[37] 23 Eliz. II, c.13, Part I (Can.).

[38] 23-24 Eliz. II, c.28, Part I (Can.).

[39] 23-24 Eliz. II, c.53 (Can.).

[40] R.S.C. 1970, c.S-19.

[41] R.S.C. 1970, c.R-12.

[42] R.S.C. 1970, c.O-1.

[43] R.S.C. 1970, c.G-14.

[44] See also Cheffins, "The Constitution Act, 1982 and the Amending Formula: Political and Legal Implications" (1982), 4 Supreme Court L. R., 43.

[45] R.S.B.C. 1979, c.62.

[46] [1976] 2 S.C.R. 373.

[47] [1959] S.C.R. 121.

[48] A. V. Dicey, *Law of the Constitution*. London: Macmillan, 10th ed., E.C.S. Wade, ed., 1965.

[49] [1981] 1 S.C.R. 753.

[50] Ibid., p. 880.

[51] Supra, note 49, p. 883.

[52] Supra, note 49, pp. 883-884.

[53] Supra, note 49.

[54] *Edwards* v. *Attorney General for Canada,* [1930] A.C. 124 (P.C.).

[55] Supra, note 46.

PRE-CONFEDERATION CONSTITUTIONAL HERITAGE AND THE BRITISH NORTH AMERICA ACT, 1867

Canada was formed by the joining together in 1867 of three British colonies, namely Canada, Nova Scotia and New Brunswick. It is important to look at pre-Confederation developments because only then is much of what later follows comprehensible. In our view, probably the most important facet of the Canadian constitutional system was developed before 1867, that is, the principle of responsible government. As we shall see throughout the course of this work, what started as a liberalizing principle brought about to reflect the wishes of the electorate, has turned into a proposition which has made Canadian government increasingly closed, oligarchic and unresponsive to public opinion. It is accordingly important to consider how we arrived at our present situation through an examination of our historical past.

The Establishment of Representative Government

It is also important to understand the development of relations between the English- and French-speaking elements in this country. Much of Canada's later constitutional and political history becomes much more meaningful if the legal and political arrangements prior to 1867 are explained and understood. Since it is impossible in a work of this nature to develop at any great length the intricate details of pre-Confederation Canada, highlights which are particularly important in understanding later constitutional developments will be emphasized. It is appropriate to start with the year 1760 when one can delineate four British possessions within the bounds of what is now Canada. These possessions were Quebec, Nova Scotia, Newfoundland and Rupert's Land. Quebec had formerly been called New France and was part of the French Empire until its conquest in September of 1759 by the British under the generalship of Wolfe. The major legal matters arising from the conquest were not finally resolved until 1763 at the Treaty of Paris, which not only brought the seven years war to an end but also concluded the long struggle for domination in North America between France and Britain. Quebec, by the Royal Proclamation of 1763,[1] was placed under a governor and an appointed council. The proclamation advised the governor to summon together a legislative assembly to assist in the rule of the colony. Governor Murray recognized that because of legal provisions in British law at that time, the assembly would fall under the control of the English-speaking minority. Murray, because of his essentially rural, conservative background, felt more empathy towards the conservative, rural French-speaking Roman Catholics than he did towards the more aggressive, commercially-minded English-speaking minority who had settled primarily in the city of Montreal. His successor, Guy Carleton, shared these sentiments and accordingly no assembly was ever elected for the old colony of Quebec.

In the meantime Nova Scotia had its first assembly summoned by Governor Lawrence in 1758. It became the essential model for governmental institutions remaining in place in Canada today. Although at this point the traditions and conventions of responsible government had not been developed, the legal entities with which we are now very familiar were being established. The government of Nova Scotia consisted of an elected legislative assembly, an appointed legislative council, and an appointed executive council. The lynchpin in all this apparatus was the governor, appointed by the Crown both as the Crown's representative and as the chief political officer of the British government in the colony. The governor appointed the legislative and executive councils which were therefore under his dominance and control. In early Nova Scotia, because of the very small population of the colony, it was common practice to have the same persons named to both the legislative council and the executive council.[2] To become law, all bills had to proceed through the legislative assembly and the legislative council and receive the assent of the governor. The governor relied on his executive council for guidance and advice on questions of policy, while keeping the general policies of the colony in line with those of the British government. Even so, there were already the beginnings of a reasonable degree of autonomy and self-government on the part of the inhabitants of Nova Scotia.[3]

In 1769 the Crown gave Prince Edward Island a separate government which was at first composed of only a governor and a council but which in 1773 was awarded a representative legislature.[4] In 1784 New Brunswick was divorced from Nova Scotia and given a similar form of government to that of Nova Scotia and Prince Edward Island. Since all of these governmental systems were established by virtue of the royal prerogative, no British legislation was required to bring about these highly important constitutional developments.

The Quebec Act, 1774

Meanwhile, in Quebec, the British parliament in 1774 passed one of the most significant pieces of legislation in the history of North America, namely the Quebec Act, 1774.[5] This Act was particularly significant not only because it recognized clearly and legally the existence of a separate French-speaking group within the British North American empire, but also because it provided another step which goaded the American colonies to rebellion. The Protestant elements in the thirteen colonies were outraged by Britain's recognition of the rights of the French-speaking Roman Catholics to their north, and jealous of the fact that the British parliament had awarded large areas of what is now the Mississippi

Valley to the colony of Quebec. The terms of this vital statute which so affected both the history of Canada and North America deserve elaboration. First, it provided that Roman Catholics were to enjoy freedom of religious worship and that the French-Canadian civil law was to be retained. Furthermore, government of the colony was to be by governor and appointed legislative council. The Act provided for a special oath so that Roman Catholics could accept seats on this council. The British government clearly recognized that any policy of assimilation into the English-speaking minority was impossible and, in fact, seemed to encourage the continuation of French-Canadian law and tradition.

The Act made no reference whatsoever to language. However, by recognizing French legal and religious traditions which involved language, the British government clearly accepted the use of the French language. The Act provided that the criminal law of the colony would be that of England, a provision which was welcomed by the colonists because the penalties of English law were considerably less severe than those of French criminal law. Perhaps the aspect of the statute which was most galling to the Americans was that it expanded the western limits of the colony to include vast areas of land as far as what is now Ohio. This meant that American colonists who wished to move westward to find farmland would have to enter a region which recognized what, to them, seemed an alien culture and an alien law. Since expansion to the west was a primary concern of many of the American colonists, they labelled the Quebec Act one of the "intolerable acts." Although not the primary piece of British legislation leading to the American Revolution, it certainly added considerable fuel to the rapidly burning political fire.

The success of the American Revolution had very significant effects for the future structure of the British North American colonies which had not joined the rebellion. A high proportion of the American colonists remained loyal to the British Crown and many of them suffered persecution at the hands of revolutionary forces and fled the thirteen American colonies. Professor Maurice Careless suggests that about a third of the population of the American colonies favoured Britain, another third supported the revolution, and the other third remained neutral.[6] Another author, Bruce Wilson, in a book called *As She Began*,[7] suggests that of the one million American colonists, half remained loyal to the British Crown. Both Careless and Wilson, however, agree that one hundred thousand loyalists found life in the United States so unbearable that they decided to leave the country. Slightly more than half of them came to what is now Canada — 45,000 to the Atlantic provinces, 2,000 to Quebec and about 7,500 to what was then called Western Quebec but is now Ontario.

These colonists changed the entire face of politics in the remaining portions of British North America. Many of them settled in that part of Nova Scotia which later became New Brunswick. In fact, it was their settlement that led to the creation in 1784 of the new colony of New Brunswick with its own legislative and executive government. Similarly, the English-speaking inhabitants of Western Quebec soon came to demand the traditional legal, constitutional and political privileges and practices which they had enjoyed in the American colonies. They wanted a representative system of government and a restoration of the traditions and rules of the English common law.

The Constitutional Act 1791 and the Rebellions of Upper and Lower Canada

In response to these demands the British parliament passed the Constitutional Act of 1791[8] which divided Quebec into the provinces of Upper and Lower Canada, each with its own system of law and with its own legislative and judicial institutions. The Province of Upper Canada was to have the immediate bestowal of the English common law as it existed at that time whereas the Province of Lower Canada was to retain its French civil law traditions. Each colony was given a constitutional structure similar to that of Nova Scotia, namely a governor, a nominated executive council, a nominated legislative council and an elected assembly. The most significant impact of the arrangement was that for the first time the French-speaking inhabitants of North America were participating in constitutional democracy. Not only were French Canadians being elected to the legislative assembly of Lower Canada but, by virtue of their numerical superiority, they were dominating this assembly. At the same time the governor was still appointing to his executive council a large number of English-speaking merchants from the city of Montreal. Thus were born the seeds of inevitable constitutional conflict. Nevertheless, the inhabitants of what had originally been New France had made gigantic strides forward under British rule. They had guarantees of their religion and law by virtue of the Quebec Act and now, by virtue of the Constitutional Act of 1791, they had assumed control of the elected assembly in their home province.

At the same time tensions inevitably developed in Upper Canada as a result of the differing views held by members of the governor's nominated council and by the elected members of the legislative assembly. Although only a small minority of the members of the legislative assembly of Ontario were in rebellion against the British connection, even moderates in the assembly with deep convictions about the British tradition began to feel the need for some restructuring of the relationship between the council and the assembly.

The leader of the rebel forces was William Lyon MacKenzie, a Scottish immigrant and a journalist by profession. His frustration with being unable to obtain control of the assembly increasingly led him on a path towards radicalism. He broke with Egerton Ryerson over the degree and method of change needed in Upper Canada. Ryerson moved to the Tory camp along with many of his influential Methodist supporters. His motivations in politics were largely religious whereas MacKenzie sought a basic restructuring of the economic and political system. For example, MacKenzie urged that there be established an elected legislative council rather than the existing council appointed by the governor. MacKenzie even fell out of step with other leading reformers such as Robert Baldwin, who preferred reform within the British context by using the technique of responsible government rather than by adopting the United States as a constitutional model. In 1836 the governor, Sir Francis Bond Head, made the forthcoming election an issue of loyalty versus republicanism and as a result MacKenzie's forces were overwhelmingly rejected at the polls. This had the effect of driving him to desperate measures and as a result he led a badly organized, almost comic opera rebellion against the existing government. The regular army supported by the overwhelming majority of the population quickly succeeded in quelling this brief attempt at revolution.[9]

In Lower Canada similar currents of unrest were flowing. Here the issues of economics and oligarchic control were underlined by tensions between the English- and French-speaking populations of the colony. The French Canadians, as a result of the electoral system introduced in 1791, had control of the legislative assembly but the governor still kept a tight grip on the executive council through his power of appointment. The result was an executive council which was still essentially under the control of the English-speaking population. The divisions were not totally along linguistic lines as some French Canadians had held official posts and generally worked with the incumbent rulers of the colony. As well, a number of English-speaking reformers joined the majority of French Canadians in urging reform of the constitutional system. Thus in November of 1837 a rebellion led by Papineau broke out against the government of the colony. This was a more serious initiative than that which occurred in Upper Canada yet it had little hope of success because of opposition by the church. The ruling elements in the clergy felt that they had reached a reasonable agreement with the British for the protection of their traditional role in French-Canadian society and they were alarmed at the prospect of what might happen to the political system should the rebels succeed. In particular, the church had doubts about Papineau's leanings towards American republicanism and the secularism that that implied. The result was the defeat of Papineau and his followers by the regular army and an end to the rebellion.

Similar reform ideas were being discussed in the Maritimes. Many of the complicating factors in existence in Upper and Lower Canada did not exist in the Maritime colonies. New Brunswick, with its strong tradition of settlement by United Empire Loyalists, rejected out of hand the idea of a government responsible to the legislative assembly. In Nova Scotia, the members of the ruling group and the participants in the executive council tended to be more liberal in outlook than in Upper and Lower Canada and, as a result, the strife there tended to be less bitter. Furthermore, in 1837 the Colonial Office ordered the separation of the executive and legislative councils in the sense that there was no longer to be overlapping membership. In addition, the British instructed the governor that four members of the executive council must be chosen from the assembly. These moves served to mitigate any movement towards armed rebellion.

Lord Durham's Report

The British government was sufficiently alarmed by the rebellions in Upper and Lower Canada to call upon John George Lambton, the first Earl of Durham, to serve as governor in chief of the British North American colonies. He was charged with the task of finding out what had prompted the Canadian rebellions and of recommending measures that would be "conducive to the permanent establishment of an improved system of government in Her Majesty's North American possessions."[10] Lord Durham travelled the country for five months hearing representations from various individuals and did gain a good grasp of Canadian affairs. He failed to share the sympathies and outlooks of the French Canadians, however, as he regarded them as a cultural throw-back to an earlier feudal time.

Durham was a typical liberal of the time and accordingly favoured a free-enterprise and free-market type of economy. He was also liberal in the sense of favouring constitutional reform which would widen the basis of participation in government. Thus when Durham handed down his famous report he stressed the need to provide for responsible government as quickly as possible. Responsible government essentially meant the appointment to the executive council of persons who sat in the elected assembly and who had the support of the elected assembly. The thrust of this proposal was to hand control of the executive government of the country to elected officials. Durham did see a continuing role for the governor in the selection from the assembly of those who would serve on the executive council, in the retention of important legal powers in terms of giving assent to legislation, and in areas such as foreign affairs and the constitution. Durham was prepared to recognize that except for constitutional matters, foreign affairs, external trade and the management of public lands, the British North American colonies would essentially be in control of their own destinies.

The report included a number of other very important recommendations, most of which were implemented and most of which have had far-reaching effects which continue to this day. For example, Durham recommended that all financial bills should originate in the assembly and should receive the consent of the Crown's representative before being introduced. This recommendation is embodied in our present constitution, in the Constitution Act, 1867,[11] and has been an important factor in the stranglehold which the executive exerts over the legislative process. Durham recommended that the initiative with respect to financial measures should come from members of the executive council which, he foresaw, would become a cabinet on the British model. This proposal was embodied in the Union Act of 1840, and was included in the Constitution Act of 1867. In essence, it requires that no financial measure can be placed before the lower house of the federal or provincial governments without a message from the Crown's representative, and by convention the message is attached to a bill only on the advice of a cabinet minister. Thus we can see that the Durham Report was intellectually the source of what is now cabinet government.

Another very significant recommendation of the report was the reunion of Upper and Lower Canada into one governmental unit to be known as the Province of Canada. There is no doubt that Durham felt the integration of the French-speaking Canadians into an English-speaking mainstream would be desirable and would enable them to join what he regarded as the progressive forces of the time, which were essentially free-market and free-trade economics and democratization of the political process. Little did he foresee that after the passage of the Union Act of 1840 amalgamating Upper and Lower Canada, the French Canadians — far from being assimilated into an English-speaking mainstream — would become an equal and equally powerful force in the government of the Province of Canada. Neither did he foresee that French Canada would begin developing the traditions of federalism within the framework of the unitary constitution of the Province of Canada. Not only is Durham in many ways the spiritual father of cabinet government in Canada, but he was also a strong advocate of the development of municipal government in Canada as we now understand it. The results of his report are still being felt by Canadians every day of their lives.

The Union Act, 1840

The Union Act of 1840 allowed the governor general of the provinces of Upper and Lower Canada to proclaim that they be joined under the name of the Province of Canada. The proclamation bringing the Province of Canada into being was not made until 1841. The Act provided for an institutional structure similar to that of all of the British North American colonies, namely, a governor, an executive council, an appointed legislative council and an elected assembly. The original assembly had forty-two members from Canada East and forty-two members from Canada West with the number being increased in 1853 to sixty-five from each of the two divisions in the colony. Although Upper and Lower Canada had been legally abolished, continuing recognition had to be given to the fact that culturally and sociologically the old provinces still remained within the new institutional structure. The next seven years in the life of the colonies of Canada, Nova Scotia and New Brunswick were some of the most exciting and probably the most important in the entire history of British North America. We see the evolution during those years of what is now cabinet government in Canada. Described here in brief skeletal form, we see a series of events leading to one party cabinet government, which has in turn led to the increasing political irrelevance of elected assemblies in determining either national or provincial policy.

The first governor, Lord Sydenham, tried to operate as both governor and premier at the same time. This was an experiment doomed to failure. Nevertheless, important consequences resulted from the effort. First, Sydenham selected the members of his executive council from persons who possessed seats in the elected assembly and had some popularity in the chamber. He was not prepared to select them from one party but instead attempted to put together a coalition of ministers or what was often looked upon as a government party. Though this was not responsible government in the full sense of what was achieved a few years later, it was an important recognition of the idea that executive government essentially had to be under the control of elected members of the assembly. Sydenham was also responsible for another very important change in government in Canada: making members of his executive council responsible for the running and conduct of different departments of government. Thus the executive council was no longer an amorphous group but was a collection of individual members of the council, each of which had to face the assembly in connection with particular policies affecting particular areas of government. Sydenham's tenure in office proved to be very brief as he died following an accident on September 19, 1841. By 1842 under Governor Sir Charles Bagot, we begin to see the emergence of a party ministry with virtually all members of the executive council coming from the reform group in the elected assembly which favoured responsible government. Not, however, until 1848 is the principle of responsible government recognized; first in January of that year in Nova Scotia, and in March of that year in the Province of Canada.

In Nova Scotia, after a general election, a direct want of confidence motion was carried in the assembly on January 25th. The executive council resigned on the 27th and the new premier, J. B. Uniacke, was asked by the governor to form a government.[12] In March of the same year the government of the Province of Canada was defeated on a want of confidence motion and an immediate change of government took place there. The principle was adopted soon after in New Brunswick and, three years later, was recognized in the colony of Prince Edward Island. Newfoundland followed shortly, achieving responsible government in 1855. This important concept, responsible government, simply means that the governor must select advisors who are members of the elected assembly and who have the support of that elected assembly. Failure to have that support means that the members of the executive council must resign.

Another significant event occurring in 1849 further illustrates and underlines the principle of responsible government as we now understand it. In that year the government introduced a bill to compensate Canadians who had suffered wanton or unnecessary injury during the rebellion of 1837 provided they had not been convicted of treason. The measure was roundly denounced by the opposition as rewarding disloyalty and, in particular, of pandering to the sentiment of French Canadians. Lord Elgin, the governor, disliked the measure as much as the members of the opposition, but he felt that it was his duty to give royal assent to the bill when advised to do so by his executive council which in turn had the support of the elected members of the assembly. He accordingly gave assent to the bill but was rewarded for his action by being pelted with rocks and debris while journeying to and from the parliamentary buildings. The buildings themselves were burned to the ground by the protesting crowds and it is probably as a consequence of this action that Montreal is not today the capital of Canada.

The significance of Lord Elgin's action in giving royal assent is that it shows that the governor increasingly felt himself obliged to follow the advice of his executive council rather than his own personal predilection. Thus we have seen emerge a system not only where the advisors to the Crown come from the popularly elected assembly, but where the representative of the Crown himself feels under an obligation to abide by the wishes of a council over which he has very limited control. By 1854 the governor had withdrawn from meetings of the executive council and thus the council turned into an informal body known as the cabinet. This body was largely a customary, conventional group given political existence only through the appointment of a premier or prime minister. For political purposes the dominant feature of the executive was the cabinet, but when acting in a legal capacity the cabinet functioned as the executive council. In effect, however, these two bodies were at that time composed of exactly the same people. The withdrawal of the governor in 1854 made it clear that he was not even to be a party to discussions leading to the formulation of government policy.

With the growth and ultimate recognition of responsible government, it was virtually inevitable that political parties of an organized and enduring nature would be formed. Until this time there had been loose alliances based on particular issues. For example, the Reform Party of Baldwin and LaFontaine began to disintegrate soon after the achievement of responsible government in 1848. What emerged was a new alliance between moderate reformers and Tories, which was to be called the Liberal-Conservative Party.[13] This particular grouping ultimately became the Progressive Conservative Party of Canada and was the dominant party in the country until the First World War. The seeds of the present Liberal party can be found in a small group of Rouges from Quebec and a rural group known as the Clear Grits from Ontario. The Rouges tended to be anti-clerical and quite often remnants of Papineau's followers, whereas the Grits tended to be anti-French, anti-Roman Catholic, agrarian populist radicals whose political roots went back to William Lyon MacKenzie. The alliance between the Rouges and the Grits was based mainly on their opposition to the governing Liberal-Conservative group.

We see in the close alliance between English-speaking conservatives from Canada West and the Bleus of George E. Cartier forming the Liberal-Conservative Party, the political pattern for much of Canada's party history until the present time. This was a party which accepted, to a large extent, the duality of Canada along linguistic and cultural lines and, at the same time, supported economic growth. Later we shall see the party become identified with the National Policy which was essentially a high-tariff policy serving the function of protecting indigenous industry. It is this Liberal-Conservative Party which generally dominated the increasingly unstable politics of the old Province of Canada.

The politics of the Province of Canada foreshadowed the political events which have dominated Canadian government since the establishment of Canada in 1867. French Canadians had been introduced to representative politics by the legislation of 1791 and now, by virtue of the Union Act of 1840, they were being introduced to the politics of controlling executive government within a parliamentary system. French-Canadian politicians soon made it clear that the province could be governed only with their cooperation and consent. Thus we see in all aspects of the government of the Province of Canada the recognition of the concept of dualism, namely, that English- and French-speaking Canadians must participate equally within the context of the political system. The result was that virtually every government had an English-speaking and a French-speaking premier, for example, the LaFontaine-Baldwin ministry of 1842, followed by the Draper-Viger ministry of 1843, and the Draper-D. B. Papineau ministry of 1846, among others. This duality was a unique experience in terms of leadership in the context of the British Empire and Commonwealth. In addition, in many of the ministries there were dual holders of offices such as that of the attorney general. Similarly, for a short period in the 1840s there were two provincial secretaries. This was followed by the practice of having the portfolio alternate between a minister from Canada East and a minister from Canada West. The same phenomenon could be observed in the bureaucracy where, for example, there were two parallel education bureaucracies. Perhaps the most important aspect of dualism was the doctrine of the *double majority*. This meant, in effect, that no legislation was acceptable unless it received the support of not only a majority in the elected assembly but also of a majority of representatives from Canada East and a majority of representatives from Canada West. This meant that one region could not impose its will on the other. Though this is not federalism in the legal sense of the term, spiritually it achieves one of the main objectives of a federal system: autonomy for different areas of a single political unit. Even attempts to make English the dominant language failed and recognition was given to the fact that the government of the province had to be carried on in virtually all respects through the use of the two languages.

One can see that when the question of a larger Canadian union was placed before the elected assembly of the Province of Canada, a large number of French-speaking legislators were very unsympathetic to the idea of Confederation. French Canada had achieved an equal and powerful place in the Province of Canada and there was considerable scepticism about whether a similar role could be achieved within a larger union. French Canadians had learned, first through the elections to the assembly of the province of Lower Canada, and then through the politics of executive government in the Province of Canada, how to more than hold their own in their relationship with their English-speaking confreres. The latter came to recognize that without the approval of French Canada, government, either in the smaller unit of the Province of Canada or in the larger entity later known as Canada, was virtually impossible. Thus one should never underestimate the incredible foreshadowing of future events in Canada by the politics and constitutional functioning of the Province of Canada.

One ironic note which can be sounded is that because of the dissatisfaction with the political system of the province, it was suggested that an elected upper house might be a solution to some of the problems. In 1856 the upper house was expanded from thirty-four members to forty-eight members through the use of elections.[14] Similarities to the American model are apparent in that members were to hold their seats for eight years and one quarter of the members were to be elected every two years. The irony is that the increasing dissatisfaction with our present cabinet-controlled political system, combined with central Canada's political dominance, has led to the suggestion that the appropriate remedy is an elected upper house. It is interesting to note that in connection with all of the various proposals suggesting an elected upper house, neither of the writers has ever seen reference to the fact that this experiment was tried once before. To be fair, however, the Canadian experience with an elected upper house was so brief that there is very little derivative comment one can make with respect to the utility for Canada of having an elected second chamber.

The Events Leading to Confederation

A series of economic, psychological, social and political factors began to force residents of the British North American colonies to consider some form of larger political unit. The presence of the United States has always been a factor with respect to Canada. Just south of this handful of sparsely populated and geographically very separated British colonies was a rapidly expanding nation increasingly bent on economic and territorial expansion. The thin red line of British control from the Province of Canada to the most remote colony of Vancouver Island established in 1849 was maintained essentially by granting control of the intervening territory to the Hudson's Bay Company. This land would undoubtedly be increasingly coveted by the rapid westward movement of American settlers.[15]

The British North American colonies had a myriad of other problems. The repeal of the British Corn Laws in 1846 and the resultant move towards free trade undermined the protected market in Britain for Canadian goods. Britain was pulling back from the idea of an Imperial economic union and was moving in the direction of free trade. All of the British colonies had to seek other outlets for their products rather than merely relying on Great Britain. It was, therefore, logical to turn towards the United States. As a result, in 1854, a reciprocity treaty was signed between the United States and British North America. Just prior to Confederation, however, the United States withdrew from the reciprocity treaty thus emphasizing the need for a wider British North American market to replace the already-lost trade with the United Kingdom and with the United States. There is no doubt that the Province of Canada, with its slowly developing industrial base, felt it needed some kind of hinterland as a market for its goods. The Province of Canada was looking both to the east and to the west. By the late 1850s and early 1860s the feeling was growing that the western regions of what is now Canada would soon have to be settled or they would be lost to the United States.

The Province of Canada no doubt saw itself as the potential lynchpin of a new empire to replace the old British Empire. When we look at the British North America Act, 1867, we see in its terms a replication in many respects of the British Empire. Ottawa is given substantial power to deal with any potential threat to central dominance. The power of reservation placed in the federally-appointed lieutenant governors of the provinces, and the absolute veto over provincial legislation, in the form of the disallowance power, are very strong evidence of the ability of the federal government to exercise the same powers which London exercised over its far-flung colonies.

The Atlantic provinces also were concerned about their geographical and economic isolation and began to feel that a larger political and economic union was an increasingly pressing necessity. Nova Scotia and New Brunswick, particularly, expected to receive economic benefits from union in the form of a common tariff, an outlet for the sale of their natural products and a source of manufactured articles. They were also particularly desirous of having a railway link with the Province of Canada, both from the point of view of military security and especially from that of achieving more expeditious transportation links for the marketing of their goods. Prince Edward Island and Newfoundland were not as influenced by economic factors although later, as we shall see, Prince Edward Island became so encumbered by debt that joining the union in 1871 became a virtual necessity in the resolution of its economic problems.

In addition to economic forces pushing in the direction of a larger British North American union, there were the ever-growing political problems of the Province of Canada. Many of these problems have been referred to earlier, namely the need for a double majority of members from Canada East and Canada West before important legislation was passed, and the existence of dual ministries for a number of the most important portfolios. The double majority was becoming increasingly difficult to obtain and thus the assembly was deadlocked on a great many serious issues. For example, between 1854 and 1864 there were no less than ten governments in office in the province. In fact, between 1841 and 1867 there were at least eighteen different governments formed to run the affairs of the province.[16]

Another pressing problem was the increasing demand by Canada West for representation by population. Under the Union Act of 1840, Canada East and Canada West each had forty-two representatives in the lower house. At that time the population of Lower Canada exceeded that of Upper Canada by several hundred thousand. By 1861 the situation was dramatically reversed and the population of Canada West was now some three hundred thousand in excess of that of Lower Canada. Some attempts at tinkering were made in 1853, by increasing the membership in the lower house to 130, but the principle of equal representation from each division of the province was not changed. Accordingly, the demands of Canada West were not satisfied. The movement from an appointed to an elected legislative council did nothing to mitigate the demands for electoral reform. Tensions were exacerbated by the rivalries between the largely English-speaking Protestant population of Canada West and the largely French-Speaking Roman Catholic population of Canada East. Putting together a government which was satisfactory to both of these two interest groups was growing more and more difficult. The double majority, though it recognized the sociology of the province, was making political viability increasingly impossible.

Another important factor which pressed British North America into union was the increasing militancy of the United States. In 1861 the Civil War between the North and South commenced with important potential ramifications for Canada. Increasingly, hard feelings developed between Britain and the United

States because many northerners felt Britain was too friendly with the southern Confederacy. It was suggested that retaliatory measures could be taken through the conquest of the British North American provinces. It must be remembered that on two previous occasions the United States had invaded portions of British North America and, in 1776, had nearly been successful in capturing all of what is now Ontario and Quebec. Only the arrival of the Royal Navy, at almost the last minute, saved Quebec City from falling into American hands.

The leadership in the colony of Quebec preferred the easy-going tolerance of Great Britain to the puritanical zeal of the United States. For English Canada, rooted as it was in a United Empire Loyalist tradition of rejecting American Republicanism, absorption by the United States was totally abhorrent. Canada, if nothing else, was a rejection of the whole concept of populist republicanism. Americans could never understand why these subjects of the British Crown rejected their visions of a new world political utopia. For example, the New York Tribune, on May 10 1867, stated "When the experiment of the 'dominion' shall have failed — as fail it must — a process of peaceful absorption will give Canada her proper place in the great North American Republic."[17] Not dissimilarly, the New York Herald trumpeted the desirability of the ultimate American takeover of the British colonies. The New York Times and the New York World were not quite as belligerent. Nevertheless, all gave voice to the view that ultimately the northern British possessions should come under the dominance of the United States.

The British North Americans were also very concerned about the fact that the United States had put together the largest conscript army known until that time, and there were fears that this army would be turned against a relatively defenceless Province of Canada. Great Britain had been astounded by the defeat of the Militia Bill of 1862, when the Province of Canada refused to vote sufficient funds to substantially increase Canadian military preparedness. Canada's unwillingness to substantially increase taxes for her own self-defence led Britain to conclude that the British North Americans should join together in order to more effectively exist with their giant American neighbour. Thus the British government threw its entire support behind the concept of British North American union. This was particularly noticeable in New Brunswick, where the British governor played a very important role in bringing about the election which brought to power a pro-Confederation government.[18]

The Eve of Confederation

The first initiatives with respect to union came from Nova Scotia.[19] The premier of that province had the legislature approve a resolution that delegates from that province should meet with appointees from New Brunswick and Prince Edward Island to consider a union of the three provinces into one governmental unit. The legislatures of the three provinces thereupon agreed to meet in September of 1864 at Charlottetown to decide upon the feasibility of union of the three Atlantic provinces.

Meanwhile, in the Province of Canada, increasing concern was being expressed about the viability of the province and the need for a wider political union. To the astonishment of many observers, George Brown, the long-time political opponent of Sir John A. Macdonald, agreed to join in a coalition with the object of seeking a general British North American federation. The leaders of the Canadian government accordingly felt that the best prospect for a wider union was to send representatives to the Charlottetown conference in the hope that some kind of political integration could be achieved between the Maritime provinces and the Province of Canada. The conference proved to be surprisingly successful and, though very little is known about what was actually agreed upon at Charlottetown, certainly it is clear that guidelines for the union were determined and generally accepted. The only exception to this proposition was the reluctance of Prince Edward Island to go along with the views of its larger neighbours. It was decided to press on towards Confederation as quickly as possible and, accordingly, the conference adjourned its sessions and quickly reconvened at Halifax, at St. John, and then at Fredericton. It must be emphasized that these were secret sessions and that what was actually decided upon is somewhat difficult to determine. Much of the mystery was swept away at the Quebec Conference of 1864 when clearly defined propositions were reached with respect to the shape and form of the new nation. These resolutions are available and one can see in them the framework of the British North America Act of 1867. Newfoundland, which had not been present at the earlier meetings, was represented by two delegates at the Quebec Conference. Each province, though it had a number of representatives, had only one vote, with the exception of Canada which was given two votes because of the long-standing tradition of Upper and Lower Canada.

The Quebec Conference re-endorsed the view accepted at Charlottetown that the system should be built along federal lines. The colonial governments were not willing to entirely submerge their existence in a unitary system. The leader of the Canadian delegation, Sir John A. Macdonald, fought hard for as centralized a form of federalism as was possible under these circumstances. He was concerned about the problems created for the United States by the division of powers inherent in a federal system. It was, however, not only necessary but desirable to follow the federal path because, as experience in the Province of Canada had illustrated, unitary government was virtually impossible. In addition, the Atlantic provinces had long-standing political and cultural traditions of their own which they were determined to maintain. In fact, Prince Edward Island and Newfoundland refused to proceed further with the idea of joining the new political confederation.

The process of consultation varied from one colony to another with respect to the series of seventy-two resolutions that emerged from the Quebec Conference. The most thorough and systematic review of these proposals took place in the legislature of the Province of Canada where, after a lengthy debate, the resolutions were accepted and the Imperial Parliament was asked to implement them. There was considerably less enthusiasm for the recommendations among the French-speaking legislators than among their English-speaking counterparts.

Many of the French-speaking parliamentarians felt that the secure position which French Canada had attained under the legal and political arrangements of the Province of Canada might be lost in the context of a larger Canadian union. In New Brunswick a general election was held on the issue of Confederation and the pro-Confederation premier suffered electoral defeat. The premier of Nova Scotia accordingly decided to avoid either an election or a straight vote on the Quebec resolutions. In April of 1866 the Nova Scotia assembly merely passed a resolution recommending the appointment of delegates to consult with the British government in order to achieve a union which would effectively guarantee the rights of the province. In the same year and in the same month the government of New Brunswick was virtually squeezed out of office by the British governor and in the consequent election the pro-Confederation party secured a majority government. The unionist forces were aided in this regard both by the support of the British government and by the financial and other contributions from political interests in the Province of Canada. After the election the New Brunswick legislature passed a resolution in almost identical terms to that of Nova Scotia.

It is quite true that by 1866 various Canadian provinces had achieved control over their purely domestic affairs. Nevertheless, in the areas of foreign trade, international relations and constitutional matters, the British government and parliament still retained ultimate control. Legally, short of declaring independence, the only method by which a new union could be achieved was by an Act of the British parliament. Accordingly, in December of 1866 the delegates from Nova Scotia, New Brunswick and the Province of Canada gathered together in London and held what came to be known as the London Conference. The early chairman of the meetings was Sir John A. Macdonald but he was ultimately replaced in January of 1867 by Lord Carnarvon, the then colonial secretary. Carnarvon's influence was to push the federation in a yet more centralist direction. However, it was the Colonial Office which blocked the attempt by Macdonald to name the new country the "Kingdom of Canada," largely for fear of alienating the United States.

The conference went through the provisions of the Quebec Resolutions in considerable detail and these ultimately evolved into what were referred to as the London Resolutions. The British parliamentary draftsmen, working from the text of the London Resolutions, then placed before the conference the first draft of what was to become the British North America Act, 1867. The passage of the bill was smooth and unspectacular. It received Royal Assent on March 29, and was proclaimed on May 22 with the provision that it was to come into effect on July 1, 1867. The only attempt to discourage the proceedings was a petition, bearing 30,000 signatures, presented to the Imperial government asking postponement of the passage of the bill until after the Nova Scotia election. Nova Scotians in very large numbers were having second thoughts about the desirability of this larger political union. In fact, the overwhelming majority of the federal members of parliament for Nova Scotia elected after the new country was created were dedicated to the repeal of the British North America Act.

Only Charles Tupper among the Nova Scotia M.P.s was completely dedicated to the support of this new constitutional statute. Similarly, in the first provincial election held in Nova Scotia after Confederation, thirty-six of the thirty-eight M.L.A.s elected were dedicated to taking the province out of the new federation. All attempts at changing the course of these events proved to be fruitless and the British government was unwilling to receive representations from the province asking that they be allowed to secede from Canada.

The Nature and Structure of the B.N.A. Act, 1867

The British parliament in 1867 essentially put into legislative form the wishes of the political representatives from the Province of Canada, New Brunswick and Nova Scotia. During the passage of the Canada Act and the Constitution Act, 1982, those involved stressed the fact that this was a 'made in Canada' constitution. What is often forgotten, however, is that the British North America Act, 1867 was also a Canadian-made constitution, both in the sense that pre-Confederation Canada had, through difficult struggle, developed a system of responsible government in the pre-Confederation colonies, and that the content of the Act was essentially devised by the political representatives of the respective pre-Confederation colonies.

Since the passage of the Constitution Act, 1982, the British North America Acts of 1867 to 1975 have been renamed and we now have the Constitution Act, 1867. The essential content of the Act, however, is the same today as when it was originally enacted. Many people seem to labour under the misapprehension that the passage of the Canada Act, 1982 and the Constitution Act, 1982 in some way obliterated the British North America Act, 1867 from the pages of our Constitution. Nothing could be further from the truth, as the Constitution Act, 1867 is still at the heart of the Canadian constitution.

The preamble to the statute spoke of a country "federally united into One Dominion under the Crown of the United Kingdom of Great Britain and Ireland, with a Constitution similar in Principle to that of the United Kingdom." Three important principles are contained in this guiding phrase, namely the desire for a federal union, a monarchy and essentially a parliamentary system similar to that of the United Kingdom. The Act is very logically organized and, after the preamble, proceeds to provide in Part II for the union of the three provinces into a Dominion to be called Canada.[20] Part II is also important because it provides for four provinces, Nova Scotia, New Brunswick, Ontario and Quebec, the latter two provinces created by the division of the Province of Canada.

Since most of the major portions of the Act will be dealt with in considerable detail throughout this work, it is unnecessary to deal with them at any length at the present time. A quick overview of the structure and general content of the Act, however, is important for the reader.

Part III of the statute deals with executive power and its key section, of course, is section 9, which vests executive government in the queen. The rest of the sections relating to executive power deal with the Privy Council. The important point to note, however, is that there is no reference to the cabinet or to the office of prime minister in this part of the Act. It seems fairly clear, however, that the phrase in the preamble referring to a "Constitution similar in principle to that of the United Kingdom" was designed to cover the fact that the traditions of parliamentary government as developed prior to Confederation would continue in existence.

Part IV of the statute deals with federal legislative power and, accordingly, creates a parliament for Canada consisting of the Senate and the House of Commons. There then follow some very detailed provisions with respect to the organization, composition and structure of the Senate and House of Commons. Also in this part of the statute are important provisions with respect to money votes and the powers of reservation and disallowance. The latter provisions granted Ottawa the power to disallow provincial legislation acting through the governor general in council. Similar powers were reserved for the British government vis-a-vis federal legislation, thus further illustrating the view that Ottawa saw itself in relation to the provinces as London had at one time stood in relation to the federal government.

Having set up the institutions of central government in Canada, the Act then, in Part V, deals with an often-forgotten subject, provincial constitutions. Here we see provisions relating to executive and legislative power in the provincial context. Part VI of the Act has been the occasion for more judicial interpretation than all of the rest of the statute combined. It is the provisions of Part VI which divide legislative jurisdiction between the federal parliament on the one hand and the provincial legislatures on the other. The phrases allocating powers were necessarily vague and thus endless conflicts have arisen over the meaning of rather ambiguous words, particularly in sections 91 and 92 though subsequent sections like 93, 94 and 95 also allocated important legislative powers.

Part VII of the Act allocates responsibility for what is referred to as the judicature. Essentially this means defining who has responsibility for creating courts, appointing, paying and removing judges, and providing administrative services for the courts so created. These provisions are relatively sparse because no court is created, the power to do so simply being allocated between the federal parliament and provincial legislatures. It was envisaged that there would continue to function, vis-a-vis Canada, the Judicial Committee of the Privy Council which, though technically not a court, essentially acted as the highest court of appeal for judicial matters coming from the British Empire to London. It was not until 1875 that the Parliament of Canada, acting under the authority of section 101, created the Supreme Court of Canada. Even then appeals could still be taken to the Judicial Committee until 1949.

Part VIII of the Act is entitled "Revenues; Debts; Assets; Taxation." These sections of the Act contain the beginnings of federal-provincial fiscal arrangements. It was obvious from the start that the central government would have to take some responsibility for the economic debts and destiny of its component parts. One section, however, particularly stands out. Section 109 vests in the provinces the revenue with respect to "Lands, Mines, Minerals, and Royalties."

Part IX is labelled "Miscellaneous Provisions." Two sections which particularly stand out here are section 132, dealing with the domestic implementation of empire treaties, and section 133, which deals with the use of the English and French languages in the federal parliament and in federally-created courts, and in the Quebec provincial legislature and provincially-created courts. This is not recognition of English and French as official languages. Nevertheless, it is a recognition that in certain arenas both of these languages are to be given equal stature.

It is interesting to note that Part XI, which consists of only two sections, deals with the admission of other colonies. It was quite clear that the Fathers of Confederation had as one of their specific objectives the formation of a "sea to sea" British North American nation. In fact, in section 146, specific processes are defined for the potential admission of Newfoundland, Prince Edward Island and British Columbia, as well as Rupert's Land and the North-Western Territory. We shall see in the next chapter how section 146 is used to bring about a much wider Canadian union.

---

[1] See Maurice Ollivier, *British North America Acts and Selected Statutes*. Ottawa: Queen's Printer, 1962, pp. 14–16.

[2] See J. R. Mallory, *The Structure of Canadian Government*. Toronto: Gage, rev. ed., 1984, p. 7.

[3] See further J. Murray Beck, *The Government of Nova Scotia*. Toronto: University of Toronto Press, 1957, chapter 1.

[4] See further R. MacGregor Dawson, *The Government of Canada*. Toronto: University of Toronto Press, 5th ed. revised by Norman Ward, 1970, chapter 1.

[5] 14 Geo. III, c. 83 (U.K.).

[6] J. M. S. Careless, *Canada: A Story of Challenge*. Toronto: Macmillan, rev. ed., 1970, p. 110.

[7] Toronto: Dundurn, 1982.

[8] See Ollivier, supra, note 1, pp. 18–20.

[9] See further Careless, supra, note 6, chapter 10.

[10] George F. G. Stanley, *A Short History of the Canadian Constitution*. Toronto: Ryerson, 1969, p. 47.

[11] Constitution Act, 1867, 30–31 Vict., c. 3, s. 54, (U.K.).

[12] See Stanley, supra, note 10, p. 67.

[13] See further Stanley, supra, note 10, chapter 3.

[14] Ibid.

[15] See further Careless, supra, note 6, chapter 13.

[16] See further Stanley, supra, note 10, pp. 73–75, and Dawson, supra, note 4, p. 21.

[17] See P. B. Waite, *The Life and Times of Confederation: 1864-1867*. Toronto: University of Toronto Press, 1962, p. 29, n.10.

[18] See Dawson, supra, note 4, chapter 2.

[19] See E. Russell Hopkins, *Confederation at the Crossroads: The Canadian Constitution*. Toronto: McClelland and Stewart, 1968, chapter 7.

[20] For a detailed commentary on the Act, see W. H. McConnell, *Commentary on the British North America Act*. Toronto: Macmillan, 1977.

4

CONSTITUTIONAL HIGHLIGHTS BETWEEN 1867 AND 1982

Entry of the Post-Confederation Provinces

The Fathers of Confederation envisaged a much wider British North American union than that achieved in 1867. Section 146 of the British North America Act, 1867 provided a specific procedure whereby Newfoundland, Prince Edward Island and British Columbia would be admitted into the new Canadian nation. It also provided a process with respect to the admission of Rupert's Land and the North-Western Territory. Section 146 provided for entry through the use of an order in council passed by the British Privy Council. Put into the crudest possible terms, this amounted to a process requiring the approval of the British cabinet and the reigning monarch of the day. An order in council by the British Privy Council could not take place, however, unless there had been approval of the Houses of the Canadian parliament and of the legislatures of the specified provinces. This meant that union could not be imposed upon Newfoundland, Prince Edward Island and British Columbia without their consent. With respect to Rupert's Land and the North-Western Territory, Her Majesty in Council would not act except after a request by the Senate and House of Commons of Canada. Thus, though the legal technique of admission was British, the process would occur only at the request of the appropriate Canadian legislative chamber or chambers as the case might be. Accordingly, the terms of union with respect to admission varied somewhat from one province to the next.

It is somewhat ironic that Canada's fifth province turned out to be Manitoba, which was not even referred to in section 146 because it did not exist as a separate colony at the time of Confederation. What is now the province of Manitoba was part of what is generally referred to as Rupert's Land and the North-Western Territory. The province of Manitoba was created by a process not mentioned in section 146, namely by Act of the Canadian parliament, in this case the Manitoba Act.[1] So doubtful was the validity of the Manitoba Act that the British parliament was asked to pass, in 1871, a statute which retrospectively granted the Parliament of Canada the power to create provinces out of territories "forming for the time being part of the Dominion of Canada, but not included in any Province thereof. . . ." By virtue of section 2 of the British

North America Act, 1871,[2] the federal parliament could also provide for "the constitution and administration of any such Province. . . ."

It was quickly recognized, however, that if parliament could create a province it could also destroy it, thus undermining the essence of federalism, namely the independence of regional and central governments. Accordingly, section 6 of the British North America Act, 1871, provided that a Canadian statute creating a new province could not be subsequently amended by the Canadian parliament. Thus prior to 1982, the Manitoba Act, the Saskatchewan Act[3] and the Alberta Act[4] were federal statutes which could not be amended by the parliament which enacted them. The Constitution Act of 1871 is now entrenched and cannot be changed except in accordance with the amendment formula in the Constitution Act of 1982. The Manitoba Act, 1870, the Saskatchewan Act and the Alberta Act are all also entrenched by the Constitution Act, 1982.

The creation of Manitoba was undoubtedly the most controversial of that of any of the provinces. In the events leading to Manitoba joining the Canadian nation, a clash between the central government in Ottawa and would-be Ontario settlers on the one hand, and the French-speaking, fur trading Metis on the other was apparent. The Metis were concerned both about their language and culture and, at the same time, their economic livelihood. The eastern Canadian settlers wanted to move an agriculturally-based Ontario society westward. The whole matter was very badly handled by the Canadian government and its representatives who, in their anxiety to add new Canadian provinces to the Canadian union, entered what is now Manitoba prematurely and began devising landmarkings following the model of Ontario farms. The result was that Louis Riel set up a provisional government to resist being overrun by eastern settlement, especially prior to the working out of suitable terms for entry into Confederation. An unfortunate and tragic consequence of these events was the shooting of Thomas Scott, one of the relatively few non-Metis settlers in the Red River colony. Despite this event and the turmoil in the small settlement which was later to become the city of Winnipeg, an accommodation was finally reached between the Metis and the government at Ottawa.

At the time the provisional government was set up by Riel, the North-Western Territory and Rupert's Land were not yet part of Canada. The Hudson's Bay Company had handed the territory to Britain but Britain had not yet passed the order in council required by section 146 to make Rupert's Land and the North-Western Territory part of Canada. The Manitoba Act, 1870 received Royal Assent on May 12, 1870 but it was not until July 15, 1870 that the imperial order in council turned over this vast expanse of western land to Canada.

The Manitoba Act set up the institutions of government for the new province. The legislature was to consist of not only the lieutenant governor but also of two houses: the Legislative Council of Manitoba and the Legislative Assembly. In 1876, however, the legislature of Manitoba voted to abolish the upper house, purportedly acting under the authority of subsection 92(1) of the British North America Act, 1867 which provides that the province can amend its own constitution "except as regards the Office of Lieutenant Governor."

The abolition of the upper house in Manitoba has gone unchallenged legally, but two other provisions of the Manitoba Act have turned out to be highly contentious both legally and politically. In recognition of the Metis' majority in the province, section 22 of the Manitoba Act guarantees the rights and privileges of denominational schools in the province. It is in essence a replication of section 93 of the British North America Act, 1867, which guaranteed denominational school rights in Ontario and Quebec. Section 22 goes somewhat further, however, guaranteeing not only legal rights with respect to denominational schools but containing the phrase in subsection (1) that the legislature must not only respect the denominational school rights obtained by law, but also by "practice in the Province at the Union." This section was a focal point in later attempts to take away important Roman Catholic school rights and led to what was referred to as the Manitoba School Crisis. The crisis was ultimately successfully resolved and denominational school rights have continued to be protected in the province.

If section 22 is particularly interesting for the political tensions and conflicts it created, section 23 is noteworthy because of the very recent case law pertaining to it. Section 23 provided that the English and French language could be used in the debates of the legislature and in the records and journals of the legislature. It also provided that either language could be used in the courts created by the province, and that the statutes of the legislature must be printed and published in both the English and French languages. In 1890 the legislature, purporting to act under the authority of subsection 92(1) of the British North America Act, 1867, made English the official language of the province. This legislation stood unchallenged until the relatively recent decision in the case of *Attorney General of Manitoba* v. *Forest*,[5] in which the Supreme Court of Canada held that the Manitoba Language Act of 1890 was unconstitutional and that the English and French rights defined in section 23 were to be protected. The result has been that Manitoba has now embarked on the very time-consuming and expensive task of translating its statutes into the French language.[6]

The next stage in the completion of Canada was the admission of British Columbia. This was achieved under the terms of section 146 of the British North America Act, 1867. British Columbia had had a turbulent history and was also in serious financial difficulties. The first British colony on what is now Canada's west coast was on Vancouver Island. Sometime later, in 1858, an influx of American miners seeking gold led to the passage of a British statute which made the mainland of British Columbia a separate colony. Although Vancouver Island had a small elected assembly, the new colony of British Columbia was governed without one. In 1866 the British parliament passed a new statute uniting the two colonies under a government composed of a governor and council, most of the members of which were appointed. A British order in council passed prior to the union with Canada provided that the majority of members should be elected. This led to the setting up of an elected assembly.[7]

One of the main reasons for British Columbia joining Canada was its desire to form a link with the rest of British North America. An attempt in 1869 to bring about the colony's annexation to the United States failed dismally when only 104 persons signed the annexation document.[8] The handful of colonists on Canada's west coast were determined to retain their link with the Crown and, feeling the desperate isolation of their situation, recognized that only a wider British North American union could stop their ultimate absorption by the United States. Accordingly, in the schedule to the order in council admitting British Columbia, the government of Canada undertook to construct a railway from the Pacific to the existing railway system of Canada. Canada also assumed the debts and liabilities of the colony prior to union. In addition, provisions for a federal subsidy were included. The terms of union also provided for the "introduction of responsible government when desired by the inhabitants of British Columbia. . . ."[9] To the best of our knowledge this is the only legal document in which one ever finds reference to the term 'responsible government.' Though it is without question one of the most, if not the most, important principles relating to the functioning of the Canadian constitution, its total absence from legal terminology is fascinating and is very reflective of the British tradition of leaving much of the actual conduct of constitutional functioning to usage and convention rather than to positive law.

British Columbia was slow in developing the rigidities of the party system as we now know it. It was not until the assumption of office by Sir Robert McBride in 1903 that strict party discipline and party labels became a fixed part of the provincial political lexicon. It must also be remembered that although explorers had reached the Pacific ocean by hazardous voyages down the rivers of British Columbia, early settlement had come by sea largely from London and San Francisco. Thus British Columbia developed a political culture which, in many ways, was more European than that of other parts of Canada. Early settlers were strongly linked to a British upper middle class and aristocratic tradition. Later, British coalminers were brought in to Vancouver Island, this being one of the factors leading to the development of probably the most powerful trade union movement in any province in Canada.

In 1873 Prince Edward Island became the seventh Canadian province by virtue of a British order in council passed under the terms of section 146 of the British North America Act, 1867. It will be remembered that Prince Edward Island delegates had participated in the Charlottetown and Quebec Conferences but had decided not to join the new nation in 1867. A combination of economic problems, absentee ownership of land and the need for transportation links with the mainland ultimately induced Prince Edward Island to join Canada.

Manitoba had been carved out of Rupert's Land and the North-Western Territory by virtue of the Manitoba Act, 1870. As population moved west it became increasingly necessary for the Dominion government to recognize the political implications of western settlement. Accordingly the federal parliament, acting under the authority of the British North America Act, 1871, in 1905 passed the Alberta Act and the Saskatchewan Act. These statutes, as did the Manitoba Act, provided for the institutions of government in those provinces and for representation in the federal parliament. Those portions of the North-Western Territory which were not given provincial status remained under federal control. They now constitute the Yukon Territory and the North West Territories. The Yukon Territory has developed a high degree of self government and during the brief Conservative regime of Joe Clark there was considerable discussion with respect to granting the Yukon provincial status. The subsequent return to power of a Liberal government halted discussion along those lines.

Newfoundland, like Prince Edward Island, had participated in the discussions at Charlottetown and Quebec but refused to go to the London Conference of 1866. Discussions were reopened in 1868 between Newfoundland and Canada. In fact, a delegation from the island visited Ottawa and worked out the general framework for union with Canada. The pro-Confederation government was defeated in 1869 however, and accordingly Newfoundland remained separate until it ultimately joined Canada in 1949. Here again economics played a very powerful role in the union. In 1934 the colony had gone into such serious debt that a commission form of government had to be struck, equally composed of representatives from Newfoundland and from Great Britain. As a consequence of this action Newfoundland fell under the ultimate control of the British parliament and accordingly received British funds to stave off financial collapse. However, by 1946 the economic situation had dramatically improved and it was quite clear that a commission form of government was growing increasingly inappropriate. In a rare departure from the Canadian practice of non-popular consultation, Newfoundland finally decided in a hard-fought referendum won only by the narrowest of margins, to join Confederation. Accordingly the British parliament passed the British North America Act, 1949[10] making Newfoundland a part of Canada. In addition, the federal parliament passed the Terms of Union of Newfoundland with Canada Act,[11] which is essentially composed of a schedule outlining the terms of union.

Newfoundland was placed on a somewhat different footing than the other provinces in a number of areas, perhaps one of the most notable being that of education. Considerable detail was also devoted to the economic arrangements between Canada and the future province, the provisions being much more specific with respect to Newfoundland than are those with respect to other provinces. Especially noteworthy is section 37 of the aforementioned schedule, which deals specifically with the subject of natural resources. Unfortunately perhaps for Newfoundland, this section does not refer to jurisdiction over offshore mineral rights, undoubtedly because the technology of the time was insufficient to conduct offshore mining and oil drilling operations. This issue has now been resolved in favour of the federal government by the Supreme Court of Canada.[12]

The British North America Act, 1949 has been renamed the Newfoundland Act and is part of the schedule of entrenched acts attached to the Constitution Act, 1982.

The Judicial Committee of the Privy Council and the Establishment of the Supreme Court of Canada

No review of the high points of Canadian constitutional history would be complete without looking at the development and impact of the Judicial

Committee of the Privy Council and the Supreme Court of Canada. Constitutions in modern times are more influenced by judicial decisions than by any other process of change. The conventions of the constitution with respect to cabinet government discussed earlier are now largely in place and will change only at a glacial pace. Similarly, though we now have a domestic amending formula, it is so rigid that we can expect only piecemeal changes from time to time.

The courts, however, right from the passage of the British North America Act in 1867, have been charged with the task of interpreting the words of constitutional documents. Until the passage of the Constitution Act, 1982, the most important of these documents was the Constitution Act, 1867. Even this proposition can be narrowed somewhat to say that most of the judicial decisions revolved around the interpretation of sections 91 and 92 of the Act of 1867 as these were the most important legal provisions dividing legislative power between the provinces and the central government. The courts will continue to wrestle with the problems posed by the division of powers but, in addition, the ambit of their authority will be increased by the interpretation and application of the Charter of Rights. It is impossible to outline in any detail the hundreds of decisions of the courts related to the Constitution. Nevertheless, some brief overview of the role of the judiciary must be part of any summary of the high points of Canada's constitutional evolution since its founding in 1867. At this point, it is appropriate to concentrate essentially on two judicial bodies with a view to reviewing their roles in Canada's constitutional evolution.

The Constitution Act, 1867 does not create any courts; rather it vests in the Parliament of Canada and in the legislatures of the provinces the power to create courts. It was assumed, as in the case of the conventions relating to cabinet government, that the practices developed before Confederation would be continued after Confederation. Accordingly, as with conventions and responsible government, there is no mention of the Judicial Committee of the Privy Council. The Judicial Committee, as its name implies, was not a court in the proper sense of the word. Instead, it was a group of legal advisors to the monarch and his or her Privy Council giving advice regarding how to dispose of appeals from the countries and colonies first of the British Empire and later of the Commonwealth. It also had and still has some domestic jurisdiction.

Most, but not all, of the countries have now ceased appeals to the Judicial Committee. Canada, by amendment to the Supreme Court Act,[13] abolished appeals to the Judicial Committee of the Privy Council in 1949. During the period from 1867 to 1949 the Judicial Committee made decisions which, in many ways, moved Canada from a quasi-federal nation to a truly federal state.[14]This means in essence that the legislative powers of the federal and provincial legislatures were put on a much more equal basis than might appear from a cursory reading of the Constitution Act, 1867. The authors, however, take the view that the highly centralized federation desired by Macdonald was unrealistic in view of the cultural diversity and geographical size of the country. The Judicial Committee seems to have been sensitive to the fact that, especially because of the presence of Quebec, the provinces must remain in control of their destinies, particularly in the private law field. This view is most clearly and dramatically expressed in the case of *Citizens Insurance Co. of Canada* v. *Parsons*,[15] where the Judicial Committee quite clearly points out its concerns with respect to the protection of the autonomy of Quebec's private law. The Judicial Committee, in what was probably its most important case on the trade and commerce power, says, in what was obviously an attempt to limit the scope of the federal power over trade and commerce, that if this power was given its widest interpretation it could

> . . . *legislate in regard to contracts in all and each of the provinces and as a consequence of this the province of Quebec, though now governed by its own Civil Code, founded on the French law, as regards contracts and their incidents, would be subject to have its law on that subject altered by the dominion legislature, and brought into conformity with the English law prevailing in the other three provinces, notwithstanding that Quebec has been carefully left out of the uniformity section of the Act.*[16]

Here Sir Montague Smith's words reflect an underlying policy concern of the Judicial Committee, namely that there was a duty to protect the autonomy and integrity of Quebec's private law. Later in the judgment he goes on to indicate that the phrase "civil rights" was used in the Quebec Act of 1774 as part of Britain's commitment to preserving the autonomy and integrity of French Canada in the midst of English-speaking British colonies. This reflects a sensitivity on the part of the Judicial Committee to the fact that Quebec was not a province like the others, and that there were fundamental guarantees to Quebec in the Act of 1867 which the Judicial Committee of the Privy Council was going to protect. It is therefore quite understandable that although Quebec did not oppose the abolition of appeals to the Judicial Committee of the Privy Council, it did not greet this move with the enthusiasm of many of the constitutional observers in the rest of Canada.[17]

In considering the substantial impact which the Judicial Committee had on the development of federalism in Canada, one cannot categorize all of their decisions as leaning in the provincial direction as this would be a gross distortion of reality. For example, in 1946, in the case of *Attorney General for Ontario* v. *Canada Temperance Federation*,[18] the Judicial Committee opened the way for extended federal power by holding that the federal parliament could use the peace order and good government clause of section 91 as a basis for federal legislation. Since that decision a number of important pieces of federal legislation have been sustained using the national interest test. Nevertheless, the real significance of the Judicial Committee was its recognition of a coordinate and equal role for the provinces with respect to the division of executive and legislative powers.

In the executive field the Judicial Committee, through its decision in the case of *The Liquidators of the Maritime Bank of Canada* v. *The Receiver General of New Brunswick*,[19] dramatically hastened the transition of the lieutenant governor from a federal officer into a representative of the monarch. In that case the Judicial Committee held that the lieutenant governor possessed all of the prerogative powers of the Crown.[20]

In the famous case of *Hodge* v. *The Queen*[21] the court held that within its legislative sphere of competence the provincial legislature was supreme. It was in no sense a delegate of either the Imperial Parliament or the Parliament of Canada. This meant in essence that if the court determined that the provincial legislature was within the designated powers outlined in the Constitution Act, 1867 then its legislation was valid.[22] These two cases were important not only for the significant legal power attributed to the executive and legislative levels of government but also because they underlined the federal nature of Canada in that they put the provinces within their sphere on an equal plane with the federal government. They were important steps in turning Canada into a genuinely federal nation, in which neither level of government was subordinate to the other.[23]

The *Maritime Bank* case, and the *Hodge* decision also coincided with an increased pressure from some provincial governments to enhance their stature and role in the federal system. It is ironic to note, in light of recent constitutional cooperation between Ontario and the federal government, that it was Ontario under the leadership of Premier Mowat that led the way in the fight for recognition of provincial autonomy in the context of the Canadian federal system. The Quebec nationalist premier Honore Mercier joined with Mowat to battle the increasing assertiveness of the dominion government under Sir John A. Macdonald. In a most significant event in Canadian constitutional history, Mercier invited the provincial governments to meet at Quebec in October 1887 to form a common front against the national government. Macdonald refused to have anything to do with the conference as did British Columbia and Prince Edward Island. Nevertheless the conference probably served as the model for one of Canada's most important institutions, namely the federal-provincial conference. The federal-provincial conference has since become one of the chief informal methods whereby important questions are resolved through political debate. Two items are of particular importance in this regard: agreement on federal-provincial financing arrangements and arrangements with respect to changes in the Canadian Constitution.

It was these important years of the 1880s and 1890s which began to slowly move Canada away from the overwhelming control of Ottawa toward a more equal relationship between the central and regional governments. This shift just prior to the turn of the century should not be overestimated because Ottawa was still the dominant government. Nevertheless, the seeds of a more balanced Canadian federalism were being planted at both the political and legal levels. The decisions of the Judicial Committee of the Privy Council were serving to underline and contribute to the changing nature of Canadian federalism.

The Supreme Court of Canada

The British North America Act, 1867 did not provide for the establishment of any court but rather assigned to the federal parliament and provincial legislatures the legislative authority to create courts.[24] In the meantime it provided that existing courts would continue until such time as parliament or the legislature had replaced them with new judicial bodies.[25] Later this work will give a fuller discussion of the structure and organization of the judiciary in Canada. It is sufficient in this brief summary of high points in Canada's constitutional development to refer to only one Canadian court, namely the Supreme Court of Canada.

The Supreme Court was created by federal statute in 1875 acting under the authority of section 101 of the Constitution Act, 1867. This section provided that "the Parliament of Canada may, notwithstanding anything in this Act, from Time to Time provide for the Constitution, Maintenance, and Organization of a General Court of Appeal for Canada. . . ." There were two attempts prior to 1875 to establish the court but these efforts proved fruitless until the passage of the Supreme Court Act in 1875. Even then there was considerable controversy as to whether the Supreme Court of Canada should have final jurisdiction with respect to appeals brought to it. The statute was so nebulous on this point that appeals to the Judicial Committee of the Privy Council continued after the creation of the Supreme Court of Canada.[26]

After the creation of the Court in 1875, bills were introduced in the House of Commons in 1879 and 1880 respectively urging the abolition of the Court. They were defeated after lively debate. A good deal of the criticism of the Court centred around the quality of the decisions rendered by it and the time taken in handing down reasons for judgment. Undoubtedly a good deal of the criticism centred on the fact that some of the initial appointments to the Court were based on factors of patronage rather than legal ability. Despite this shaky beginning, the Court remained in existence, although it was overshadowed until 1949 by the existence of the Judicial Committee of the Privy Council. It must be noted that it was possible for litigants to by-pass the Supreme Court of Canada entirely and bring an appeal directly from the highest court of the province to the Judicial Committee. In fact, it has been noted that about one third of Canada's constitutional cases between 1867 and 1949 did not go to the Supreme Court of Canada at all but rather proceeded directly to the Judicial Committee.[27] Although the Judicial Committee frequently expressed its desire that cases should go through the route of the Supreme Court of Canada, it was customary for litigants to try to obtain leave from the highest provincial appeal court or from the Judicial Committee itself to avoid the extra cost of going to the Supreme Court of Canada.

The Court was originally made up of six judges with a seventh judge added to the roster in 1927. It was not until 1949, appropriately coinciding with the abolition of appeals to the Judicial Committee, that two more judges were added, bringing membership on the Court to its present figure of nine. Originally it was provided that two of the judges must come from Quebec; it is now required by statute that three of the judges must come from that province.[28] The purpose of this provision was to ensure that there would be enough judges on the Court who were sufficiently trained in the Quebec Civil Law to hear matters from the province of Quebec. It is now traditional usage that three of the other judges come from Ontario, two from the four western provinces and one from the four Atlantic provinces.

In this very brief survey of the high points of Canadian constitutional development it is difficult to synthesize in a few words the impact of the Supreme Court of Canada. It is certainly easy to underline the fact that the Supreme Court of the United States has been incomparably more powerful in the American constitutional system than has the Canadian Supreme Court in relation to the Canadian constitutional structure. A number of reasons can be advanced for this proposition and have already been catalogued by one of the authors.[29]

The primary reason advanced then was the concept of the supremacy of parliament; namely. . .

> the notion that, as long as the federal and provincial legislatures are acting within their assigned legislative spheres their enactments cannot be rendered invalid by the courts. This, of course, can be compared with the American concept which allows the courts to declare invalid any legislation which transgresses those entrenched portions of state and federal constitutions protecting human rights. This, in effect, has meant that there is no Act of either the United States Congress or a state legislature which cannot be overruled as being unconstitutional by at least some part of the American judiciary.[30]

This meant essentially that the Supreme Court of Canada's constitutional role was confined to determining whether a particular statute fell within the appropriate legislative sphere as defined by the Constitution Act, 1867. This did give the court considerable scope in striking down legislation which it felt to be undesirable. Nevertheless, it did not allow the court the scope possessed by the United States Supreme Court. The passage of the Constitution Act, 1982 will change this situation dramatically and will put the Supreme Court of Canada on the same footing with the United States Supreme Court, in that it will be able to strike down legislation both on the ground that it is beyond the legislative powers of the appropriate legislative body and that it transgresses the Charter of Rights.

We are still left with the question, however, of what the impact of the court on the years between 1949 and 1982 has been. Has the court dramatically altered the direction of Canadian federalism? Two of the most distinguished scholars of the Canadian constitution take very different positions on this challenging question. Professor Peter Hogg writing in the Canadian Bar Review states

> My conclusion is that the Supreme Court of Canada has generally adhered to the doctrine laid down by the Privy Council precedents; and that where the court has departed from those precedents, or has been without close precedents, the choices between competing lines of reasoning have favoured the provincial interest at least as often as they have favoured the federal interest. There is no basis for the claim that the court has been biased in favour of the federal interest in constitutional litigation.[31]

Professor Ken Lysyk, however, (now Mr. Justice Lysyk of the British Columbia Supreme Court) states:

On the surface, the court's track record since 1949 resembles that of the Privy Council less than it does that of the United States Supreme Court, where a successful challenge to an Act of Congress on the basis that it has trespassed upon the exclusive domain of the states has become an increasingly rare event.

With respect to what has been seen as the Supreme Court of Canada's restrictive approach towards provincial power and an expansionist view of federal authority, perhaps the single most important area has been in connection with recent decisions involving the federal power to regulate trade and commerce. [32]

Professor Hogg freely admits from his study of the statistics that a much higher proportion of provincial statutes have been held unconstitutional than have federal statutes. [33] Professor Hogg, despite these statistics which appear to show a bias in the federal direction, urges extreme caution in the interpretation of this data, arguing that "this situation stems from the nature of the Canadian federal system, not from any bias on the part of the judges." He looks at the fact that there are ten legislative bodies enacting provincial laws and that the provinces are accordingly often innovative "social laboratories" with a tendency to experiment more readily with radical political ideas. He also argues that because of the geographical limits of the provinces they are more vulnerable to challenge on the basis of extra-territorial impact. In addition he feels that technological developments have served to make the courts more sympathetic to federal regulations than to provincial control.

Professor Lysyk, as he then was, tends to stress the quality of the decisions rendered by the Supreme Court of Canada. He is particularly concerned by relatively recent decisions of the Supreme Court of Canada with respect to provincial control of natural resources. In particular he cites two decisions in which the court struck down legislation enacted by the provincial legislatures with respect to oil and with respect to potash. [34] He sees an increasing threat to provincial control over agriculture manifested in the decisions striking down provincial legislation in the case of *Burns Foods Ltd. v. Attorney General for Manitoba* [35] and in the case of *Attorney General for Manitoba v. Manitoba Egg and Poultry Association.* [36] Professor Lysyk sees these decisions among others as increasingly whittling down the authority of the provinces in the economic sphere in favour of the federal parliament. He also resorts to a number of recent decisions in the field of communications which he feels dramatically reflect excessive sympathy for federal positions at the expense of those of the provinces. [37] He is also concerned about the decision in the *Anti-Inflation Reference* case where he felt the court was too ready to accept parliament's judgment as to those circumstances which would allow it to enact sweeping powers to regulate the national economy under the guise of an emergency. [38]

The authors have of necessity very briefly synthesized the views of these two distinguished scholars. Readers who wish to pursue this matter further are urged to read these articles in full. The authors' view is to lean more in the direction of the position taken by Professor Lysyk than in that of the position adopted by Professor Hogg. It is especially in the area of trade and commerce that the trend has seemed to favour the federal position. Professor Hogg admits that the decision regarding the Manitoba egg marketing scheme and the striking down of Saskatchewan's scheme to control the production and price of potash constitutes a shift away from the fairly considerable autonomy granted to the provinces to control local trade. Certainly the decision in the *Canadian Industrial Gas and Oil Ltd.* case was regarded by Saskatchewan as such a blow to provincial control over natural resources that the province pressed successfully for an amendment to section 92, allowing for indirect taxation in the area of natural resources and some degree of legislative control over interprovincial export of natural resources.

Conversely, although the anti-inflation legislation of the federal parliament was sustained, the court sustained it on the very narrow ground of emergency rather than the much broader and easier to satisfy test of a national interest or national dimension. It is also clear that the Supreme Court has been more than fair to the provinces in restricting through a number of decisions, the jurisdiction of the Federal Court of Canada. These decisions have gone a long way towards preserving the integrity of Canada's traditional judicial structure. Certainly the decision in the *Reference re Upper House* case[39] was a severe warning to the federal government to be cautious about unilateral moves to amend the Constitution. This view was reinforced in the *Reference re Amendment of the Constitution of Canada*[40] whereby the court, though it held that a unilateral request for parliamentary action by the United Kingdom was legally valid, found that such a request was contrary to convention. This decision slowed federal initiatives and contributed to bringing about federal-provincial agreement, except for Quebec, before proceeding to London.

Provincial critics of the decision, however, would probably underline the fact that the court, by saying that agreement of a substantial majority of Canadian provinces was sufficient, very much undermined the traditional position of Quebec. Nevertheless, this decision is probably regarded by most observers as generally being in the interests of the provinces. Thus, except for the area of trade and commerce, the position taken by Professor Hogg is probably valid, but it is also our view that Professor Lysyk is completely correct in pointing out that although the Supreme Court of Canada uses the same tests with respect to trade and commerce as did the Judicial Committee of the Privy Council, the members of the court have been prepared to narrow the definition of what constitutes local trade.

The future impact of the court deserves comment. It seems almost axiomatic that with the entrenchment of a Charter of Rights binding both the provincial legislatures and federal parliament, the scope for judical review will be broadened dramatically. This means that now not only must the federal parliament and provincial legislatures satisfy the court that they are within their appropriate legislative spheres but also that their legislation does not violate the Charter of Rights. This will give the court considerably more opportunity to strike down legislation with which it disagrees. It is generally recognized that in the past the division of powers often served as a means whereby legislation could be held unconstitutional, but the court is now equipped with another important legal weapon in the form of the Charter.

Statute of Westminster, 1931

One of the highlights relating to Canada's legal autonomy with respect to the United Kingdom was the passage by the British parliament of the Statute of Westminster, 1931.[41] In 1865 the British parliament had passed the Colonial Laws Validity Act[42] which provided that no Canadian or other colonial law would be invalid if it clashed with a British statute unless that statute applied to the overseas colony either specifically or by clear implication in the British statute. This Act was liberating in that prior to 1865 the pure theory was that any colonial statute in conflict with a British statute was void on the ground of repugnancy. This was a technical term meaning that a clash between two statutes rendered the colonial statute void. In practice this was an impossible principle to fulfil because it so constricted the area of legislation available to the colonial legislatures. Accordingly the doctrine of repugnancy was in fact ignored in most areas of law. It turned out, however, that one of the judges in the Australian colonies began to apply literally the doctrine of repugnancy, and in order to clarify the situation the British parliament passed the Colonial Laws Validity Act. This meant that conflicting domestic laws were void or repugnant only if the British parliament clearly intended the British legislation to apply overseas.

The doctrine of repugnancy was essential in the maintenance of Canada's federal system. If either the central or provincial governments could unilaterally alter each other's jurisdiction then the basic principles of federalism would be violated. Federalism by definition means that the federal and provincial legislatures are independent within their spheres and that one cannot alter the other except through the use of some extraordinary process involving joint federal-provincial participation or, as in Australia, the use of a plebiscite. Thus, the British North America Act, 1867 and all the subsequent British North America Acts remained under control of the British parliament because any attempt by Canadian legislatures to legislate contrary to their terms would be held void on the grounds of repugnancy.

This doctrine had not proved to be a source of difficulty or embarrassment for Canada until the first attempt to partially cut off appeals to the Judicial Committee of the Privy Council. In *Nadan* v. *The King*[43] the Judicial Committee of the Privy Council had held that the attempt to abolish appeals in criminal matters by the federal parliament was unconstitutional in that it clashed with two British statutes, namely the Judicial Committee Acts of 1833 and 1844[44] and was therefore void on the grounds of repugnancy. In addition, the Judicial

Committee held that Dominion legislatures still did not have the power to legislate extra-territorially, that is, beyond their borders, and that therefore on these two grounds the federal revisions abolishing criminal appeals were unconstitutional. In order to remove some of these fetters the British parliament asked for consultation with the representatives of Canada, Australia, New Zealand, South Africa, the Irish Free State and Newfoundland, who ultimately agreed to the passage of the Statute of Westminster. The Statute provided in section 2 that the Colonial Laws Validity Act, 1865 should no longer apply to the parliament of a dominion: henceforth no law passed by "the Parliament of a Dominion shall be void or inoperative on the ground that it is repugnant to the law of England, or to the provisions of any existing or future Act of Parliament of the United Kingdom. . . ." This meant, in effect, the abolition of the doctrine of repugnancy, meaning that Canada would be free, as would the provincial legislatures, to operate without fear of having their legislation found void on the grounds of clashing with the United Kingdom statute.

This provision immediately created anxieties for the provinces and as a result of the efforts of Premier Ferguson of Ontario there was included in section 7 of the Act the following provision: "Nothing in this Act shall be deemed to apply to the repeal, amendment, or alteration of the British North America Acts, 1867 to 1930, or any order, rule or regulation made thereunder." This meant that for the British North America Acts, the doctrine of repugnancy still applied. Premier Ferguson and his provincial allies had quickly recognized that if the doctrine of repugnancy was not maintained for the British North America Acts, the federal parliament, or for that matter the provincial legislatures, could immediately pass legislation repealing or varying the division of powers as provided for in the British North America Act, 1867, without any fear of this legislation being declared invalid. Accordingly, the inclusion of subsection 7(1) was necessary to preserve the federal principle, namely that there could be no unilateral action on the basic constitutional statutes without some consultative process. It must be remembered that it was generally accepted at this time that the Canadian government would not request parliamentary action by Britain without the agreement of the provinces. Thus a de facto kind of amending formula involving federal-provincial agreement had developed through usage and practice rather than through specific legal provision as in the case of the United States.

The Statute also contained other important provisions. It recognized in its preamble that the established tradition was that the United Kingdom Parliament would not legislate with respect to the dominions except on their request and with their consent. This convention was put into specific language in section 4, which provided that no United Kingdom statute would apply to a dominion "unless it is expressly declared in that Act that that Dominion has requested, and consented to, the enactment thereof." In addition, section 3 of the Statute provided that henceforth any dominion could pass laws having extraterritorial effect, thus removing the only other important legal barrier to the dominions attaining sovereign power. It was also provided in the preamble that since the Crown was the unifying symbol of the British Commonwealth of Nations, no change in the law governing succession to the throne or with respect to the royal style and titles should be made without the agreement of the parliaments of all of the dominions. This proved to be an important factor in the abdication of Edward VIII in that the British government refused to act unilaterally with respect to his abdication without first obtaining the advice and agreement of the dominions to whom the Statute of Westminster applied.

In conclusion, the passage of the Statute of Westminster meant that in the case of Canada the British could not act except at Canadian request, and that Canadian legislation could not be struck down on the grounds that it was contrary to British law. However, the British North America Act, 1867 and the amendments thereto were still subject to the doctrine of repugnancy, that is to say they could not be altered by Canadian federal or provincial legislative action but only through a request by Canada to the United Kingdom Parliament. In all other respects Canada was left legally autonomous.

Constitutional Review and the Road to the Constitution Act, 1982

There were no special provisions in the British North America Act, 1867 for its amendment. The Act was a statute of the United Kingdom Parliament, and it was accordingly assumed that it would be amended in the same manner as any other British statute. Included in the Act were phrases which stated that particular sections were to remain in effect "until the Parliament of Canada otherwise provides,"[45] or "until the Legislature of Ontario or of Quebec otherwise provides."[46] These were relatively minor provisions — dealing, for example, with the duration of the legislative assembly[47] — where it was envisaged that domestic arrangements would have to be made. Similarly, subsection 92(1) provided that a provincial legislature could amend its provincial constitution with the exception of the office of lieutenant governor. This meant that although the provincial legislature could not actually amend the British statute it could, through its own enactment, render sections of the British North America Act, 1867 spent. The most dramatic illustration of this was the abolition of Quebec's upper house and the changing of the name of the Quebec legislative assembly to that of the National Assembly, both accomplished by Quebec statute.[48] In summary, the powers of both the federal parliament and the provincial legislatures to render portions of the British North America Act, 1867 spent were still relatively minor, and by and large amendment of this fundamental constitutional document remained in the hands of the United Kingdom Parliament.

It must have been understood in 1868[49] that the British parliament would not act without Canadian initiative. This first occurred prior to the passage of the British North America Act, 1871 when the Canadian government requested the amendment which legitimized the creation of the province of Manitoba. A new element entered the amendment equation when the House of Commons unanimously adopted a resolution stating that the executive government of

Canada should not seek changes by the British parliament without the approval of the Canadian parliament. The cabinet responded to this resolution by obtaining from the Senate and House of Commons a joint address approving the content of the bill to be passed by the British parliament. Accordingly it became accepted practice that the Canadian government would not request British parliamentary action without the approval of the Senate and the House of Commons.

A further change occurred in 1906 when the federal government called together a federal-provincial conference to discuss a change in the financial subsidies paid to the provinces. The original provisions in the British North America Act, 1867 were now dated and in addition new provinces had joined confederation. The conference produced an agreement between the federal government and all of the provinces except British Columbia. The Canadian government felt, however, that despite the objections of British Columbia (which wanted more federal funds) it had sufficient support to revise federal-provincial fiscal relations, and after receiving approval of the Senate and House of Commons requested and obtained the passage by the British parliament of the British North America Act, 1907.[50] Subsequent changes to the constitution were enacted by Great Britain with only federal approval. However, these changes primarily related to matters of concern to the federal government only and did not substantially alter relationships between the federal and provincial governments. All amendments to the Constitution which in direct and clear language altered the division of powers were only passed by the British parliament at the request of federal and provincial governments, and after a joint resolution of the Senate and the House of Commons. The 1930 amendment, which transferred control over natural resources to the western provinces, received the approval of only those provinces directly affected.[51]

Surprisingly, two amendments did not receive provincial assent although it could be argued that they substantially affected federal-provincial relationships. These statutes were the British North America Act of 1949 and British North America (No. 2) Act, 1949.[52] These amendments respectively provided for the entry of Newfoundland into Confederation and granted authority to the federal parliament to amend the federal government's own constitution. With respect to the latter amendment, the then prime minister, Mr. St. Laurent, argued that he was merely putting the federal government in the same position with respect to its own internal constitution as the provinces were with respect to theirs. He was referring, of course, to the power of the provinces to amend their constitutions under subsection 92(1) of the British North America Act, 1867. Of more interest perhaps is the British statute admitting Newfoundland into Confederation. A resolution was moved in the House of Commons urging that this step should not take place without consultation with the provincial governments, but the federal government took the position that this statute did not affect the division of powers and therefore was dissimilar to amendments such as that of 1940, which vested control of unemployment insurance in the federal parliament.[53]

Nevertheless by 1965 the federal government, issuing a paper on the amendment process in Canada, under the name of the Honourable Guy Favreau, stated that four clear principles had now emerged. The first of these principles to be stated in the Favreau White Paper was that no legislative action would be taken by the United Kingdom Parliament except upon formal request from Canada. Secondly, parliamentary approval should be obtained before a request to the British parliament was made. Thirdly, the British parliament should not act upon a request from a Canadian province, recognizing that the only appropriate vehicle for making such a request was the federal government. The final and undoubtedly most important principle was that the Canadian parliament would not request an amendment ". . . directly affecting federal-provincial relationships without prior consultation and agreement with the provinces."[54] This latter proposition turned out to be the most controversial one when the federal government attempted unilateral action with respect to the Constitution in 1981.

The Favreau White Paper was issued in connection with the attempts in 1964 and 1965 to find a purely domestic amending formula. These were not the first attempts to do so, as in 1927 a federal-provincial conference gathered to discuss the subjects of patriation and an amending formula. Similarly, in 1935 and 1936 there were once again federal-provincial discussions with respect to finding a purely Canadian method of amending the Constitution. The most serious efforts made prior to the unilateral action of Mr. Trudeau in 1981 were the so-called Fulton-Favreau formula generated in 1965 and the so-called Victoria Charter which ultimately emerged in June of 1971. The Fulton-Favreau formula dealt exclusively with finding a domestic amending formula whereas the Victoria Charter included not only an amending formula but other substantial changes to the Constitution. Both of these attempts failed because of the objections of Quebec. Essentially Quebec took the view that patriation should not take place until some of Quebec's demands regarding the division of powers were met. The thrust of Quebec's objections in both 1965 and 1971 was that the province should have greater autonomy, and that until this demand was satisfied there should be no resolution in legal form of the amendment question.

Prior to 1967 the thrust of formal constitutional change centred around the finding of a domestic amending formula. With the coming to power in 1960 of the Lesage Liberals in Quebec there was an even greater push for provincial autonomy than there had been under the regime of the previous Union Nationale government. Premier Duplessis, the long-time leader of the Union Nationale, had tended to stress the greater autonomy of the province in terms of a higher proportion of tax revenue rather than any thrust toward a redrafting of the Constitution. He accordingly fought a running battle with the federal government during the federal-provincial conferences on the distribution of tax revenues.

When Premier Lesage came to power he was basically concerned with reform of the governmental, social and economic structure of Quebec. Certainly the government did not seem to develop any clear cut strategy with respect to obtaining dramatic changes in the country's constitutional structure. They obviously recognized that many of Quebec's needs could be satisfied within the context of the existing constitutional system. Nevertheless, the Lesage government rejected the Fulton-Favreau formula because they felt it imposed a constitutional strait jacket on Quebec and that prior to the formulation of an amending procedure it was desirable that Confederation be reshaped. The Fulton-Favreau formula imposed unanimity for amendment of large areas of the Constitution, and Quebec took the view that its aspirations for a wider legislative jurisdiction could be forestalled by the opposition of merely one province.

The year 1966 brought back the Union Nationale to power in the province of Quebec. The new premier, Daniel Johnson, requested an early and wide-sweeping revision of the Constitution with greater recognition of Quebec's role in Confederation. The government of Ontario became increasingly alarmed over the prospect of escalating tensions between Quebec and the federal government and accordingly took the initiative in calling an interprovincial conference on the future of Confederation. The Confederation for Tomorrow Conference accordingly met in November of 1967 in the city of Toronto. Although the federal government was unhappy with this provincial initiative, it nevertheless sent four federal officials to act as observers. The federal government at that time did not regard revision of the Constitution as a matter of priority, but did in effect resent these initiatives coming from the provincial level of government. Accordingly the federal government called together a constitutional conference in February of 1968 for the purpose of reviewing the Constitution. The federal government felt that three areas should be considered, first protection of human rights, second, central institutions of Canadian federalism, and third, the always difficult problem of the division of powers between the federal parliament and the provincial legislatures. A series of federal-provincial conferences was held after that initial meeting in February of 1968, culminating in the June, 1971 meeting in the city of Victoria, from which emerged the "Victoria Charter."

That charter was only the beginning of what was hoped to be an overall review of the Constitution. It contained a formula for patriation and amendment of the Canadian Constitution. It elucidated the entrenchment of certain human rights, although in much briefer form than ultimately emerged in the Charter of Rights enacted in 1982. It contained important provisions with respect to the English and French language in both the Parliament of Canada and all of the provincial legislatures except Saskatchewan, Alberta and British Columbia. It also had provisions with respect to the use of the English and French languages in federally-created courts and in the courts of Quebec, New Brunswick and Newfoundland. A good deal of the charter was taken up with a very complicated process for selecting judges for appointment to the Supreme Court of Canada. This process required consultation with the provinces. The existing provisions in the Constitution with respect to the reservation and disallowance of provincial legislation were to be removed.[55] Once again Quebec refused to accept the charter, advancing as its rationale that the provisions with respect to social welfare did not coincide with Quebec's objectives. Many, however, felt that Quebec opposed the charter for reasons very similar to its opposition to the Fulton-Favreau amending formula, namely a feeling that Quebec's future role in Confederation should be more clearly defined before putting in place a rigid domestic amending formula.

After the failure to achieve consensus with respect to the terms of the Victoria Charter, constitutional review was not discussed at the senior governmental levels until Mr. Trudeau indicated in 1974 that he was prepared to look at the question of patriation alone. He suggested that patriation be achieved on the basis of the Victoria Charter amending formula. At the interprovincial conference held in August of 1975 the premiers restated that patriation was a "desirable objective" but that this issue should be dealt with "in the context of a general review of the distribution of powers, control of resources, duplication of programs and other related matters."

In March of 1976 Mr. Trudeau, in a letter to the premiers, indicated that he was prepared to take on the task of a modified constitutional review involving either 1) patriation alone, 2) patriation with the Victoria amending formula, or 3) patriation with the Victoria amending formula and a series of other issues including language rights, Supreme Court provisions, and regional disparities among others. At the interprovincial premiers' meetings in August and October of 1976 the premiers wrote to the prime minister urging the desirability of constitutional patriation and attaching the stipulation that a great many matters affecting provincial legislative powers should also be reviewed. These included greater provincial involvement in immigration, language rights, provincial jurisdiction in the area of taxation of natural resources, and the use of the declaratory power only with the permission of the province or provinces concerned. In addition the premiers felt that a number of other matters, such as communications, the Supreme Court, spending power and Senate representation, should be examined. In a telex from the prime minister to the premiers on January 20, 1977 the prime minister indicated that he was once again prepared to embark on an extensive constitutional review if the premiers so wished. It must be remembered that this constitutional review was certainly stimulated by the election to power in Quebec of the Parti Quebecois. Though the party did not fight the 1976 election on the basis of independence, the rationale of its existence was to achieve either complete independence or an extraordinary degree of autonomy in the context of an almost common market arrangement with the rest of Canada.

The year of 1978 turned out to be a frenetic one with respect to constitutional review. Not only were there exchanges between the federal and provincial governments but also there were statements from other organizations, such as the Canada West Foundation's paper entitled "Alternatives" indicating changes it felt should be made in Canada's constitutional functioning. In April of 1978 the Ontario Government's Advisory Committee on Confederation issued its first report indicating what it felt were desirable changes in the Constitution. Perhaps the highlight of that year was the sudden emergence of Bill C-60, prepared by a special committee of the federal government. This bill was drafted in such a way as to form a model for a comprehensive redrafting of the Canadian

Constitution. It was, of course, legally impossible for the federal parliament to pass this bill because much of what was contained within it was a direct impingement on the legislative jurisdiction of the provincial legislatures, but presumably it was designed to provoke a broad rewriting of the Canadian Constitution. Federal government spokesmen certainly agreed that portions of the bill dealt with matters of provincial concern. However, they took the view that certain parts of it could be implemented by the federal parliament as they dealt solely with matters of federal concern.

Parliamentary critics of the bill focussed their fire on the question of whether the federal parliament could alter or abolish the structure of the Senate and redefine the role and powers of the monarchy. Ultimately the federal government felt that it would place before the Supreme Court of Canada the question of whether parliament alone could pass an enactment dealing with either abolition or reform of the Senate of Canada. In what must have been something of a shock to the federal government, the Supreme Court of Canada unanimously upheld the view that the federal parliament could not by itself change the nature of the Senate of Canada, it being beyond the control of the federal parliament as a result of subsection 91(1) of the British North America Act, 1867.[56] This subsection provided that although certain constitutional matters could be dealt with by the Parliament of Canada, a number of categories of subjects could be dealt with solely by the British parliament. The first and most important of these categories was, of course, "classes of subjects by this Act assigned exclusively to the Legislatures of the provinces." The statute went on to say that only the British parliament could pass amendments to the Constitution with respect to "rights or privileges by this or any other Constitutional Act granted or secured to the Legislature or the Government of a Province." The Supreme Court of Canada held that the Senate was one of the rights or privileges of provincial governments and accordingly unilateral action by the federal parliament was unconstitutional. This decision was a clear warning to the federal government that it could not, through federal parliamentary action, encroach upon the legislative jurisdiction or other rights of the provinces.

In 1979 and 1980 other reports and documents appeared with various proposals for changes in the Canadian Constitution. In July of 1977, the federal government had created a task force on Canadian unity, generally referred to as the Pepin-Robarts Committee, which was charged with hearing briefs from citizens and groups across the country with a view to making recommendations for changes in the constitutional system. The Committee's report appeared in January 1979 and, much to the surprise of the federal government, it advocated a highly decentralized Canadian federation giving very considerable recognition to the claims of Quebec for more autonomy. Needless to say, Prime Minister Trudeau was to some extent embarrassed by the report and it was obvious that it was destined for a speedy burial.

Meanwhile, in the latter part of 1979 the government of Quebec issued an important document entitled "Quebec-Canada: A New Deal." The subtitle of this work was "The Quebec Government Proposal for a New Partnership between

Equals: Sovereignty-Association." This work was in large part a review of Canadian history from a Quebec nationalist perspective and an argument that Quebec's destiny would best be served by forming a loose association with Canada using the euphemism of "sovereignty-association" rather than independence. Its proposals in effect amounted to a form of common market with Canada and certain shared institutional structures relating to matters such as currency. In essence, however, if the proposals contained in this document had been carried out, Quebec would have been virtually an independent sovereign nation.

This document was part of the build-up towards the referendum held in May of 1980 in which the Quebec voters were asked whether they wished to enter into negotiations on sovereignty-association with the rest of the country. In the course of the campaign leading to the vote, the provincial Liberal party issued its own detailed document called "A New Canadian Federation." This document, which became very closely identified with the leader of the then Liberal party, Claude Ryan, soon came to be known as the Beige Paper. It proposed an even more decentralized Canada than had been advocated in the Pepin-Robarts Commission. During the course of the campaign leading to the referendum on sovereignty-association, Prime Minister Trudeau pledged changes in the Canadian Constitution but carefully avoided giving any specific detail. It is possible that many voters assumed that the reconstructed Canadian federalism would follow some of the lines indicated in the Pepin-Robarts Commission or the Beige Paper. It was accordingly quite a shock to people like Claude Ryan when the prime minister finally introduced his package of constitutional change.[57]

Through the summer of 1980 there were a series of ministerial meetings leading to a First Ministers Conference in Ottawa in September of that year. Substantial negotiations took place on twelve subjects and a high degree of accord was achieved on a number of these items. Prime Minister Trudeau, however, did not seem satisfied that sufficient agreement was achieved and accordingly on October 6 he introduced into the House of Commons "A Proposed Resolution for a Joint Address to Her Majesty the Queen Respecting the Constitution of Canada." This format was a resolution, namely a statement of support in principle, for a request to the Queen in her capacity as head of state in Great Britain to lay before the parliament of the United Kingdom a bill which would translate the resolution into law. Attached to the resolution was the exact bill which Canada wished the United Kingdom Parliament to pass. It was assumed that the British parliament would not in any way alter the text of the resolution but would in essence act as a legal rubber stamp. The problem with this action by the federal government was that, as indicated in the earlier part of this chapter, there had arisen a tradition that where provincial matters were concerned the federal government would make no request for amendment to the United Kingdom Parliament without provincial consent. The fourth principle of the Favreau White Paper was a clear endorsation of this principle of federal-provincial unanimity.

Eight of the provinces immediately protested this unilateral action by the federal government. Nevertheless, the resolution was passed by the Liberal-dominated House of Commons and Senate in April of 1981. The April 1981 version of the amendment, however, was never sent to the United Kingdom for enactment because in the meantime the provinces had mounted a challenge in the courts regarding the legality of unilateral action by the federal government. Two provinces, namely Ontario and New Brunswick, supported the position of the federal government. Three of the eight opposing provinces, namely Manitoba, Quebec and Newfoundland, had in the meantime sought judicial rulings on the constitutionality of the federal government's unilateral action.

By April 1981 the decisions in the three Courts of Appeal had been rendered[58] and an appeal was taken from the Manitoba decision to the Supreme Court of Canada. The Courts of Appeal of Quebec and Manitoba ruled that the federal action was legal whereas the Court of Appeal of Newfoundland held the opposite. It perhaps should be noted that the Manitoba decision was narrowly decided with the court dividing three to two on the correctness of the federal government's position. The Supreme Court of Canada heard arguments between April 28 and May 4, 1981 and ultimately rendered its decision on September 28, 1981. The Supreme Court held by a majority of seven to two that legally the federal government could proceed unilaterally with a request for United Kingdom parliamentary action. However, the court held by a majority of six to three that a "substantial degree" of provincial consent was required by convention before any request could be made to the United Kingdom Parliament to alter the Constitution relating to federal-provincial relationships.[59]

The decision of the Supreme Court of Canada forced Prime Minister Trudeau to seek a "substantial degree" of support for his package before sending it to the United Kingdom Parliament for enactment. Ultimately, with the exception of Quebec, agreement was achieved between the provinces and the federal government in November of 1981. Quebec continued to dissent and refused to enter into any kind of agreement with the federal government and the other provinces. A new resolution was placed before the House of Commons embodying the changes agreed upon by Ottawa and the provinces in November of 1981. Essentially this involved certain trade-offs, whereby the provinces accepted the idea of a Charter of Rights in exchange for the right to opt out of certain portions of the Charter of Rights, and the inclusion in the resolution of a provincially-drafted amending formula. The ultimate version of the resolution was passed by the House of Commons and Senate in December of 1981.

The United Kingdom Parliament passed the legislation in March of 1982, with Royal Assent being given by Her Majesty Queen Elizabeth II on March 29, 1982. The legislation was called the Canada Act, 1982, and attached was a schedule referred to as the Constitution Act, 1982. With the giving of Royal Assent on March 29th the Canada Act, 1982 became law for Canada. However, it was provided in the Constitution Act, 1982 that that Act would not come into force until proclaimed by the Queen in her capacity as Queen of Canada. Accordingly Queen Elizabeth came to Ottawa and on April 17, 1982 signed the Proclamation bringing the Act into force as of that day. In essence that Act involves some important changes to the existing Canadian constitutional structure but it is certainly a long way from being a substantial rewriting of the Canadian Constitution.[60]

The Nature and Structure of the Canada Act, 1982 and the Constitution Act, 1982

It is now appropriate to give an overview of the results of the events which led to the passage of the Canada Act, 1982. Because a substantial portion of the rest of this book will refer in detail to specific provisions of this legislation, it is unnecessary to examine it in detail here. Instead, the writers will attempt to summarize the essence of the legislation and to determine where it fits into the overall structure of the Canadian Constitution. The Act starts out with a preamble to the effect that Canada has requested and consented to the passage of legislation by the United Kingdom Parliament giving legal effect to the provisions of the Canada Act, 1982 and the Constitution Act, 1982. The essence of the Canada Act, 1982 is contained in section 2 which provides that "No Act of the Parliament of the United Kingdom passed after the *Constitution Act, 1982*, comes into force shall extend to Canada as part of its law." As a result, the United Kingdom Parliament will no longer legislate for Canada. The provision is often colloquially referred to as the "signing-off clause." The remainder of the Canada Act, 1982 establishes the legality of the Constitution Act, 1982 and the fact that the English and French versions will be of equal validity.

The Constitution Act, 1982 was attached to the Canada Act, 1982 and entitled Schedule B to the aforementioned Act.[61] It is rather unusual to see another entire Act as a Schedule attached to an Act. However, presumably it was intended that in time the Canada Act, 1982 would be increasingly forgotten in the course of the study of the Canadian Constitution. Perhaps another reason for enacting the Constitution Act as a schedule was that the Canada Act came into force immediately upon the assent of Queen Elizabeth II in her capacity as Queen of the United Kingdom whereas it was provided in the Constitution Act, 1982 that it would only come into force upon proclamation of Her Majesty.

The Constitution Act, 1982 opens with a preamble that states: "Whereas Canada is founded upon principles that recognize the supremacy of God and the rule of law." It then goes on to elucidate what is referred to in section 1 as the Canadian Charter of Rights and Freedoms. Part I of the Act, the Charter, encompasses sections 1 to 34 and includes a number of subdivisions such as fundamental freedoms, democratic rights, mobility rights, legal rights, equality rights and official languages of Canada.[62] These are preceded by a clause indicating that none of these rights are unlimited in that they are ". . . subject only to such reasonable limits prescribed by law as can be demonstrably justified in a free and democratic society." [63] Furthermore, section 32 provides that the Charter applies to the parliament and government of Canada, including the Yukon Territory and the Northwest Territories and in addition, to the legislature and government of each province. It should be noted, however, that section 33 indicates that parliament or the legislature of a province can expressly declare that a statute or a provision of a statute can operate without being subject to the provisions of section 2 or sections 7-15 of the Charter. This is often referred to as the *non obstante* clause and was inserted at the request of the provinces as part of the accord reached between the federal government and the nine provincial governments.

Part II of the Act deals with the aboriginal and treaty rights of Canada's aboriginals, who are defined as the Indian, Inuit and Metis peoples of Canada. Part III deals with equalization and regional disparities. Part IV provides that there shall be a constitutional conference one year after the coming into force of the Charter of Rights and Freedoms and that one of the responsibilities of this conference will be to identify and define the rights of the aboriginal peoples of Canada. Part V of the Act is a procedure for amending the Canadian Constitution and the terms of this part of the Act will be analyzed in the next chapter. Part VI of the Constitution Act provides for the addition of a new section, namely section 92A to the Constitution Act, 1867, and it provides for wider provincial jurisdiction with respect to non-renewable natural resources.

Part VII consists of sections 52-60, the most important provision being subsection 52(1), which makes it clear that "the Constitution of Canada is the supreme law of Canada, and any law that is inconsistent with the provisions of the Constitution is, to the extent of the inconsistency, of no force or effect." Subsection 52(2) defines what is meant by the Constitution of Canada. It includes

(a) the *Canada Act, 1982*, including this Act;
(b) the Acts and orders referred to in the schedule; and
(c) any amendment to any Act or order referred to in paragraph (a) or (b).

Attached to the Constitution Act, 1982 is a Schedule of Acts and orders in council that are accordingly entrenched by section 52, which means that they can only be changed by the use of the amending formula. These are the documents referred to in section 52 as the supreme law of Canada. Any law inconsistent with the provisions of this legislation is accordingly illegal or, to use the constitutional term, *ultra vires*. The Schedule to the Act provides that the names of most of these British statutes still applicable to Canada have been changed as have the names of the orders in council admitting Prince Edward Island and British Columbia. For example, the order in council admitting British Columbia is to be henceforth referred to as the British Columbia Terms of Union. In almost every instance where the words "British North America Act" were used in the name of a statute they have replaced by the words "Constitution Act." Finally a few very minor changes are made with respect to other pieces of legislation. These changes are indicated in Column II of the Schedule to the Constitution Act, 1982. In particular, section 4 of the Statute of Westminster is repealed along with subsection 7(1). Thirty legal documents are listed in the schedule and all are, by section 52, defined as entrenched. As will be noted in the next chapter, however, questions can be raised as to whether other pieces of legislation become entrenched by virtue of the provisions of the Constitution Act, 1982. In conclusion, one can see that the legislation of 1982 did not provide for a new Canadian Constitution but merely added another building block to the existing Canadian constitutional structure.

---

[1] 33 Vict., c. 3 (Can.).

[2] 34-35 Vict., c. 28 (U.K.).

[3] 4-5 Edw. VII, c. 42 (Can.).

[4] 4-5 Edw. VII, c. 3 (Can.).

[5] [1979] 2 S.C.R. 1032; see also Bilodeau v. Attorney General of Manitoba, [1981] 5 W.W.R. 393 (Man.C.A.).

[6] See Cheffins and Tucker, "Provincial Constitutions," The Provincial Political Systems. Toronto: Methuen, David J. Bellamy, Jon H. Pammett and Donald C. Rowat, eds., 1976, p. 257. For further information with respect to Manitoba, see W. L. Morton, Manitoba: The Birth of a Province. Altona, Man. : Manitoba Record Society, W. D. Smith, ed., 1965.

[7] R. MacGregor Dawson, The Government of Canada. Toronto: University of Toronto Press, 5th ed., revised by Norman Ward, 1970, p. 17.

[8] J. M. S. Careless, Canada: A Story of Challenge. Toronto: Macmillan, rev. ed., 1970, p. 263.

[9] See item 14 to the schedule to the order in council admitting British Columbia, which can be found in Maurice Ollivier, British North America Acts and Selected Statutes. Ottawa: Queen's Printer, 1962, pp. 174, 178.

[10] 12-13 Geo. VI, c. 22 (U.K.).

[11] 13 Geo. VI, c. 1 (Can.).

[12] Reference re Jurisdiction over the Seabed Offshore Newfoundland, [1984] 1 S.C.R. 86.

[13] Now, R.S.C. 1970, c.S-19.

[14] See K. C. Wheare, Federal Government. Toronto: Oxford University Press, 4th ed., 1963.

[15] (1882) 7 A.C. 96 (P.C.).

[16] Ibid., per Sir Montague Smith, p. 111.

[17] For the most fully developed defence of the Judicial Committee of the Privy Council see Cairns, "The Judicial Committee and its Critics" (1971), 4 Can. J. Poli. Sci., 301.

[18] [1946] A.C. 193 (P.C.).

[19] [1892] A.C. 437 (P.C.).

[20] For a fuller description of this case, see R. I. Cheffins and R. N. Tucker, The Constitutional Process in Canada. Toronto: McGraw-Hill Ryerson, 2nd ed., 1976, pp. 88-89.

[21] (1883) 9 A.C. 117 (P.C.).

[22] For a fuller comment on this case see Cheffins and Tucker, supra, note 20, pp. 31-32.

[23] It must be remembered that the federal government still had the power to disallow provincial legislation, but by the turn of the century this power was beginning to fall into increasing disuse. However, the federal government resorted to its use eleven times in its struggle with the Alberta government in the years between 1935 and 1942.

[24] Sections 92(14), 101.

[25] Section 129.

[26] For a detailed history of the developments preceding and following the establishment of the Supreme Court of Canada, see MacKinnon, "The Establishment of the Supreme Court of Canada" (1946), 27 Can. Hist. Rev., 258.

[27] See Peter H. Russell, Leading Constitutional Decisions. Ottawa: Carleton University Press, 3rd ed., 1982, p. 6, n.8.

[28] Supreme Court Act, R.S.C. 1970, c.S-19, s.6.

[29] See Cheffins, "The Supreme Court of Canada: The Quiet Court in an Unquiet Country" (1966), 4 Osgoode Hall L. J., 259.

[30] Ibid., p. 263.

[31] Hogg, "Is the Supreme Court of Canada Biased in Constitutional Cases?" (1979), 57 Can. B. Rev., 721, 739. A more recent examination of this question has been undertaken by Professor

Peter Russell, "The Supreme Court and Federal Provincial Relations: The Political Use of Legal Resources" (1985), 11 Can. Public Policy, 161. Russell states at p. 168:

> *In recent years, it is my assessment that despite a reasonable balance in terms of doctrine, as well as quantitatively, Supreme Court decisions on the division of powers have been more useful to federal than to provincial politicians in the struggle over constitutional change. This perhaps has had more to do with the skill and coherence of federal players in the constitutional game than with the inherent value of the resources the Supreme Court has given them.*

[32] Lysyk, "Reshaping Canadian Federalism," *William Kurelek Memorial Lectures.* Toronto: University of Toronto Press, 1978, p. 16.

[33] In his study of the period beginning in 1950 and extending until June 1, 1979, Professor Hogg finds that sixty-five provincial statutes were challenged before the Supreme Court of Canada and that twenty-five of them were held to be unconstitutional either in their entirety or in part. During the same period he points out that thirty-seven federal statutes were challenged but that only four of them were held to be unconstitutional either in some respect or in total: supra, note 31, pp. 727-729.

[34] *Canadian Industrial Gas and Oil Ltd.* v. *Government of Saskatchewan,* [1978] 2 S.C.R. 545; *Central Canada Potash Company Ltd.* v. *Government of Saskatchewan,* [1979] 1 S.C.R. 42.

[35] [1975] 1 S.C.R. 494.

[36] [1971] S.C.R. 689.

[37] Supra, note 32, p. 18.

[38] Supra, note 32, p. 21.

[39] [1980] 1 S.C.R. 54.

[40] [1981] 1 S.C.R. 753.

[41] 22 Geo. V, c.4 (U.K.).

[42] 28-29 Vict., c.63 (U.K.).

[43] [1926] A.C. 482 (P.C.).

[44] 3-4 Will. IV, c.41 (U.K.); 7-8 Vict., c.49 (U.K.).

[45] See, for example, s.40.

[46] See, for example, s.83.

[47] Section 85.

[48] Legislative Council Act, Stats. Que. 1968, c.9.

[49] That is, when the province of Nova Scotia attempted to withdraw from Confederation; see Guy Favreau, *The Amendment of the Constitution of Canada.* Ottawa: Queen's Printer, 1965, p. 15.

[50] 7 Edw. VII, c.11 (U.K.).

[51] British North America Act, 1930, 20-21 Geo. V, c.26 (U.K.).

[52] 12-13 Geo. VI, c.22 (U.K.); 13 Geo. VI, c.81 (U.K.).

[53] British North America Act, 1940, 3-4 Geo. VI, c.36 (U.K.).

[54] Favreau, supra, note 49, p. 15.

[55] For readers interested in a much fuller discussion of the Victoria Charter, see Donald V. Smiley, *Canada in Question: Federalism in the Eighties.* Toronto: McGraw-Hill Ryerson, 3rd ed., 1980, pp. 76-79.

[56] Supra, note 39.

[57] It should be remembered that Prime Minister Joe Clark was sworn in as prime minister on June 4, 1979 and handed back the reigns of power to Pierre Trudeau on March 3, 1980, after an election in which Clark's Conservative government was defeated. Mr. Clark was not particularly interested in constitutional revision of any general kind although he did indicate that he was prepared to look favourably upon a wider role for the provinces with respect to offshore natural resources.

[58] *Reference Re Amendment of the Constitution of Canada,* (1981) 117 D.L.R. (3d) 1 (Man. C.A.); *Reference Re Amendment of the Constitution of Canada (No. 2),* (1981) 118 D.L.R. (3d) 1 (Nfld. C.A.); *Reference Re Amendment of the Constitution of Canada (No. 3),* (1981) 120 D.L.R. (3d) 385 (Que. C.A.).

[59] Supra, note 40.

[60] For readers wishing a detailed analysis of the legitimacy of the events of 1982, as well as further details on the history of attempts to amend the Canadian Constitution, see Strayer, "The Patriation and Legitimacy of the Canadian Constitution," *Dean Emeritus, F.C. Cronkite, Q.C. Memorial Lectures*. Saskatoon: College of Law, University of Sask., 1982. For even more detail on the events of 1980 through April 1982, see Peter W. Hogg, *Canada Act 1982 Annotated*. Toronto: Carswell, 1982, pp. 1-3.

[61] It should be noted that Schedule A is the French version of the Canada Act, 1982.

[62] Readers who would like a detailed section by section analysis of the Constitution Act, 1982 should see Hogg, supra, note 60.

[63] Section 1.

THE AMENDMENT FORMULA — FREEZING THE SYSTEM

The chief thrust of nearly all of the conferences on revision of the Canadian Constitution centred on the question of finding a purely domestic amending formula. It will be remembered from earlier in this work that the British North America Act, 1867 was a British statute and thus was amendable in the same manner as all other British statutes. Put in its simplest terms, this meant passage through the House of Commons and the House of Lords and the granting of Royal Assent. The drafters of the British North America Act, 1867 did, however, foresee that certain matters would require purely Canadian action and thus one sees throughout that statute the phrase "until the Parliament of Canada otherwise provides" or the phrase "until the Legislature of Ontario (or Quebec) provides." Most of the sections containing these phrases were of a relatively minor nature dealing largely with questions of the electoral map and electoral representation. In addition, subsection 92(1) provided that the legislatures of the province could provide for "the Amendment from Time to Time, notwithstanding anything in this Act, of the Constitution of the province, except as regards the Office of Lieutenant Governor." It was quite obvious that this section did not give the provincial legislatures the power to actually repeal or change the wording of the British North America Act, 1867, because only the British parliament could do so. Through their utilization of the authority of subsection 92(1), however, the provincial legislatures were in effect given the authority to render spent certain provisions of the Act. Thus the actual words remained in the British statute, but they were of no further force or effect because they had been superceded by provincial legislation which was valid under the terms of subsection 92(1).

One of the best illustrations of the foregoing was the enactment by the Quebec legislature of a statute which not only changed its name to that of the National Assembly but also abolished the Quebec Upper House. This meant that although section 69 and sections 71 to 79 all remained in the British North America Act, 1867 and still remain in the Constitution Act, 1867, they had in effect been rendered spent and accordingly superceded by Quebec legislation[1] which changed the constitution of the province of Quebec. Despite this particularly sweeping example of the power to render spent provisions of the British North

America Act, 1867, the basic amending power remained with the British parliament.

This formal authority of the British parliament was tightly ruled by conventions of the Constitution which made the British parliament essentially an instrument of Canadian will. These conventions of course required an initiative by the Canadian government, a joint resolution of the Senate and the House of Commons, and on matters involving the distribution of powers, the unanimous consent of the provinces. At least the general consensus seemed to be that unanimity was required until the decision was handed down in the *Reference Re Amendment of the Constitution of Canada* case.[2] That case of course dealt with the amendment of the Canadian Constitution and provided that "substantial consent" was all that was needed. Nevertheless, by a series of evolutionary steps, a process of amendment had been laced together involving the provinces, the federal executive, the federal parliament and ultimately, as an enacting legal automaton, the parliament of Great Britain.

In an earlier chapter we reviewed the attempts to find a domestic amending formula prior to 1982. When Prime Minister Trudeau introduced the package which was ultimately to become the Constitution Act, 1982, he included in it essentially the formula for amendment which had been specified in the Victoria Charter of 1971. The provinces had very serious doubts about this formula as they felt it was much too susceptible to federal manipulation. They accordingly set about the task of devising an amendment formula of their own, largely led in this regard by the province of Alberta, but in the later stages of draftsmanship obtaining support and advice from other provinces. Ultimately, Prime Minister Trudeau compromised by accepting the provincial amending formula and a provision for opting out of certain sections of the Charter of Rights in exchange for the binding imposition of the Charter of Rights on both the federal and provincial governments.

The subject of amendment is bound up with the concept of entrenchment. By entrenchment we mean that there are certain provisions in the constitution which are beyond the normal control of either the federal parliament or the provincial legislatures. That is to say, certain provisions of the constitution are regarded as so significant and so important that they can only be changed by an extraordinary process. In the United States the entire document known as the Constitution of the United States is entrenched and it can only be changed by the formula which is provided in that constitutional document: put in its crudest terms, the approval of two-thirds of Congress and three-quarters of the States. The situation in Canada, however, is much more complex because we first have to determine what is subject to the amending formula; in other words, which portions of Canada's constitutional rules can be changed only by resort to the amending formula specified in Part V of the Constitution Act, 1982.

Part V refers to the process necessary to amend the "Constitution of Canada. . . ." What is meant by the Constitution of Canada? This phrase is often used in a very broad sense as including constitutional conventions, judicial decisions, and important provincial and federal statutes dealing with electoral matters and the creation of courts. In the context of amendment, however, the words "Constitution of Canada" are used as a term of art. That is to say, they are used in a precisely defined way. Accordingly, it was necessary to place in the Constitution Act, 1982 a definition of the phrase the "Constitution of Canada." It is accordingly appropriate when studying the process of formal constitutional amendment to look first at section 52 of the Constitution Act, 1982.

This section provides that the Constitution of Canada is the supreme law of the country and that any law inconsistent with the provisions of the Constitution of Canada is *ultra vires*. Subsection 52(2) states that

> the Constitution of Canada includes (a) the *Canada Act*, 1982, including this Act; (b) the Acts and orders referred to in the schedule; (c) any amendment to any Act or order referred to in paragraph (a) or (b).

Thus we see that the entire Constitution Act, 1982 is entrenched and accordingly no portion of it can be changed without the use of the amending formula. We also know that because of paragraph 52(2)(b), all the Acts and orders referred to in the Schedule to the Act are entrenched.

The first thing that strikes one upon examining the schedule is the relatively large number of documents which are brought under the rubric of section 52. Thirty documents are listed as being entrenched by virtue of this section.[3] What is somewhat more troubling, however, is that when we look at the amending formula in Part V, we see that there are also other matters which come within the phrase "Constitution of Canada." Certainly upon reading section 52 it should be noted that it provides that "the Constitution of Canada includes. . ." thus suggesting that the later mentioned provisions are not exhaustive. This means that there are possibly matters other than those listed in the Schedule which are subject to the amending formula. The use of the word "includes" is certainly prophetic because we shall soon see that at the very least the Supreme Court Act, an Act of the Parliament of Canada, which is not mentioned in the Schedule to the Constitution Act, 1982, is very probably now entrenched and largely, if not entirely, amendable only through the use of the amending formula.

Thus the first point to be recognized is the relatively sweeping nature of entrenchment in our existing constitution, which decreases the possibility of rapid change in the basic structures of the Canadian constitutional system. When one combines the number of areas entrenched by the constitutional formula for amendment with the proposition that at least for some of these matters the unanimous agreement of both the federal and provincial legislatures is required, one can see that the degree of entrenchment in Canada is very substantial. Before discussing the latter point in any detail we will look at the actual provisions of the amending formula contained in Part V of the Constitution Act, 1982.

Subsection 38(1) contains the basic amendment formula. Required for an amendment to the Constitution of Canada are resolutions of the Senate and of the House of Commons and resolutions passed by the legislative assemblies of at least two-thirds of the provinces that have, according to the latest general census, fifty percent of the population. Where the amendment derogates from the legislative rights and powers of a provincial legislature or government then according to the terms of subsection 38(3) this amendment will not have effect in a province which, through a resolution of its legislative assembly, has expressed in clear terms its dissent with respect to the amendment. Thus if the transfer of an important legislative subject matter from the provincial legislature to the federal parliament was attempted, a dissenting province could by its dissent preclude the amendment from applying to that province. For example, if it was decided to transfer Workers' Compensation jurisdiction to the federal parliament and the province of Manitoba dissented, the result would be that the federal parliament would have jurisdiction over Workers' Compensation in every province but Manitoba.

It must be remembered however that by virtue of section 40 it is only when the transferred provincial power deals with education or "other cultural matters" that the province shall receive a reasonable compensation for the subject matter lost. Thus, in the example of Workers' Compensation, Manitoba would retain jurisdiction but would not receive any recognition in terms of federal-provincial fiscal arrangements to sustain what would then be a distinct and extraordinary matter of provincial jurisdiction. Thus finance becomes an important factor working against what was often referred to as the "checkerboard effect."[4]

Certain matters were regarded as being sufficiently important that no change should be made to them unless the unanimous agreement of all eleven legislatures was obtained. These matters are, respectively, in shortened form, the monarchy and its representatives at the provincial and federal level, the assurance that no province will have less members of the House of Commons than it will have senators, the use of the English or the French language, the composition of the Supreme Court of Canada, and finally the requirement that the amending formula cannot be changed except with the unanimous agreement of all eleven legislatures.

This requirement of unanimity is indeed ironic in that one of the main arguments advanced in favour of constitutional review was the inflexibility of a tradition that required unanimous federal and provincial consent before proceeding to the United Kingdom Parliament for an amendment to the British North America Act, 1867. Politicians never seemed to grow tired of raising the hue and cry that Canada's constitutional progress could be blocked at the whim of Prince Edward Island. No suitable evidence was ever put forward as to this possible perfidious action by that province and yet it was continuously presented as an example of why the rules of the Canadian constitutional game had to be rewritten. Furthermore, we have undoubtedly created at least one area where previously the unilateral action of the federal parliament was all that was required to effect change but which now requires federal-provincial unanimity: the composition of the Supreme Court.

It was obviously felt necessary that certain federal institutions or federally controlled institutions should be dealt with according to the provisions of subsection 38(1) already outlined. Some of these matters, although they are federal institutions in the sense that they are part of the Ottawa government, have a subject matter and nature such as to affect the entire country. This list has six categories and includes proportionate representation, the powers of the Senate, the method of selection of senators and the representation in the Senate that a province is entitled to have, "subject to paragraph 41(d), the Supreme Court of Canada," extending provinces into the territories and the establishment of new provinces.[5] This last is a further illustration of the imposition of greater rigidity: where previously the Parliament of Canada had the authority to create new provinces, now the creation of a new province requires the approval of eight legislatures along the lines outlined in subsection 38(1). It should also be noted that by virtue of section 47, the Senate can be by-passed after the passage of a designated period of time. Thus the Senate could not block reforms to its functioning and powers.

The scope of entrenchment is probably somewhat wider than initially appears from the provisions of the amending formula. For example, it requires unanimous agreement under section 41 to change the office of the queen, the governor general, and the lieutenant governor of a province. At first glance this does not seem to be particularly significant in terms of the scope of the provision. However, after reflecting upon the decision in the case of *Re the Initiative and Referendum Act*,[6] one realizes that the phrase 'office' involves more than dealings with the office holder, encompassing also the powers relating to the office. That decision held that any change in these powers involved an amendment to the office. At issue in that case was the legal requirement that no bill could become legislation without the assent of the lieutenant governor of the province. The attempt to by-pass the office through referendum legislation was held to be unconstitutional as a violation of subsection 92(1), which allowed the province to amend its constitution except with regard to the office of lieutenant governor. Taken to its logical conclusion, this result means that any change in the powers of the Crown and its representatives requires the unanimous agreement of the legislatures of the eleven governments.

The legal powers of the governor general and lieutenant governor include such things as the appointment of the first minister, the appointment of ministers and the dissolution of the elected chamber, to name just a few of the more significant powers. In fact, the legal powers of the Crown are intrinsically interwoven with the system of cabinet government and thus any attempt to change cabinet government would invariably change the legal powers relating to the office of governor general or the lieutenant governor of a province. In essence, the authors contend that by virtue of paragraph 41(a) this means that the cabinet system of government has become entrenched. Consider, for example, section 54 of the Constitution Act, 1867, which provides that all money bills must be accompanied by a message from the lieutenant governor or the governor general. By convention a message is given only to a member of the cabinet. The question therefore arises as to whether such a convention is, in effect, frozen by virtue of paragraph 41(a). This further illustrates that the functioning of cabinet government and the functioning of the monarch's representatives are closely and invariably interlinked.

We have already indicated that the Supreme Court of Canada is mentioned in both sections 41 and 42 of the Constitution Act, 1982. Paragraph 41(d) outlines that the composition of the Supreme Court of Canada can only be changed with the approval of the Senate, the House of Commons and the legislative assembly of each province. At the very least the word "composition" seems to include the number of members of the court and probably the fact that at least three of the judges must come from the province of Quebec. Somewhat more puzzling however is the phrase in paragraph 42(1)(d): "subject to paragraph 41(d), the Supreme Court of Canada." Are we to conclude from this that most of the provisions of the Supreme Court Act are entrenched? These would include matters such as appointment of the court and, especially important, the jurisdiction of the court. Perhaps when this phrase is ultimately interpreted by the courts, they will reach some kind of compromise to the effect that housekeeping matters are within the jurisdiction of the Parliament of Canada, but that matters of real substance such as removal, appointment and jurisdiction are subject to the application of the amendment formula. The provisions with respect to the Supreme Court are some of the most important in illustrating the increased rigidity now introduced into the system.

Paragraph 42(1)(f), which provides that the approval of eight governments is required for the establishment of new provinces, is another example of the introduction of further rigidity into the constitutional functioning of Canada. As one of the authors stated in an article written prior to this chapter:

While the details of this amendment process will be looked at shortly, the crucial point is that this amending formula has brought us a good deal more rigidity than apparently existed under the previous constitutional structure. Matters that prior to the adoption of the amending formula now before us could have been dealt with by the federal parliament alone, now require either unanimous or seven province approval. It is also true that many more of the existing Canadian political institutions are entrenched by this amending formula than might be apparent at first glance. [7]

As the author of that article stated there:

In conclusion, let me reiterate that the tragedy of the constitutional compromise of 1982 is that it did not really address the question of constitutional reform. The heart of what should be reformed, in my opinion, is the system of parliamentary government, and yet far from addressing this subject, the revised Canadian constitution freezes a system which, as already suggested, is unresponsive, inflexible, and nonrepresentative of regional viewpoints. [8]

[1] Legislative Council Act, Stats. Que. 1968, c.9.

[2] [1981] 1 S.C.R. 753.

[3] See chapter 2 for a detailed analysis of these documents.

[4] Section 40 was placed in the Act in order to attempt to induce Quebec to support the amendment formula.

[5] Subsection 42(1).

[6] [1919] A.C. 935 (P.C.).

[7] Cheffins, "The Constitution Act, 1982, and the Amending Formula: Political and Legal Implications" (1982), 4 Supreme Court L. R., 43, pp. 47-48.

[8] Ibid., p. 54.

EXECUTIVE AUTHORITY

The events of 1982 did not change the fact that Canada remains a monarchy with its traditional form of cabinet government. As previously indicated, the changes in the Constitution Act, 1867 were minimal, and certainly no changes were made with respect to the formal role of the Crown and its representatives. Section 9 of that Act provides that "the Executive Government and Authority of and over Canada, is hereby declared to continue and be vested in the Queen." This means that government is carried on in the name of the monarch and all of the traditional rules relating to the monarchy are still in existence. The Constitution Act, 1982 contained one reference to the office of the monarch, the governor general and the lieutenant governors of the provinces: it provided in section 41 that no change could be made in these offices without a resolution authorized by the Senate, the House of Commons and the legislative assembly of each province. Thus the likelihood of Canada moving from a monarchical to a republican form of government in the immediate future is extremely remote. Furthermore, since the decision in *Re the Initiative and Referendum Act*[1] the word "office" also includes the powers relating to the office, any attempt to change the major legal powers of these office holders would need the unanimous consent required by the section 41 amending process.

One of the most perplexing features of the Canadian constitutional system is the subtle line distinguishing the formal executive, the monarch and her representatives, from the purely informal executive, the cabinet, to which the law makes relatively little reference. An exhaustive search through all of the documents defined in section 52 of the Constitution Act, 1982 as being included in the "Constitution of Canada" reveals no reference to either the office of prime minister or to the cabinet. Nevertheless, in our constitutional and political system, power has shifted inexorably in the direction of first the cabinet and, increasingly in recent years, the first minister, whether at the federal or provincial level. It is our view that one of the unfortunate consequences of constitutional review in 1982 was the failure to examine and reform the excessively executive-dominated parliamentary system. The chances of any substantial revision of the cabinet and the parliamentary model of government now practised in Canada is unlikely.

Perhaps, however, the model is particularly suitable to a country which leading students of sociology and political culture such as Seymour Lipset and Gad Horowitz[2] regard as deferential and geared to an interventionist statist model of society. The Tory touch as defined by Horowitz means that Canada has adopted from Great Britain a system involving a high degree of state intervention in all aspects of human life. Our executive-dominated system thus blends very satisfactorily with a sense of deferential hierarchy with which Canadians feel both familiar and comfortable. As Van Loon and Whittington point out,[3] lobbyists in Canada spend very little time talking to M.P.s and M.L.A. s, but instead try to convince the bureaucracy, recognizing its substantial impact on decisions made by the cabinet. It is because of this executive dominance that the provincial premiers have become the only viable alternative, other than the courts, to the incredible power vested in the office of the prime minister of Canada.

The Crown

Executive government in Canada can be viewed from two perspectives, the formal executive and the political executive. They are of course closely interlinked but the formal executive is much more defined by legal rules than is the political executive. As indicated earlier, the head of the formal executive is the queen of Canada, who is at the time of writing Queen Elizabeth II. She is represented in Canada by the governor general at the federal level and by the lieutenant governors at the provincial level. Her powers derive from two sources, namely the prerogative powers of the Crown, that is, the residue of traditional authority which the monarch has had over the years, and a few provisions of the Constitution Act 1867.

It is the prerogative powers of the Crown which are, in many respects, the most important of the powers vested in the monarch. These prerogative powers are referred to in the Letters Patent of 1947 which, along with its precursors, is the document which delegated to the governor general the prerogative powers of the Crown. In fact, the creation of the office of governor general was done by Letters Patent and is accordingly a prerogative action of the monarch. As we shall see, the governor general, like the monarch, derives powers from two sources: prerogative powers delegated from the monarch and a series of designated powers in the Constitution Act, 1867. Undoubtedly the two most important statutory powers mentioned in the Constitution Act, 1867 relating to the monarch are, as already indicated, section 9 which vests executive authority in her person and section 17 which provides that "there shall be One Parliament for Canada consisting of the Queen, an Upper House styled the Senate and a House of Commons." As we shall see, these powers are exercised on her behalf by the governor general.

The Office of Governor General

No exhaustive analysis of the role of the Crown and its representatives in Canada will be made here as this has already been done in several other books on the

Canadian government and constitution.[4] The office of governor general was not created by the Constitution Act, 1867, but instead was created by the prerogative powers of the monarch. The prerogative powers vested in the monarch are those residual powers, recognized by the common law, which have not been taken away by statute. These powers of course find their antecedents in early times and have only continued through the sufferance of parliament. Parliament in the United Kingdom, if it wishes, can remove prerogative powers of the Crown, or it can put them into statutory form; thus the continued existence of the power depends upon the whim of parliament. Nevertheless, despite a continual whittling away of the prerogative powers of the Crown by parliament, a substantial number of these powers still exist and are of considerable importance in the Constitution of Canada.

In an earlier era all governors of British colonies were appointed by prerogative authority of the Crown as direct representatives of the monarch in the overseas milieu in which they served. It is to this historical origin, therefore, that the office of governor general owes its existence. Though the office is not created by statute, many of the most important powers vested in the governor general are in fact specifically elucidated in the Constitution Act, 1867. We can thus say that the office of governor general is created by the royal prerogative and has a combination of legal powers derived from two sources, namely through delegation by the monarch and in addition through specific provisions of Canada's fundamental constitutional document, the Constitution Act, 1867.

There have been a series of letters patent issued by the monarch relating to the office of governor general and allocating monarchical authority to the governor general to be exercised in Canada on behalf of the monarch. The most recent of these letters patent were those issued in October 1947, which provided that "there shall be a Governor General and Commander-in-Chief in and over Canada, and appointments to the Office of Governor General and Commander-in-Chief in and over Canada shall be made by Commission under Our Great Seal of Canada." The unique feature of the Letters Patent of 1947 was that for the first time in Canadian history the letters patent delegated all of the monarch's prerogative powers with respect to Canada. This authority was expressed in these words, "We do hereby authorize and empower our Governor General, with the advice of Our Privy Council for Canada or any members thereof or individually, as the case requires, to exercise all powers and authorities lawfully belonging to Us in respect of Canada. . . ." The Letters Patent then go on to outline by specific example the authority vested in the governor general through this delegation of authority from the monarch, including the power to appoint a number of important Canadian officials.

The most significant of the prerogative powers assigned to the governor general is of course the power to ask someone to undertake the position of prime minister of Canada and accordingly to form a government in the monarch's name. This prerogative power also includes the authority to appoint ministers of the Crown as recommended by the prime minister. The letters patent go on to provide that the governor general is authorized "to remove from his office, or to suspend from the exercise of the same, any person exercising any office within Canada under or by virtue of any Commission or Warrant granted, or which may be granted, by Us in Our name or under Our Authority." This would, of course, allow the governor general to legally remove either the prime minister or cabinet ministers from office. This has never happened in the history of Canada at the federal level but it is an important weapon in the hands of the prime minister in the face of a recalcitrant minister who is not prepared to resign. The prime minister would be entitled to go to the governor general and recommend, as his first minister, that the minister in question be removed from office.

It is clear that, in legal theory although highly unlikely in practice, the governor general could dismiss the prime minister if he or she thought fit. This happened in Australia in 1975 when a deadlock between the Liberal-dominated upper house and the Labour-dominated lower house produced a stalemate over the budget introduced by the labour government. Sir John Kerr, the governor general, took it upon himself to first dismiss the prime minister, order the dissolution of the House, thereby precipitating a general election, and to call upon the leader of the opposition to form a government. These dramatic actions by Kerr, who, it should be noted, was an appointee of the Crown on the advice of the Labour government, are unique in the history of the major Canadian dominions forming part of the former British Empire and colonies. They of course precipitated a good deal of critical comment in Australia as well as street demonstrations. Nevertheless, John Fraser, the newly appointed prime minister, was maintained in office by the general election which followed the actions of Kerr.[5]

The primary function of the Crown and its representatives is to make certain that there is always a first minister in office assigned the responsibility of advising the Crown on the conduct of government in the country. In addition to this important prerogative power is the authority to prorogue and dissolve parliament and thus precipitate a general election. It should be remembered that this important power of dissolution, in all but the most unusual circumstances, is exercised on the advice of the first minister. One of the two incidents in which a governor general refused to act on the advice of a first minister centred around the refusal, by Lord Byng, to grant a dissolution of the House of Commons to the then Prime Minister Mackenzie King. There were very solid constitutional traditions which justified the action by Lord Byng. There had been a recent general election and in addition there was, within the House of Commons, an alternate government capable of carrying the responsibility of office. The situation was a rather unusual one in that the election of October 29, 1925, resulted in a House composed of 101 Liberals, 116 Conservatives and 24 Progressives, plus assorted Independents. Prime Minister King chose to remain in office despite having fewer seats than the opposition Conservative party. When faced with a vote of non-confidence based on a serious customs scandal, Mr. King went to the governor general and asked for dissolution of the House. Lord Byng, acting on the aforementioned principles, refused to grant him dissolution and called on Opposition Leader Arthur Meighen to form a government. This government was only briefly in office, being defeated by one vote when a member of the opposition broke his pair with a member of the government.

This extraordinary turn of events led to another general election won by Mackenzie King, although again he did not obtain a majority in the House of Commons. He was able, through the support of the smaller parties, including the Progressives, United Farmers, Labourites and Independents, to carry on a stable government until his defeat in the general election of 1930. The leading scholar on the Crown in Canada has written a major book justifying the position of Lord Byng. Readers further interested in this subject should see the work, by Dr. Eugene Forsey: *The Royal Power of Dissolution of Parliament in the British Commonwealth.*[6]

The prerogative powers of the Crown also allow the governor general on behalf of Her Majesty to enter into treaties on behalf of Canada, to declare war and peace, and to name ambassadors to other countries. Naturally these legal powers are only carried out on the advice of the prime minister. In the case of a declaration of war it would be virtually unthinkable for the prime minister to render this advice to the governor general without debate in the House of Commons and a resolution approving the prime minister's action. Historically, the summoning of the House of Commons was a prerogative act of the Crown, but in Canada it is provided for by section 38 of the Constitution Act, 1867.

There are also a number of other very important legal powers vested in the governor general through the Constitution Act, 1867. For example, section 11 provides that the Queen's Privy Council for Canada is "chosen and summoned by the Governor General and sworn in as Privy Councillors, and Members thereof may be from Time to Time removed by the Governor General." Every cabinet minister is sworn in as a member of the Privy Council, though it should be noted that it is quite possible for persons to be summoned to the Privy Council without being members of the cabinet. The governor general will, however, only select persons to serve as members of the Privy Council on the advice of the prime minister. For example, it is quite common for the leader of the opposition, even though he has never been a member of cabinet, to be sworn in as a member of the Privy Council and thus be entitled to the use of the term "Honourable." The chief justice of Canada is also a member of the Queen's Privy Council for Canada. When parliament delegates powers in reality to the cabinet this is always done using the legal form of the governor in council. This simply means that selected members of the cabinet sign the order in council in their capacities as members of the Privy Council and then the approval of the governor general is obtained. Almost all major pieces of legislation contain some form of delegation. Probably the most frequent recipient of delegated authority is the governor in council.

As has already been noted, one of the crucial sections of the Constitution Act, 1867 is section 17, which provides that the Parliament of Canada shall consist of the Queen, the Senate and the House of Commons. This, in effect, means that no bill can be turned into law until it has been approved by votes in the House of Commons and the Senate and then given Royal Assent. Since the governor general is the queen's representative, Royal Assent is given on behalf of Her Majesty by the governor general. It is theoretically possible for the governor general to refuse assent but this is most unlikely. No governor general has ever refused assent to a bill after its passage through the Senate and House of Commons.

Another very significant legal power of the governor general is outlined in section 24 of the Constitution Act, 1867, which provides that the governor general, acting in the queen's name, will "summon qualified Persons to the Senate. . . ." These appointments are only made by the governor general on the advice of the prime minister. An interesting provision of the Act is section 26, which allows the governor general, if the Queen thinks fit, to appoint four or eight extra members to the Senate. This was obviously intended as a dead-lock breaking mechanism in case the upper house refused to pass a bill sent to it by the House of Commons. It has never been used because the general pattern of the Canadian Senate has been for one party to be overwhelmingly represented in the upper house at the expense of all other parties and independents.

Another interesting provision with respect to the power of the governor general is that provided by section 34, that he or she shall appoint the speaker of the Senate and, if necessary, remove the speaker. The speaker of the House of Commons, at least in theory, is elected by the members of that chamber, but the oligarchic position of the Senate is reflected not only in the method of appoint-ment of its members but also in the selection of its spokesman. It almost goes without saying that the governor general will only select a speaker of the Senate upon the advice of the prime minister.

An often-neglected provision of the Constitution Act, 1867 which has very important consequences is section 54. Summarized in its briefest form, it provides that no measure can be introduced into the House of Commons dealing with the raising or expenditure of public funds without a ". . . Message of the Governor General in the Session in which such Vote, Resolution, Address, or bill is proposed." The significance of this particular provision is that Canadian tradition dictates that the governor general will give a message in relation to financial measures only to a member of the cabinet. This has the effect of prohibiting government back benchers and members of the opposition from introducing any measures, including private members' bills, which deal with fiscal matters. It does not take a great deal of acumen to realize that the scope provided for ordinary members to take legislative initiative is thus very limited. This provision is another reason for the executive dominance in the Canadian political and constitutional system.

Section 55 provides that where a bill has passed the two houses of the Canadian parliament, the governor general shall give Royal Assent in the queen's name or that assent can be withheld or the bill reserved for the pleasure of Her Maj-esty. As already indicated, the governor general has never, since 1867, refused Royal Assent and an Imperial Conference[7] recognized that the governor general's power of reservation would never be used. Under extremely unusual circum-stances, it might perhaps be defensible to refuse assent, but certainly it would never be justifiable to utilize the technique of reservation.

Other than the aforementioned Byng crisis, there has been only one other occasion in which a Canadian governor general has refused to act on the advice of the prime minister. This occurred in 1896 with the defeat of the Conservative government of Dr. Charles Tupper. After the defeat the prime minister recommended to the governor general, Lord Aberdeen, that he appoint a number of prominent Conservatives to the judiciary and to the Senate. The governor general took the position that although the prime minister was technically still in office, he had been repudiated by the electorate and it was inappropriate for him to find jobs for party supporters before the swearing in of the Laurier government. Unlike the furor which raged with respect to the King-Byng crisis, the actions of the governor general in this instance seemed, to most observers, appropriate and within the spirit of constitutional democracy.

The Office of Lieutenant Governor

The provincial equivalent of the office of governor general is the position of lieutenant governor. The lieutenant governor fulfils within his provincial context the same role and function as does the governor general within the federal context. The office of lieutenant governor, unlike that of governor general, is created by the Constitution Act, 1867. Section 58 provides that there shall be a lieutenant governor in each province, "appointed by the Governor General in Council by Instrument under the Great Seal of Canada." Section 59 provides that he or she holds office at the pleasure of the governor general, and can only be removed during his five-year appointment for some specifically defined cause. On a few occasions the lieutenant governor's five-year term has been extended by an additional one or two years. Section 60 provides that the salary of the lieutenant governor is designated and provided for by the Canadian parliament. Readers will undoubtedly recognize the close linkage, at least in law, between the office of lieutenant governor and the federal government. This close relationship certainly substantiates the position taken by Professor John Saywell in his book *The Office of Lieutenant Governor*,[8] that originally the lieutenant governor was more a federal officer than a representative of the monarch. In fact, it was envisaged that the lieutenant governor would represent federal interests within the provincial context and assure that provincial policies were not altogether out of line with those of the federal government. The function of a lieutenant governor as a federal officer probably made sense at a time when the provinces were far-flung and all forms of transportation and communication were difficult.

The legal role of the lieutenant governor was clarified with the decision of the Judicial Committee of the Privy Council in the case of *The Liquidators of the Maritime Bank of Canada v. The Receiver General of New Brunswick*.[9] The court had to decide the question of whether the lieutenant governor was the representative of the sovereign in such a way that all the privileges, powers and immunities of the Crown passed to the lieutenant governor of the province. The court held that the lieutenant governor was the representative of the Crown and that the prerogative rights of the Crown, insofar as they related to the province, passed to the holder of that office. This meant that, like the governor general, the lieutenant governor possessed all the prerogative powers of the monarch, such as the summoning and dismissal of a premier or cabinet minister and the dissolution of the legislature, in addition to those statutory powers set out in the Constitution Act, 1867.

It is sometimes forgotten that the prerogative includes special rules which apply only to the Crown and the Crown's representatives. For example, in the *Maritime Bank* case the Province of New Brunswick had deposited money in the Maritime Bank of Canada, which found itself in serious difficulty and had to wind up its financial affairs. The question arose as to whether the province enjoyed the traditional priorities of the Crown such that it could have its claims satisfied prior to other depositors and simple contract creditors of the bank. The province would only have a prior claim if it enjoyed the privileges of the royal prerogative. The court held that the lieutenant governor was, in fact, the representative of the Crown and enjoyed all the rights and privileges of a representative of the monarch. Thus, in this case, the province of New Brunswick was able to stand first in line when creditors had to be satisfied out of the limited assets of the bank.

This decision handed down in 1892 begins the redefinition of the office of lieutenant governor from that of federal officer to representative of the monarch. In the first fifty years after Confederation, lieutenant governors were involved in a good deal of political controversy largely because of the uncertainty over their role. For example, lieutenant governors have reserved seventy bills for the pleasure of the governor in council, thirteen of which ultimately received Royal Assent in the form of a federal order in council. Forty-two of these reservations took place in the first twenty-one years after Confederation and only one has been reserved since 1937.[10]

Everyone was astonished when Lieutenant Governor Bastedo of Saskatchewan in April of 1961 indicated that he was reserving for the pleasure of the governor in council a bill passed by theLegislative Assembly of Saskatchewan. The federal government indicated its surprise that the lieutenant governor would take this action without consultation with the prime minister, and through federal order in council gave speedy Royal Assent as provided for by section 57 of the Constitution Act, 1867.[11]

It should be noted that section 90 of the Constitution Act, 1867 makes sections 53, 54, 55, 56 and 57 applicable to the provinces. Thus, since the lieutenant governor is a component part of the legislature of each province, he is legally entitled when presented with a bill passed by the legislative assembly, to give or refuse Royal Assent or to reserve the bill for the pleasure of the Queen's Privy Council for Canada. As already indicated, lieutenant governors have reserved seventy bills for the pleasure of the governor in council, but it should also be noted that there have been twenty-eight refusals of assent. In twenty-seven of these cases assent was withheld on the advice of, or at least with the approval of, the provincial cabinet. There has been only one instance where a lieutenant governor unilaterally withheld assent to a bill passed by the legislative assembly of a province, namely Prince Edward Island.[12] There have been five occasions on which lieutenant governors have dismissed premiers, and three occasions on which lieutenant governors have refused requests by the premier of the day for a dissolution of the legislative assembly.[13]

It must be stressed that the generally turbulent times of lieutenant governors are certainly over. It would be extraordinary today for a lieutenant governor to refuse assent, a dissolution of the legislature or any other prerogative of the Crown without the advice of his or her first minister. It is now safe to say that the lieutenant governor plays within the provincial political structure the same role that the governor general fulfils within the federal political structure. Both are representatives of the monarch and both are assigned the traditional responsibilities of representing the Crown in their own constitutional baili-wick. Their first and most important responsibility is to make certain that the Crown is advised, that is to say, that someone is given a commission to form a government.

It is in the selection of a first minister that the governor general or lieutenant governor might have some discretion, depending upon the circumstances. For example, if a first minister should die in office then it is the responsibility of the Crown's representative to ask someone to form a government. Usually this does not present a problem, because if a political party has won the majority of seats in a general election then obviously their leader is asked to become prime min-ister or premier. If a prime minister should resign after the political party which is in power has had a convention and selected a new leader, then obviously the governor general or lieutenant governor will select the choice of the party. An element of discretion enters the picture, however, when a prime minister or premier dies in office. It then becomes the duty of the Crown's representative to ask a member of the ruling party to form a government. The queen's representative is entitled to consult with anyone that he or she wishes and, in fact, should consult as widely as possible. Ultimately, however, the choice of selecting a successor devolves upon the governor general or lieutenant governor. Should the new first minister not be chosen as party leader then, of course, he or she would have to resign to make way for the new leader of the majority party.[14]

The role of the Crown was vividly illustrated in Great Britain in 1956 when Sir Anthony Eden resigned as prime minister and Her Majesty Queen Elizabeth II was faced with the task of choosing between Mr. Harold Macmillan and Mr. R. A. B. Butler. After consultation with leading Conservatives, she called upon Mr. Macmillan to form a government.

The foregoing indicates the immense legal powers of the governor gen-eral and lieutenant governors, but as has been continually reiterated these powers, except in the most exceptional circumstances, are exercised on the advice of the appropriate first minister. This logically brings us to an analysis of the role, structure and function of a cabinet in the Canadian political system, and in particular points to the very special role of the first minister of that cabinet.

The First Minister and the Cabinet

The engine room of the Canadian governmental system at both the federal and provincial levels is the cabinet. Readers will remember that there had developed before 1867 the concept of responsible government. This is still undoubtedly the most important principle of Canada's constitutional structure. There are carefully defined conventions of the Constitution which determine who is called upon to form a government. Normally the leader of the party with the largest number of seats in the House of Commons is given by the governor general the queen's commission to form a government. It is then the responsibility of this person to submit to the governor general a list of ministers, to which the governor general will give his approval. Thus, legally, the first minister and cabinet are appointed by the governor general acting under the prerogative authority of the Crown. Those persons who can be designated as the first minister and ministers of the Crown are, of course, determined by convention.

This collective group of ministers and first minister is known as the cabinet, and remains as the cabinet only so long as a first minister is in office. In the event that a prime minister or premier should die, cabinet ministers remain ministers but a cabinet is no longer in existence. It is for this reason that the Crown's representative has a discretion as to whom he or she can call upon to form a government. This, in essence, is because only the first minister can give constitutional advice which is binding on the representative of the Crown. This is why it is so important that the representative of the Crown discharge the task of asking someone to form a government as quickly as possible after the resignation or death of a prime minister or premier. There is no lawful requirement that a prime minister or premier must have a seat in either the Senate or the House of Commons. However, it would be considered improper for a first minister not to seek a seat as soon as possible. An example of this, of course, was the governor general asking Mr. John Turner to form a government, even though he was not at the time a member of the House of Commons.

It should be noted that nowhere in the entrenched documents of the Canadian Constitution is there any mention of the office of prime minister or that collectivity known as the cabinet. In their judgment in the case of *Reference Re Amendment of the Constitution of Canada*,[15] the majority of the judges suggested that the phrase in the preamble to the Constitution Act, 1867, "with a Constitution similar in Principle to that of the United Kingdom," might well involve a recognition of the principle of responsible government. Though that phrase has been given other interpretations by the courts, such as the concept of parliamentary supremacy or the recognition of civil liberties, the judges are probably correct in identifying the ideas of responsible government as being at the heart of what was intended by that phrase.

Other than the foregoing, there is no specific mention in any of our legal documents of the responsibility of the office of prime minister, premier or cabinet. However these offices do not go unrecognized in other statutory provisions governing salaries and the residence of the prime minister at the federal level. The latter, though important, do not define in any way the nature and structure of the office of the first minister and his cabinet. Similarly, at the provincial level, most provinces have statutes called the Executive Council Act or, in the case of British Columbia, the Constitution Act, which refer to the executive council of the province and, in some cases, to the premier.

All of this legislation, however, at both federal and provincial levels, totally ignores the real authority and functioning of the cabinet in the Canadian constitutional context. Certainly under Prime Minister Trudeau, the cabinet seemed to become less important than under a number of other regimes, in that the ministers seemed to have less latitude and scope for individual initiative. It has been suggested that in recent years more and more authority has been vested in various standing committees of the cabinet. As Van Loon and Whittington suggest in their book on the Canadian political system, more and more decisions are being made at the committee stage of cabinet, rather than by the cabinet meeting to collectively determine solutions. All of the committee decisions must be funnelled through cabinet, but the outcomes are in essence determined by the appropriate committee.[16]

The development of a committee system has in turn strengthened the role of the bureaucracy in determining the force of policy in Canada. Each of these committees has assigned to it full-time civil servants who are members of the Privy Council Office. It is the function of these civil servants to brief and guide members of the committee in their deliberations. The size of the Privy Council Office grew dramatically during the regime of Prime Minister Trudeau. Alongside the Privy Council Office is the Prime Minister's Office which, as Van Loon and Whittington indicate, grew to include over one-hundred members by the latter years of the Trudeau administration. The result of these factors has been to dramatically increase the power of the prime minister at the expense of individual ministers and of parliament itself. The sheer number of cabinet ministers has lessened their individual importance.

This is not to say, however, that the office of prime minister was not traditionally a very powerful one, since a Privy Council minute, P.C. 3374, issued by the cabinet on October 25, 1935, stated that

> *the following recommendations are the special prerogative of the prime minister: dissolution and Convocation of Parliament: Appointment of— Privy Councillors; cabinet Ministers; lieutenant governors (including leave of absence to same); Provincial Administrators; Speaker of the Senate; Chief Justices of All Courts; Senators; Sub-Committees of Council; Treasury Board;. . .[17]*

This minute alone would be sufficient to give the reader some indication of the stranglehold which the prime minister has on power in the context of the federal government. This means, in effect, that especially by using the powers of the governor general, the prime minister has effective control of the appointment of all of the Senate, the speaker of the Senate, the appointment of cabinet ministers and their removal, the summoning, prorogation and dissolution of parliament, the selection of a speaker for the House of Commons, control of the appointment of deputy ministers, appointment of members of boards and commissions and effective control of the appointment of judges of all the federal courts and of all provincially created courts, starting with those of the county court right through to the court of appeal of each province. A brief refinement should probably be made with respect to the appointment of members of the judiciary, as the fundamental responsibility for making recommendations other than those of chief justices rests with the minister of justice. Nevertheless, one can be fairly certain that if the prime minister strongly objected to a recommendation of the minister of justice, the likelihood of that appointment being made is extremely small.

Considering further the powers of the cabinet, it must be remembered that the cabinet dictates the functioning of the legislative process. As already indicated, the cabinet determines when parliament sits and the order of business before the House. Its members control the budget and, by virtue of section 54 of the Constitution Act, 1867, no money bill is ever introduced in the House of Commons without a message from the governor general. Convention dictates that no message is ever provided by the governor general except to a minister of the Crown on the advice of the cabinet.

The question of the delegation of legislative authority through the executive will be dealt with in the following chapter on the role of the federal parliament and provincial legislatures. It is important, however, to recognize that another major source of cabinet authority is the delegation of rule-making power from parliament to the governor in council. This, in effect, means that power is delegated to a small group of ministers whose decisions are then approved by the governor general, as most orders in council are not discussed by the cabinet as a whole. No order in council can be passed unless the authority has been delegated by parliament. However, this authority is so wide and often so vague that it allows tremendous scope for law making by the governor in council. It must be remembered that an order in council has the same legal effect as if it was contained in the statute itself. Thus, not only do the cabinet and prime minister control the legislative process but they also can decide whether parliament itself delegates power back to the governor in council, thereby, to all intents and purposes, by-passing parliament in the making of law. Since the provincial constitutional systems are in essence identical to the federal system, the same points apply.[18]

Surely in the review of Canada's constitutional structure nothing calls out more for reform than the excessive dominance of the system by the cabinet. By definition, however, since constitutional review was carried out by the federal first minister and the ten provincial first ministers, the chance of any reform of a cabinet dominated system was extremely unlikely. Even if we had made some moderate changes with respect to appointments, such as those to the Senate, judiciary, boards and commissions, this would have done something to alleviate the excessive dominance of the executive. At least one can point to the Victoria Charter which provided for a joint federal-provincial role in the appointment of judges of the Supreme Court of Canada.

Similarly, as was pointed out in the chapter on the amending formula, as so many of the functions and responsibilities of the cabinet are inexorably linked with the monarchy and its representatives, changes in the system of cabinet government would probably require utilization of the unanimity rule in many instances. For example, the dissolution of the Parliament of Canada for the purpose of calling a general election is a legal power of the governor general acting on advice of the first minister. Surely a step in the right direction would have been to require elections to be held at fixed periods of time rather than allowing this manipulation of election dates to be undertaken by the government in office. Since the passage of the amending formula, however, any change in the office of governor general, which includes the powers of the governor general, would require the unanimous approval of all eleven legislatures as provided by paragraph 41(a) of the Constitution Act, 1982. Thus the chance for any substantial reform of the cabinet system and its resultant dominance of the legislature has now probably passed for many years to come. Having decided to rewrite the constitution, surely it would have been preferable to undertake a full and comprehensive re-evaluation of the system rather than to adopt the hastily patched together package of 1982.

Currently there is considerable discussion of providing for greater regional representation and more popular input through the revision of Canada's upper house. We view these proposals with scepticism and feel that they are unlikely to redress the imbalance now weighted so heavily in favour of the executive in its relationship with parliament. It is now opportune to examine the legal positions of parliament and the legislatures in the context of the Canadian constitutional system.[19]

---

[1] [1919] A.C. 935 (P.C.).

[2] "Conservatism, Liberalism, and Socialism in Canada: An Interpretation" (1966), 32 Can. J. Econ. Poli. Sci., 143.

[3] Richard J. Van Loon and Michael S. Whittington, *The Canadian Political System*. Toronto: McGraw-Hill Ryerson, 3rd ed., 1981.

[4] See R. I. Cheffins and R. N. Tucker, *The Constitutional Process in Canada*. Toronto: McGraw-Hill Ryerson, 2nd ed., 1976, chapter 4; R. MacGregor Dawson, *The Government of Canada*. Toronto: University of Toronto Press, 5th ed., revised by Norman Ward, 1970; J. R. Mallory, *The Structure of Canadian Government*. Toronto: Gage, rev. ed., 1984, chapter 2.

[5] For an exposition of the position of Sir John Kerr see John Kerr, *Matters for Judgment: An Autobiography*. New York: St. Martin's Press, 1979.

[6] Toronto: Oxford University Press, 1943. For a brief synthesis of this crisis see Cheffins and Tucker, supra, note 4, pp. 83–84; Forsey, "Was the Governor General's Refusal Constitutional?" *Politics: Canada*. Toronto: McGraw-Hill Ryerson, 5th ed., Paul W. Fox, ed., 1982, p. 431. A further analysis of this incident can be found in Roger Graham, ed., *The King-Byng Affair, 1926; A Question of Responsible Government*. Toronto: Copp Clark, 1967.

[7] Held in 1887.

[8] Toronto: University of Toronto Press, 1957.

[9] [1892] A.C. 437 (P.C.).

[10] G. V. La Forest, *Disallowance and Reservation of Provincial Legislation*. Ottawa: Department of Justice, 1955.

[11] For a more detailed account of this incident, see Mallory, "The Lieutenant-Governor's Discretionary Powers: The Reservation of Bill 56" (1961), 27 Can. J. Econ. Poli. Sci., 518.

[12] This event took place in 1945 in connection with a measure designed to liberalize the liquor law of the province. See further Saywell, supra, note 8, p. 222.

[13] For further details with respect to the office of lieutenant governor see Saywell, "The Lieutenant-Governors," *The Provincial Political Systems*. Toronto: Methuen, David J. Bellamy, Jon H. Pammett and Donald C. Rowat, eds., 1976, p. 297.

[14] Professor J. Mallory describes the rather unusual course of events which followed the deaths of Premiers Duplessis and Sauve in Quebec, whereby all the members of the Union Nationale caucus signed a petition to the lieutenant governor indicating who they wanted to succeed the deceased premier; see Mallory, "The Royal Prerogative in Canada: The Selection of Successors to Mr. Duplessis and Mr. Sauve" (1960), 26 Can. J. Econ. Poli. Sci., 314.

[15] [1981] 1 S.C.R. 753.

[16] Van Loon and Whittington, supra, note 3, at p. 493.

[17] This minute can be found in Heeney, "Functions of the Prime Minister," *Politics: Canada*. Toronto: McGraw-Hill, 3rd ed., Paul W. Fox, ed., 1970, p. 347.

[18] See Cheffins and Tucker, "Constitutions," in *The Provincial Political Systems*, supra, note 13, p. 257.

[19] See further, with respect to the role of the cabinet and its functioning in the Canadian governmental structure, Van Loon and Whittington, supra, note 3, chapters 14–18; Mallory, supra, note 4, chapters 2 and 3; Dawson, supra, note 4, parts 3 and 4; Bellamy, Pammett and Rowat, eds., supra, note 13, especially Cheffins and Tucker, "Constitutions," p. 257, Saywell, "The Lieutenant Governors," p. 297, and Bryden, "Cabinets," p. 310. For a useful work on the provincial government of British Columbia, see J. Terence Morley, Norman J. Ruff, Neil A. Swainson, R. Jeremy Wilson and Walter D. Young, *The Reins of Power*. Vancouver: Douglas and McIntyre, 1983.

LEGISLATIVE AUTHORITY

In pure constitutional theory, the major losers as the result of the passage of the Constitution Act, 1982 were the federal parliament and the provincial legislatures. The Constitution Act, 1982 provides in subsection 52(1) that:

> The Constitution of Canada is the Supreme Law of Canada, and any law that is inconsistent with the provisions of the Constitution is, to the extent of the inconsistency, of no force or effect.

This means that every piece of legislation enacted by either the federal parliament or a provincial legislature must be considered in light of what is defined in subsection 52(2) of the Constitution Act, 1982 as the Constitution of Canada. In brief, and at the very least, it includes the thirty legal documents in the schedule attached to the Constitution Act, 1982. As noted earlier in the chapter on the amending formula, it also probably includes at least some portions of other statutes, in particular, the Supreme Court Act. This means that any enactment of the federal parliament or provincial legislature is open to challenge on the grounds that it is inconsistent with "the Constitution of Canada." The definition of what is illegal as a result of violating the provisions of the Constitution of Canada will lie with the courts. In particular, not only will legislative enactments have to be judged to be within the appropriate legislative sphere of the legislature concerned, but they must also not violate the Charter of Rights and Freedoms. Although these are the major hurdles facing legislators, it must also be remembered that legislators cannot enact legislation violating any of the provisions included in any of the documents listed in the Schedule to the Constitution Act, 1982.

Since 1867 we have had judicial review of the validity of legislation by the courts. Prior to 1982, however, the courts restricted themselves to determining whether the legislation was within the area of authority assigned to the federal parliament or the provincial legislatures. These definitions of the legislative purview of the federal parliament and provincial legislatures are found in sections 91, 92, 93, 94, 94A, 95, 101, 117 and 132 of the Constitution Act, 1867.[1]

Supremacy of Parliament

Prior to 1982, it was appropriate to state that Canada still relied upon the doctrine of the supremacy of parliament. This notion of parliamentary dominance was inherited from Great Britain and was the most fundamental and overriding principle of our law prior to 1982. Let us first look at the doctrine of parliamentary supremacy as it operates in the United Kingdom.

> *In that country it means that, to the judiciary, the power of Parliament is unlimited. In other words, Parliament can make any law that it wishes, or repeal any law that it wishes. It means, in essence, that the courts have no authority to declare illegal any statute passed by Parliament. It means that no Parliament is bound by an act of its predecessors, consequently giving every Parliament the right to change or undo the obligations established by preceding Parliaments.[2]*

It should be recognized, however, that despite the sweeping legal power vested in the parliament of the United Kingdom, the exercise of that power was and still is mitigated by a host of political, cultural, psychological and other factors. Notwithstanding the doctrine of parliamentary supremacy, the United Kingdom has remained in the forefront of those nations recognizing civil liberties. In fact, Jeremy Bentham, the great English philosopher, regarded parliamentary supremacy as an integral legal weapon in the struggle to reform the legal system of England. He wanted to forestall any suggestion that parliament could not act because previous practices or law were unchangeable or immutable. The opposition to the dead hand of the past put the Utilitarians, led by Bentham, in the vanguard of the supporters of the idea of parliamentary supremacy.[3]

The leading case in Canada on the subject of legislative supremacy is that of *Hodge* v. *The Queen.*[4] In that case Hodge had been found to be in violation of a regulation passed by the Board of Licence Commissioners for the City of Toronto, which had been created and given legislative authority by the Ontario legislature in relation to liquor control in the City of Toronto. Hodge argued that the Ontario statute was beyond the authority of the provincial legislature and that the provincial legislature did not have the constitutional authority to delegate power of a rule-making nature to a regulatory body. The case ultimately reached the Judicial Committee of the Privy Council, which held not only that the legislation was within the authority of the provincial legislature, but also that the provincial legislature had the authority to delegate rule-making power to a body which they had created. The Judicial Committee rejected any idea that the Ontario legislature was merely a delegate of the British parliament by virtue of the British North America Act, 1867 and instead held that provincial legislatures had

> *authority as plenary and as ample within the limits prescribed by sect. 92 as the Imperial Parliament in the plenitude of its power possessed and could bestow. Within these limits of subjects and area the local legislature is supreme, and has the same authority as the Imperial Parliament,*

or the Parliament of the Dominion, would have had under like circum-
stances, to confide to a municipal institution or body of its own creation
authority to make by-laws or resolutions as to subjects specified in the
enactment.[5]

This meant that within a defined legislative sphere the provincial legislatures were supreme; that is, that once it had been established that the legislatures were within the legislative jurisdiction assigned to them by the Constitution Act, 1867, their legislative enactments could not be challenged before the courts.

In the case of *British Coal Corporation* v. *The King*[6] the Judicial Committee stated with respect to the Dominion Parliament that it was supreme and was endowed "with the same authority as the Imperial Parliament, within the assigned limits of subject and area, just as it was said in *Hodge* v. *The Queen* that s.92 of the Act had that effect in regard to the Provincial Legislatures." [7]

Thus, prior to 1982 three legislatures possessed a totality of power. These bodies were the United Kingdom Parliament, the Parliament of Canada and the legislatures of the provinces. As indicated, the allocation of legislative power between the federal parliament and the provincial legislatures was defined in the sections of the Constitution Act, 1867 already referred to. The jurisdiction of the parliament of the United Kingdom was limited and at the same time defined in 1949 by the passage of the British North America (No. 2) Act, 1949. This enactment was inserted into the then British North America Act, and became subsection 91(1) of that Act. It reserved for the United Kingdom Parliament six classes of subject matter on which that parliament alone could legislate. The most important thrust of this subsection was the requirement that any changes with respect to the division of powers or the "rights or privileges by this or any other Constitutional Act granted or secured to the Legislature or the Government of a province. . ." must be made by the United Kingdom Parliament. This phrase became the substance of a constitutional reference on the legislative authority of the Parliament of Canada to change the method of appointment of senators and the structure of the Senate. In the *Reference Re Upper House* case[8] the Supreme Court of Canada held unanimously that it was not within the jurisdiction of the Parliament of Canada to change the structure and composition of Canada's upper house. They held that since the upper house was designed to protect regional interests, it was one of the "rights or privileges" of the provinces. Accordingly, the Court made it clear that any change in the Senate would have to be undertaken by the Parliament of the United Kingdom.

Thus in summary, the British parliament, the federal parliament and the legislatures of the provinces possessed between them a totality of legislative power, and the role of the courts was to determine whether legislation was properly within the areas laid down in the British North America Act, 1867.

The Doctrine of Supremacy of Parliament since 1982

As indicated at the beginning of this chapter, the previous description of Canada's constitutional structure has shifted from a doctrine of legislative supremacy to one of judicial supremacy. Section 52 underlines, as already indicated, that the "Constitution of Canada is the supreme law of Canada. . . ." This means that the judiciary is now equipped with the significant weapon of the Charter of Rights in order to strike down any legislation that is inconsistent with the provisions of the Charter. As we shall see in a later chapter, the provisions of the Charter are very broad and provide the courts with considerable leeway in invalidating legislation. In this respect our courts are now placed in a situation comparable to that of the courts of the United States. The extent to which they will use the courts of that country as a model with respect to holding legislation invalid will be examined in a later chapter.

The essential reason for the opposition of the eight provinces to the constitutional proposals of Prime Minister Trudeau was their unwillingness to abandon the doctrine of legislative supremacy. They were led in this regard by Premier Sterling Lyon of Manitoba, who felt that the will of the legislature should not be superceded by that of the courts. As a result of these provincial concerns, subsection 33(1) was included in the Constitution Act, 1982, and provided that

> Parliament or the legislature of a province may expressly declare in an Act of Parliament or of the legislature, as the case may be, that the Act, or a provision thereof shall operate notwithstanding a provision included in section 2 or sections 7 to 15 of this Charter.

This means that if parliament or a provincial legislature wishes to restore the doctrine of parliamentary supremacy, at least with respect to sections 2 or 7 to 15 of the Charter, it can do so by including an express statement in the legislation. This is commonly referred to as the *non obstante* clause of the Constitution; providing that an Act or part of an Act may operate notwithstanding the aforementioned sections of the Charter. Shortly after the passage of the Constitution Act, 1982 and its proclamation by Her Majesty, the National Assembly of Quebec, utilizing section 33, passed a statute which made section 33 applicable to all Quebec legislation.[9] The Quebec government, of course, refused to agree to the constitutional accord accepted by the federal government and the other nine provinces and therefore used section 33 to express to the greatest extent possible its dissent from the whole process which led to the passage of the Constitution Act, 1982. Leaving Quebec aside, no other legislature in Canada, or the federal parliament, has at the time of writing used the option outlined in section 33. It is, however, an interesting attempt to retain important elements of legislative supremacy as we knew it prior to 1982.

The Structure of the Federal Parliament and the Provincial Legislatures

The Constitution Act, 1867 provides in section 17 that the Parliament of Canada shall consist ". . . of the Queen, an Upper House styled the Senate, and the House of Commons." In order for legislation to be passed by the federal parliament it must be approved by the House of Commons and the Senate, and Royal

Assent must be given by the queen's representative, the governor general. A frequent misconception is that the Senate can be by-passed when the federal parliament is enacting statutes. This is untrue and Senate approval is equally as necessary for the passage of legislation as is that of the House of Commons. It should be remembered, however, that amendments to the Constitution can be achieved without approval of the Senate. Undoubtedly, this provision was included so that the Senate could not block its own reform. Members of the House of Commons are of course elected whereas members of the Senate of Canada are, by virtue of section 24 of the Constitution Act, 1867, appointed by the governor general, on the advice of the prime minister.[10]

At the provincial level the legislative models are essentially identical in that the legislature of each province is composed of the lieutenant governor and an elected lower house. Seven of the provinces, namely, New Brunswick, Prince Edward Island, Ontario, Manitoba, Saskatchewan, Alberta and British Columbia, refer to their elected body as the Legislative Assembly. In both Nova Scotia and Newfoundland it is referred to as the House of Assembly and in Quebec it is referred to as the National Assembly. Nevertheless, despite the differences in names, the law and practice of all provincial constitutions is identical in that before a provincial bill can become law it must pass through three readings of the elected assembly and receive the approval of the lieutenant governor. Half of Canada's provinces at one time had appointed upper houses but these were all abolished by provincial legislative enactment. The most interesting of these events was in Quebec, which was the last to abolish what was called the Legislative Council of Quebec. The appointment and composition of the Legislative Council of Quebec was provided for by the British North America Act, 1867. Quebec, through an amendment to its Legislature Act in 1968, not only abolished the Legislative Council but also changed the name of the Legislative Assembly to that of the National Assembly.[11]

No constitutional challenge was mounted against this action by the Quebec legislature because it was obviously politically impractical to do so. Nevertheless there is a strong case for upholding the validity of Quebec's action on the grounds that it was authorized to do so by virtue of what was then subsection 92(1) of the British North America Act, 1867, which gave to the legislature of the province the power to provide for "the Amendment from Time to Time, notwithstanding anything in this Act, of the Constitution of the province, except as regards the Office of Lieutenant Governor." This phrase, especially the words "notwithstanding anything in this Act" in our view legitimized the actions of the Quebec legislature. It should be noted that although subsection 92(1) has now been repealed it has, in essence, been replaced by section 45 of the Constitution Act, 1982, which provides that "subject to section 41, the legislature of each province may exclusively make laws amending the constitution of the province." Notwithstanding the fairly wide latitude seemingly given to the provinces with respect to their own constitutions, the amount of experimentation with respect to legislative functioning has been very limited in each of the different provinces. In fact, one of the authors concluded in an article on provincial constitutions that ". . . the basic constitutional institutions and functions within each of the provinces remain consistent with the traditional practices inherited from the United Kingdom and pre-Confederation Canada."[12]

As we did not make any attempt to develop in detail the internal procedures and processes with respect to the federal parliament, neither will we do so with regard to the provincial legislatures. We are, however, fortunate in that there is a growing body of literature dealing with the functioning of provincial governments and provincial legislatures in particular.[13] The executive dominance which prevails in the federal parliament similarly exists in the provincial legislatures. It must also be remembered that as a result of section 90 of the Constitution Act, 1867, section 54 of the Act is applicable to the provinces. This means that all bills involving the raising or expenditure of public funds must be accompanied by a message from the lieutenant governor which, as already pointed out, is given only to a member of the cabinet. This, combined with the other principles of responsible government already defined in chapters 3 and 6, serve to underline executive dominance in the provincial context.

Subordinate Legislation

Probably the most effective and important legal device for modern government is the ability to delegate authority to subordinate bodies. As the business of government became increasingly complex, it became less and less possible for legislatures to draft statutes with the detail and precision necessary to fulfil their intent. Accordingly the practice has developed of drafting statutes in general terms and delegating to subordinate bodies the power to pass regulations fleshing out the often-skeletal provisions of the statutes.

What must first be examined is what is meant by and implied in the concept of delegation. The classic definition was advanced by Mr. Justice Wills in *Huth* v. *Clarke*[14] where he outlined that

> *delegation, as the word is generally used, does not imply a parting with power by the person who grants the delegation, but points rather to the conferring of an authority to do things which otherwise that person would have to do himself.*

He went on to state that

> *it is never used by legal writers, so far as I am aware, as implying that the delegating person parts with his power in such a manner as to denude himself of his rights.*

Thus, the federal parliament and the provincial legislatures are, in the course of legislation, able to vest in subordinate bodies the power to make laws which have the same effect as if contained in the statute. Used responsibly this is a vital and necessary part of the process of modern government. Used irresponsibly it can be a very valuable tool in the hands of the executive for avoiding the scrutiny of parliamentary debate. In fact, as far back as the late 1920s in Great

Britain, a famous British judge, Lord Hewart, wrote a book entitled *The New Despotism* in which he advanced the theory that there was a conspiracy within the civil service to promote widespread delegation of legislative powers, having the effect of ultimately increasing the power of the bureaucracy.[15] The British government was so alarmed by the publication of this book that they set up the most famous royal commission ever established in the British Commonwealth on this subject, namely, the Committee on Ministers' Powers. The essence of the Committee's report[16] was that delegation was inevitable in modern society yet should be subject to a number of recommended controls.

Despite Lord Hewart's concerns, the practice of delegation has grown at an incredible pace and there seems to be little indication of any mitigation or moderate abatement of this process. Let us, however, make clear that while delegation is inevitable in the modern state, there are clearly decisions to be made as to when delegation is appropriate and the extent to which the delegating legislature has control of the process.

There is little doubt that the ever-increasing demands for government involvement in all aspects of our lives have increased the pressure on legislatures to delegate responsibility to subordinate bodies. New technological developments require new bureaucratic mechanisms for their regulation. In an earlier work by one of the authors there is a lengthy analysis of how the development of radio and television resulted in the creation of both a new regulatory body and a government-owned corporation, namely the Canadian Broadcasting Corporation, to compete in the field of television and radio. It was obvious, as a result of the complexities of regulating radio and television, that no statute could be sufficiently comprehensive to deal with the myriad of details required to regulate the complex industries of radio and television. It seems as if every new industry has produced a new regulatory body entrusted by parliament with the responsibility of drafting laws which have the same effect as if contained in a parliamentary enactment. The problems created by the regulation of the transportation industry, particularly railways and the aircraft industry, are sufficient to illustrate this point.[17]

The Recipients of Delegated Power

Foremost among those who receive delegated legislative authority are, at the federal level, the governor in council, and at the provincial level, the lieutenant governor in council. This, in essence, means delegation to the representative of the monarch and the appropriate cabinet. First, it should be underlined that neither the federal governor in council nor the provincial lieutenant governor in council possesses any inherent authority. The prerogative powers of the Crown are vested exclusively in the Crown's representative and these have been specifically recognized by the courts through time. As the *Reference re Anti-Inflation Act* case[18] made clear, the lieutenant governor in council in Ontario could not enter into an arrangement with the federal government whereby the federal Anti-Inflation Act applied to Ontario without first receiving delegated authority from the legislature of Ontario to make the federal legislation applicable to that province. Thus the often hazy notion that the governor in council or, at the provincial level, the lieutenant governor in council, possesses some kind of amorphous authority was put to rest once and for all. In the case of the Anti-Inflation Act and Ontario mentioned above, the situation was remedied by a retroactive Act of the Ontario legislature making valid the agreement between Ontario and Canada which made the Anti-Inflation Act applicable to the Ontario provincial public sector.

A very high proportion of federal and provincial statutes delegate authority to the governor in council or the lieutenant governor in council. The troublesome aspect of this delegation is that, as already indicated, it forces parliament to deal with what is often virtually skeletal legislation, and then to let the details be filled in by the executive. What is particularly alarming is the fact that, at the federal level, an order in council requires the signature of only four cabinet ministers and later the signature of the governor general. There is, accordingly, no requirement for extensive debate with respect to the merit of the order in council under consideration. The Honourable Perrin Beatty states:

> *But it often happened when I was in the Cabinet. . . that a messenger would come from the Privy Council and say, 'We need your signature on this. We need signatures from four ministers.' 'What's it about?' you would ask, and the messenger would say, 'Don't ask me.'*
>
> *So you would find ministers being asked to sign Orders in Council, creating law without the benefit of any full discussion or briefing. And the minister assumes that his colleagues know what he is doing, so he goes ahead and signs it.*
>
> *The belief that Cabinet gives adequate scrutiny to delegated legislation is false. The extent to which a bureaucrat is able to write law is very great.*[19]

For example, in July of 1981 by order in council, the cabinet ordered cuts in railway service to large parts of the country, affecting 1,200,000 passengers. All of this was done without public debate, reference to parliament or to the Canadian Transport Commission.[20]

The statute which best illustrates the ultimate in delegation of parliamentary authority is of course the War Measures Act.[21] This statute provides that

> the Governor-in-Council may do and authorize such acts and things, and make from time to time orders and regulations, as he may by reason of the existence of real or apprehended war, invasion or insurrection, deem necessary or advisable for the security defense, peace, order and welfare of Canada. . .

The Act then goes on to specify the myriad of matters about which the governor in council may pass regulations, including censorship and the control of publications, arrest, detention, deportation, extensive control over harbours, ports, transportation, trading, production and manufacturing. The Act states that the issue of a proclamation by the governor in council

... shall be conclusive evidence that war, invasion, or insurrection, real or apprehended, exists and has existed for any period of time therein stated, and of its continuance, until by the issue of a further proclamation it is declared that the war, invasion or insurrection no longer exists.[22]

The Act has been proclaimed on three occasions and has involved the most sweeping kind of delegation to what is in practice the cabinet. Two of the occasions for the proclamation of the Act were the First and Second World Wars and the third proclamation took place on October 16, 1970 in connection with the kidnapping of a Quebec cabinet minister and a British diplomat. Since these events already have been chronicled in considerable detail there is no need to go over this ground again except to draw the reader's attention to this most extreme illustration of the use of delegation.[23]

Provincial cabinets have benefitted similarly from the technique of delegation as provincial statutes are replete with examples of widespread powers delegated to the lieutenant governor in council of the province. Each of these provincial operations is considerably smaller than that of the federal government. There is more likelihood that orders in council will be considered and debated by the appropriate provincial cabinet. Nevertheless, at least in British Columbia, the discussion of orders in council takes place after the general consideration of cabinet business and is like all other cabinet business conducted in private and protected by the oath of secrecy.[24]

Other important recipients of delegated authority are boards, commissions and Crown corporations. These bodies exist at the federal and provincial level and have all been established by legislation, and are invariably recipients of delegated legislative authority. Sometimes the delegation involves merely the discharge of responsibilities assigned by statute, but usually there is delegation of rule-making power. The rules made by these bodies are usually referred to as regulations, and once made by the boards or commissions have the same authority as if enacted by the legislature. It is perhaps important to note that the nomenclature for various rules passed by delegatees varies: orders in council, regulations, or in the case of cities, bylaws; nevertheless, from a legal perspective the nomenclature merely describes the source of the rule rather than the nature of its legal impact. Irrespective of how the rule is named, the effect is identical. Namely, the delegatee acting on authority from the delegating legislature has the power to pass rules having the same effect as if those rules were contained in the statute itself.

Boards, commissions and Crown corporations are invariably set up by government so as to place them outside the normal departmental structure. Sometimes this is because one of these bodies is given an adjudicatory function, or because it has had vested in it the responsibility of running a business. It has accordingly been deemed appropriate to remove this body from the normal chain of departmental authority. For example, the term 'Crown Corporation' usually refers to some form of enterprise owned wholly or partially by the state. John Langford and Kenneth Huffman list in an article written in 1983, 454 federal public corporations. They indicate that the Government of Canada has either "a continuing ownership or membership involvement" in all of the legal entities named. These entities deal in everything from buying and selling agricultural products to running an airline and a railroad, and supporting a national hockey team to represent Canada in international ice hockey competitions.[25]

There are, of course, a wide variety of boards and commissions whose only function is to regulate the activities of economic enterprises, whether they be government-owned or privately owned. The classic example of this is the Canadian Radio and Telecommunications Commission which has the responsibility of regulating both publicly and privately owned radio and television in Canada. It not only has the adjudicatory role of deciding who is to have a television or radio licence, but also must determine whether the conditions of that licence have been fulfilled. In addition, the commission is also charged with laying down regulations as to the appropriate content of radio and television broadcasts. There is in fact very little in the way of Canadian business activity that is not tightly regulated by some form of governmental regulation, usually emanating from a board or commission. A classic example of this is, of course, the entire field of agriculture, which is closely regulated at both the federal and provincial levels by large numbers of different agricultural marketing bodies.

Other recipients of delegated authority include cities, professional associations, universities and, on occasion, judges for the purpose of creating rules of civil procedure.[26] As noted above, regulations issued by municipalities and cities are invariably referred to as bylaws, but their legal effect in no way differs from that of orders in council or regulations. In fact, it may come as a surprise to many to learn that every city, municipality, town or village owes its existence to provincial legislation as the authority in this area is vested by the Constitution Act, 1867 in the legislatures of the provinces. Accordingly, cities can be amalgamated, created and abolished as the provincial legislature sees fit.[27]

The above list of delegatees is by no means exhaustive as there is little to restrain the federal parliament or a provincial legislature in deciding who may receive delegated authority. Cabinet ministers have been delegated authority as well as various public officials such as the commissioner of the Royal Canadian Mounted Police.[28] In fact, the general presumption is that the legislature can delegate any power within its jurisdiction to whomever it wishes, subject to two or possibly three exceptions to this general rule, described below.

It has been clearly laid down by the courts that the federal parliament and provincial legislatures cannot delegate power to each other. This was the result of the decision in *Attorney General of Nova Scotia* v. *Attorney General of Canada*.[29] However, this did not stop the Supreme Court of Canada a short time later from declaring valid a scheme whereby the Prince Edward Island legislature and the Parliament of Canada both delegated authority to a provincially-created marketing board.[30] The effect of this decision was really to make interdelegation between legislatures unnecessary as the same result could be achieved by delegating to legal entities created by the appropriate legislature.[31]

The only substantial blockage to delegation has arisen by virtue of the use of section 96 of the Constitution Act, 1867. This section provides that the appointments of judges of the ". . . Superior, District, and County Courts in each Province. . ." are made by the governor general. A series of cases has forestalled attempts by provincial legislatures to vest, in provincially created tribunals or provincially appointed courts, traditional powers of section 96 court judges. The rationale behind these decisions is to make certain that the purpose of section 96 cannot be undermined by a province delegating to administrative tribunals or assigning by legislation to provincially appointed courts, the functions of federally appointed judges. The courts have been fearful that the traditional section 96 courts could therefore end up being denuded of power by provinces using end-run methods of increasing the jurisdiction of administrative tribunals and provincially appointed courts. Thus, for example, an attempt by Ontario to transfer jurisdiction over disputes with respect to landlord and tenancy matters to a provincial commission was declared unconstitutional by the Supreme Court. The Court took the view that matters of landlord and tenant law were traditional functions of section 96 courts and that any attempt to remove them from the jurisdiction of courts with federally appointed judges was a violation of the constitution.[32]

Similarly, attempts to widen the jurisdiction of provincially appointed judges so as to encroach on the functions traditionally exercised by section 96 court judges have been held invalid by the courts.[33] A recent attempt by the federal parliament to delegate the traditional criminal law jurisdiction of county and superior court judges to provincially appointed magistrates in New Brunswick has also been declared unconstitutional as a violation of section 96. This is the first occasion in which section 96 has been used to forestall an attempt at allocating power by the federal parliament.[34]

Though section 96 has in a few instances served to block delegation of legislative authority, in the overall scheme of things it has not proved to be a major hindrance to the utilization of delegation as an important instrument in our governmental system. Generally speaking the courts have been cautious in the use of section 96 and it is only when they have felt that a flagrant violation of the traditional turf of section 96 courts has occurred that they have resorted to this approach.[35]

Another possible restriction on what can be delegated is imposed by the terms of sections 53 and 54 of the Constitution Act, 1867, which provide that bills relating to the raising and expenditure of public funds must originate in the House of Commons and be accompanied by a message from the governor general. As already pointed out these sections are applicable to the provinces by virtue of section 90, therefore money bills must be accompanied by a message from the lieutenant governor. Accordingly, it is our conclusion that any attempt to delegate taxing powers to a subordinate body is quite likely unconstitutional and in violation of sections 53 and 54. It is impossible, however, to provide a definitive answer to this question as no case decided by our courts has ever addressed this issue. In the case of *Reference re Regulations (Chemicals)*[36] the

Supreme Court of Canada asked itself whether sections 53 and 54 would provide an obstacle to delegation involving the raising or expenditure of public funds, yet declined to provide an answer.

Conclusion

Both federal-provincial conferences on constitutional review and various reports have tended to focus on reform of the Senate rather than the House of Commons. It is our view that considerably more attention should have been devoted to the interaction between the executive and the elected members of the House of Commons. It is, however, not surprising that first ministers were not particularly interested in legislative reform which might lead to the diminution of the power of the cabinet in the system. Therefore, the focus was on changing the upper house, particularly with a view to giving the provinces more voice in the affairs of the central government. This objective was frequently seen as being achieved by having senators appointed by the provincial government and thus becoming spokesmen for regional interests. Even a federal commission, namely the Task Force on Canadian Unity, popularly known as the Pepin-Robarts commission, suggested that "in the place of the existing Senate we propose that there be established a Council of the Federation composed of provincial delegations to whom provincial governments could issue instructions, each delegation being headed by a person of ministerial rank or, on occasion, by the premier."[37]

This idea was basically derived from the proposals of the British Columbia government, who in turn based their suggestions on the German constitutional model whereby the Bundesrat essentially is composed of representatives of the regional governments. Prime Minister Trudeau, as indicated earlier, was generally shocked by the decentralizing nature of the proposals of the Pepin-Robarts committee and accordingly ignored the report. However, probably to counteract the many suggestions that the upper house be provincially appointed, Prime Minister Trudeau encouraged the establishment of a joint committee of the Senate and House of Commons to look into the question of Senate reform. The joint committee reported in January of 1984 and suggested that Senators be elected for nine-year terms.[38]

The prospects for Senate reform in the immediate future do not appear particularly bright, as any change in the Senate requires the utilization of the amending formula as outlined in subsection 38(1) of the Constitution Act, 1982. The chances of seven provincial legislative assemblies and the Senate and the House of Commons agreeing on a different structure for the Senate are probably somewhat remote. It is quite possible that at some future time the agreement of seven provinces could be obtained to abolish the Senate. However, all federal governments have found it a useful dumping ground for friends of the governing party and worn-out members of the House of Commons, so the prospect of federal agreement to abolition of the Senate is unlikely.

None of the federal-provincial conferences on constitutional reform dealt with reform of either the functioning of the House of Commons or of the legislative assemblies of the provinces. The Pepin-Robarts commission did suggest introducing a degree of proportional representation into the process of electing members of the House of Commons. They suggested that ". . . the current mode of election to the House of Commons should be modified by introducing an element of proportionality to complement the present simple-majority single-member constituency system." They went on to say that the number of members in the House should be increased by sixty and that "[t]hese members should be selected from provincial lists of candidates prepared by the federal parties in advance of a general election, with the seats being distributed between parties on the basis of percentage of popular votes."[39] The commission, however, did not go on to deal with the whole question of the executive dominance of the legislative process.

In our view, one of the most important changes needed in the Canadian constitutional and governmental system is the revitalization of the parliamentary process, particularly by giving M.P.s and M.L.A.s a more vigorous and creative role in the system. Here again the chance of dramatic change is small as, in an executive-dominated system, the executive is most unlikely to accede to proposals which substantially increase the power of elected members at the expense of the cabinet.[40]

---

[1] For a brief discussion of the subject matters covered by these sections, see R. I. Cheffins and R. N. Tucker, *The Constitutional Process in Canada*. Toronto: McGraw-Hill Ryerson, 2nd ed., 1976, pp. 25–30. For a fuller analysis of the judicial material interpreting the scope of the legislative powers, see Peter W. Hogg, *Constitutional Law of Canada*. Toronto: Carswell, 2nd ed., 1985, chapters 15–27.

[2] Cheffins and Tucker, supra, note 1, p. 16.

[3] The leading defence of positivism and its link with utilitarianism and parliamentary supremacy can be found in an article by Hart, "Positivism and the Separation of Law and Morals," *Jurisprudence; Readings and Cases*. Toronto: University of Toronto Press, 2nd ed., Mark R. MacGuigan, ed., 1966, p. 193.

[4] (1883) 9 A.C. 117 (P.C.).

[5] Ibid., p. 132.

[6] [1935] A.C. 500 (P.C.).

[7] Ibid., pp. 519–520. For further details with respect to this case and the events leading up to it, see Cheffins and Tucker, supra., note 1, pp. 31–32.

[8] [1980] 1 S.C.R. 54. See also the case comment by Hogg, "Constitutional Law — Federal Power to Amend the Constitution of Canada — Reform of the Senate" (1980), 58 Can. B. Rev. 631.

[9] For a detailed analysis of Quebec's use of section 33, see Scott, "Entrenchment by Executive Action: A Partial Solution to 'Legislative Override'" (1982), 4 Supreme Court L. R., 303.

[10] It is not appropriate in this work to go into extensive detail with respect to the internal processes of the federal legislative system. Among the many important works on this subject readers are referred to Robert J. Jackson and Michael M. Atkinson, *The Canadian Legislative System*. Toronto: Macmillan, 2nd rev. ed., 1980. The role of the prime minister in his legislative context as well as in other respects can be pursued in a book by R. M. Punnett, *The Prime Minister in Canadian Government and Politics*. Toronto: Macmillan, 1977. See also Richard J. Van Loon and Michael S. Whittington, *The Canadian Political System*. Toronto: McGraw-Hill Ryerson, 3rd ed., 1981, pp. 616–665. This is a lengthy and interesting chapter but it is noteworthy that in a book consisting of nineteen chapters on the Canadian political system, only one chapter is devoted to parliament. The authors are not suggesting that this is inappropriate but rather that it reflects the relatively

insignificant role played by parliament in formulating public policy at the federal level. For a more formal and traditional but very valuable work on parliament, see J. R. Mallory, *The Structure of Canadian Government*. Toronto: Gage, rev. ed., 1984, chapter 6 on the Senate and chapter 7 on the House of Commons.

[11] Legislative Council Act, Stats. Que. 1968, c.9.

[12] See Cheffins and Tucker, "Constitutions," *The Provincial Political Systems*. Toronto: Methuen, David J. Bellamy, Jon H. Pammett and Donald C. Rowat, eds., 1976, pp. 257, 268. This article develops in greater depth the points made in the preceding paragraph.

[13] See especially Laundy, "Legislatures," *The Provincial Political Systems*, supra, note 12, p. 280. See also J. Terence Morley, Norman J. Ruff, Neil A. Swainson, R. Jeremy Wilson and Walter D. Young, *The Reins of Power*. Vancouver: Douglas and McIntyre, 1983, chapter 2, "The Legislature," by Morley, p. 11.

[14] [1890] 25 Q.B.D. 381, 395.

[15] G. Hewart, *The New Despotism*. London: E. Benn, 1929.

[16] Committee on Ministers' Powers, *Report*. London: Her Majesty's Stationery Office, 1932.

[17] For a fuller exposition of the interrelationship between the development of regulatory bodies and new technology, see Chapter 3 of Cheffins and Tucker, supra, note 1, pp. 52-55.

[18] [1976] 2 S.C.R. 373.

[19] This quotation is contained in an excellent and extensive article on the utilization of orders in council by David Lancashire, "One Slice at a Time," *The Globe and Mail*, October 3, 1981, p. 10.

[20] Ibid.

[21] R.S.C. 1970, c.W-2.

[22] Supra, note 21, s.2.

[23] See Cheffins and Tucker, supra, note 1, pp. 61-63. A series of books was written immediately after the October crisis; they were mostly critical of the invocation of the War Measures Act. See Cheffins and Tucker, supra, note 1, p. 135, n.29-30, where the reader will find summarized the books written on the subject of the October crisis.

[24] For a discussion of cabinet government in British Columbia, see Morley, Ruff, Swainson, Wilson and Young, supra, note 13, chapter 3, "The Premier and the Cabinet," by Young and Morley, p. 45. As that article quite rightly points out, the lieutenant governor in council probably produces more law, in terms of quantity at least, than the legislature.

[25] Langford and Huffman, "The Uncharted Universe of Federal Public Corporations," *Crown Corporations in Canada*. Toronto: Butterworths, J. Robert S. Prichard, ed., 1983, p. 219. This work by Professor Prichard is of invaluable use for anyone interested in a detailed examination of the role, and especially the economics, of Crown corporations at both the federal and provincial levels. For example, with respect to the provinces, see chapter 5 by Vining and Botterell, "An Overview of the Origins, Growth, Size and Functions of Provincial Crown Corporations," p. 303.

[26] The judges of the Supreme Court of Canada can, by virtue of section 103 of the Supreme Court Act, lay down rules of procedure applicable to the conduct of proceedings before the Supreme Court: see R.S.C. 1970, c.S-19, s.103.

[27] Constitution Act, 1867, 30-31 Vict., c.3, s.92(8) (U.K.).

[28] For further detail with respect to recipients of delegated power, see Cheffins and Tucker, supra, note 1, pp. 70-71.

[29] [1951] S.C.R. 31.

[30] *P.E.I. Potato Marketing Board* v. *H.B. Willis Inc. and Attorney General of Canada*, [1952] 2 S.C.R. 392.

[31] The best summation of the law relating to interdelegation between the federal parliament and provincial legislatures is in an article by Lysyk, "Constitutional Law — the Interdelegation Doctrine: A Constitutional Paper Tiger?" (1969), 47 Can. B. Rev., 271.

[32] *Re Residential Tenancies Act of Ontario*, [1981] 1 S.C.R. 714.

[33] See *Attorney General for Ontario and Display Services Co. Ltd.* v. *Victoria Medical Building Ltd.*, [1960] S.C.R. 32; *Seminary of Chicoutimi* v. *Attorney General and Minister of Justice of Quebec*, [1973] S.C.R. 681; *Re Family Relations Act of British Columbia*, [1982] 1 S.C.R. 62.

[34] *McEvoy* v. *Attorney General for New Brunswick and Attorney General of Canada*, [1983] 1 S.C.R. 704.

[35] For a further exposition of the case law relating to section 96, see Hogg, supra, note 1, pp. 152-161. See also Cheffins and Tucker, supra, note 1, pp. 72-74.

[36] [1943] S.C.R.1.

[37] Task Force on Canadian Unity, *A Future Together: Observations and Recommendations*. Ottawa: Minister of Supply and Services Canada, 1979, p. 97.

[38] Government of Canada, *Report of the Special Joint Committee of the Senate and of the House of Commons on Senate Reform*. Ottawa: Queen's Printer, 1984.

[39] Supra, note 37, p. 131.

[40] Readers interested in a very thoughtful series of proposals with respect to the Canadian legislative system should read Jackson and Atkinson, supra, note 10, pp. 191-215. For a much more impassioned critique of the parliamentary system at the federal level, we recommend an article by a former minister in the government of Prime Minister Joe Clark: James Gillies, "The Parliamentary Imperative," *Saturday Night*, June, 1984, p. 52. He argues that both the House of Commons and the Senate are in need of dramatic and drastic reform. As he points out, however, "a government is unlikely to sponsor reform because no government will voluntarily surrender power. Most M.P.s are afraid to propose reform because they aspire to become ministers or at least parliamentary secretaries; calling for parliamentary reform is not the surest route to a seat in the cabinet," p. 56.

JUDICIAL AUTHORITY

The Expanding Role of the Judiciary

In pure constitutional theory the major winners as a result of the passage of the Constitution Act, 1982 were the judiciary. Subsection 52(1) of the Constitution Act, 1982 provides that "the Constitution of Canada is the supreme law of Canada, and any law that is inconsistent with the provisions of the Constitution is, to the extent of the inconsistency, of no force or effect." The impact of this section has already been described and analyzed in the opening pages of the chapter on legislative authority and accordingly need not be dealt with here in detail. It is probably sufficient to remind the reader that now pieces of legislation and governmental actions can be challenged in the courts on the ground that they are inconsistent with the "Constitution of Canada." As the result of historical development, the task of determining whether legislation is contrary to the Constitution of Canada will rest with the judiciary. Furthermore, the judiciary is now armed with subsection 24(1), which provides that "anyone whose rights or freedoms, as guaranteed by this Charter, have been infringed or denied may apply to a court of competent jurisdiction to obtain such remedy as the court considers appropriate and just in the circumstances." It is quite clear that this equips the courts with all of their traditional remedies, especially the power to declare a piece of legislation *ultra vires* (unlawful), as well as other administrative remedies, but it also hints that the courts can now go beyond the traditional remedies that they have utilized in the past.

In the area of pure constitutional law the chief weapon of the courts has been the utilization of the concept of *ultra vires*, namely the proposition that the provincial legislatures, the federal parliament and the British parliament must each stay within the field of legislative jurisdiction vested in them by the Constitution. In practice this meant defining whether legislation was valid according to the defined heads of power in what was formerly the British North America Act, 1867, especially sections 91 and 92. There have been, since Confederation, several hundred decisions of the Judicial Committee of the Privy Council and the Supreme Court of Canada interpreting the words of that Act in order to define the appropriate boundaries of provincial and federal legislative action. Knowledgeable scholars and lawyers agree that quite frequently the division of powers was used by the courts to strike down legislation towards which they were unsympathetic. For example, in *Switzman* v. *Elbling*[1] the Supreme Court of Canada held that a statute which entitled the attorney general of Quebec to padlock premises being used for what was called the dissemination of "Bolshevik propaganda" was beyond the legislative power of that province. On purely analytical legal grounds there was probably good reason for the court to take the position that this was an invasion of the criminal law power. Nevertheless, it is clear from *dicta* in the judgment that there was considerable antagonism to the spirit of this legislation. One judge went so far as to suggest that if it hadn't been struck down on the basis of violating the criminal law power of the federal parliament, it would have violated the spirit of the preamble of the British North America Act, 1867, which provides that Canada shall have a "Constitution similar in Principle to that of the United Kingdom."

The main new weapon in the hands of the judiciary, however, is the first thirty-four sections of the Constitution Act, 1982: the Canadian Charter of Rights and Freedoms. These freedoms, which include democratic rights, mobility rights, legal rights, equality rights, language and educational rights, are very far-reaching in their scope. Furthermore, they are couched in very general language, giving the judiciary considerable opportunities for rendering legislation unconstitutional on the ground that it violates the Charter of Rights and Freedoms. One has only to look at section 2 of the Act to realize that any legislation which violates "freedom of conscience and religion; freedom of thought, belief, opinion and expression including freedom of the press and other media of communications; freedom of peaceful assembly; and freedom of association" is in violation of the Constitution of Canada and can be struck down by the courts as *ultra vires*. This raises a number of questions. For example, do the hate literature provisions of the Criminal Code restrict freedom of "thought, belief, opinion and expression" as provided in paragraph 2(b)? Does compulsory membership in a trade union, referred to frequently as the "closed shop," violate freedom of association if someone's religious beliefs preclude the joining of a union? Is restriction of the use of the imperial measurement system by a retailer contrary to freedom of expression? A provincial judge in Ontario took the view that it was, but on October 16, 1984, a county court judge ruled otherwise.

The foregoing gives merely an inkling of the plethora of problems with which the courts will have to deal in deciding whether governmental enactments or actions are in violation of the Charter. Already the legal rights sections of the Charter, namely sections 7-14, have prompted a whole host of cases dealing with the problems of unreasonable search and seizure, the right to counsel and arbitrary detention, among others. The equal rights provision contained in section 15 which took effect on April 17, 1985 is another section of the Act of very considerable importance when weighing the authority of the legislature against that of the Constitution as interpreted by the judiciary.

The Authority to Create Courts

When the British North America Act was passed in 1867 it did not create any courts but rather vested in the Parliament of Canada and in the provincial legislatures the power to create courts. The most useful starting point is subsection 92(14), which provides that the provincial legislatures have jurisdiction over "the Administration of Justice in the Province, including the Constitution, Maintenance, and Organization of Provincial Courts, both of Civil and Criminal Jurisdiction, and including Procedure in Civil Matters in those Courts." The federal parliament, on the other hand, under the authority of section 101 was given power to

> . . . provide for the Constitution, Maintenance, and Organization of a General Court of Appeal for Canada, and for the Establishment of any additional Courts for the better Administration of the Laws of Canada.

Accordingly, the provinces have passed statutes under the authority of subsection 92(14) creating different courts within their jurisdiction. The traditional practice has been to provide for either two or three levels of trial courts and a supervising body in the form of a court of appeal. All provinces have a provincial court with provincially appointed judges, but, at the time of writing, only about half of the provinces still retain a system of county courts whose judges are appointed and paid by the federal government under the authority of sections 96 and 100 of the Constitution Act, 1867. All of the provinces have a court of general jurisdiction, sometimes referred to as a supreme court, a superior court or a high court. As indicated, every province also provides for a court of appeal to hear appeals from one or more of these trial courts. Usually a case is heard at trial by one level of trial court and then appealed directly to the court of appeal, although occasionally there are provisions for appealing a case from the provincial court to the county court or highest trial court and then appealing to the court of appeal of the province. This, however, illustrates an important and fundamental principle of subsection 92(14), namely, that the creation of these courts and the determination of their civil procedures and jurisdiction is vested in the provincial legislatures. It should be noted, however, that subsection 91(27) of the Constitution Act, 1867 excludes criminal procedure from provincial jurisdiction and hands it to the federal parliament.

The federal parliament has created three courts under its authority as outlined in section 101. Undoubtedly the most important is the Supreme Court of Canada, established in 1875 after very considerable debate and trepidation as to the advisability of this step. The other courts created by the federal parliament are the Federal Court of Canada and the Tax Court of Canada. These latter two courts, however, can only be vested with jurisdiction to deal with matters relating to ". . . the better Administration of the Laws of Canada." This has achieved the accepted meaning of vesting in those courts only authority to deal with laws created by and within the jurisdiction of the federal parliament. In other words, the phrase "Laws of Canada" means federal laws.

With respect to these three federally created courts, the appointment, salary and removal of these judges is completely within the jurisdiction of the federal parliament. The appointment is made by the governor in council as provided by the statutes creating these courts.

With respect to the provincially created courts, the situation is somewhat more complex. Section 96 of the Constitution Act, 1867 provides that the judges of the ". . . Superior, District, and County Courts in each province . . ." shall be appointed by the governor general. This means, in quick summary, that all judges from the county court level right through to the court of appeal are appointed and paid by the federal government. It is true that the official appointment is made by the governor general but this takes place on advice of the federal cabinet. The payment of judges is provided for in a federal statute, namely the Judges Act.[2] The removal of a county court judge is much easier than is that of a superior court judge. By virtue of federal statute, a county court judge can be removed for "misbehaviour or . . . incapacity or inability to perform his duties properly by reason of age or infirmity."[3] With respect to superior court judges, however, the process of removal dates back to the restoration of William and Mary in 1689. At that time the members of the House of Commons and House of Lords were determined that judicial tenure not be within the unilateral control of the Crown and therefore tenure during good behaviour subject to removal only by the upper and lower houses of parliament was established as a fundamental principle of the British constitution. This notion has been carried forward into Canada by subsection 99(1) of the Constitution Act, 1867 which provides that ". . . the Judges of the Superior Courts shall hold office during good behaviour, but shall be removable by the Governor General on Address of the Senate and House of Commons." It is also well understood that the Senate and House of Commons would not take the dramatic step of removing a judge without a thorough investigation by a parliamentary committee.

The Independence of the Judiciary

In the United States the separation of powers between the executive branch, the legislative branch and the judicial branch is a constitutional imperative. The courts must, under the terms of the United States constitution, keep as clear a delineation as possible between these three branches of government. The situation in Canada is, of course, largely different in that members of the cabinet must obtain a seat in the provincial legislature or federal parliament as soon as possible. The concept of the separation of powers, however, is meaningful in Canada in terms of the place and role of the judiciary in the constitutional system. It is well recognized in both law and practice that the judiciary should be independent and as free as possible from the control, influence and dominance of either the executive or legislative parts of government. This independence is achieved in a number of ways. First, as has already been pointed out, it is very difficult to remove judges as compared with other office holders.

Superior court judges and those of federally created courts can only be removed through joint address of the Senate and House of Commons. In addition, judges' salaries are specified by separate statute in order to recognize the distinction between the judiciary and other parts of the public bureaucracy. Thus in the case of federally appointed judges, any alteration to their salaries must proceed through the regular processes of parliamentary legislative procedure. Therefore, attention would quickly be drawn to any attempt to reduce judicial salaries on account of political dissatisfaction with the role of the courts.

Furthermore, no minister of the Crown is held accountable in either the federal parliament or the provincial legislatures for the decisions rendered by the judiciary. A minister cannot be called upon to justify, explain, repudiate or affirm a decision of the judiciary. This long-held tradition of judicial independence is a substantial part of the political consciousness of Canada and any attempt to interfere with it would be bitterly resented. The citizenry of Canada, in our view, remain confident that the courts stand apart from political manipulation and coercion. In turn, the courts in Canada generally have been responsible in trying to maintain a reasonable balance between the needs and necessities of governments on the one hand and the requirements that individual and group interests be protected from government on the other hand.

The Appointment of Judges

One area of concern in recent years has been the process of making judicial appointments. There is no reference in the Constitution Act, 1867 to the role of the provinces with respect to judicial appointments. However, appointments to magistrates' courts were traditionally made by the provinces and the matter was resolved in the case of *R. v. Bush*,[4] in which it was decided conclusively that the power to appoint magistrates is validly vested in the lieutenant governor in council of the province, acting under the authority of subsection 92(14). Thus every province has created, at the bottom of its judicial hierarchy, some form of purely provincial court, that is to say in which every aspect of the court's functioning is under provincial legislative jurisdiction. This means that the determination of matters that can come before the court (other than criminal law matters), court officials, buildings and the appointment and payment of judges are within provincial authority.

The higher courts have made certain that the jurisdiction of purely provincial courts has not been extended so as to invade the traditional realm of county and superior courts.[5] The Supreme Court of Canada, however, has been willing to recognize that the fiscal jurisdiction of the provincial courts must increase in dollar terms to accord with ever-present inflationary trends.[6]

Although the appointment of judges to the purely provincial courts rests in the hands of the lieutenant governor in council, it is sometimes the practice to have a judicial council which sends forward several names for ultimate selection by the lieutenant governor in council. Appointments to all other courts in Canada rest with the federal authorities. As already indicated, with respect to county courts, superior courts and courts of appeal, we enjoy a very interesting blend of federal and provincial jurisdiction. All of these courts are provincially created and except for criminal matters their jurisdiction is provincially determined. Their civil procedure is provincially delineated and the buildings and administrative offices provided for these courts are under provincial authority. Furthermore, the number of judges sitting in county, superior and appeal courts is determined by the provinces, even though the appointment of these judges is, by virtue of section 96, vested in the governor general of Canada. Thus a considerable degree of goodwill is required in the relations between the federal and provincial governments in order to blend what are provincial courts but federally appointed judges. Generally this has worked quite well. However, in the closing days of the government of Prime Minister Trudeau, the Saskatchewan attorney general utilized his power of determining the number of judicial positions to forward the idea that the province should have some consultative part in the process of appointing judges to Section 96 courts.

The federal position has varied over the years with respect to the internal mechanisms used to effect the governor general's appointment powers. When former Prime Minister John Turner was justice minister in the early 1970s, he tried assiduously through the use of a specially appointed official to find highly qualified persons for judicial appointment irrespective of political affiliation. A considerable spirit of goodwill developed among the federal government, the Canadian Bar Association and the provincial governments. It seems that if this essentially unified Canadian judicial system is to function effectively, a maximum degree of cooperation and consultation is required between federal and provincial levels of government. No one is questioning the ultimate authority of the federal government to make judicial appointments, yet surely it is not unreasonable to suggest that the provinces have some voice in the selection of judges to provincially created courts. In fact, late in 1984, Minister of Justice John Crosbie announced his intention of consulting the provincial attorneys general.

With respect to the federally created courts, that is, the Supreme Court of Canada, the Federal Court of Canada and the Tax Court of Canada, the power to appoint judges is vested in the governor in council. This means in effect that the basic responsibility for recommending names to the cabinet rests with the minister of justice, although it is commonly accepted that recommendations with respect to the chief justice of Canada and the chief justices in the various provinces lie within the ambit of the prime minister. Since the Federal Court of Canada is vitally involved in determining that the processes of federal administrative tribunals are within proper legal guidelines, it is important to ensure that appointments to this court be made after as wide a search as possible for appropriate judicial talent.

It is, however, with respect to appointments to the Supreme Court of Canada that the provinces have been most concerned. They see that court as the ultimate umpire in deciding major legislative disputes between the provincial legislatures and the federal parliament. Responsible scholars such as Professor K. M. Lysyk (as he then was) have asked in a quiet but subtle way whether the court has pushed too far in the direction of increasing federal legislative authority at the expense of that of the provinces.[7]

The provinces were so concerned about what they viewed as the possible bias of the Supreme Court of Canada that in the final draft of the Victoria Charter an elaborate scheme was proposed which allowed the provinces a substantial role in the appointment of judges to that court. Quebec, however, for other reasons, rejected the charter and this elaborate process was abandoned, although at subsequent constitutional conferences the question of judicial appointment was continuously raised and debated. It seems unlikely now, in view of the rigidity of the amending process, that any substantial change will be made in the way judges are appointed in Canada. Any effective change will thus probably come about not through legal amendments, but rather through a greater sensitivity on the part of federal officials with respect to consultation not only with provincial governments, but also, if feasible, with other elements of the community.

Many critics of the present situation are reluctant to move to the American model whereby the federal appointment of judges must be approved by the Senate of the United States. The criticism frequently voiced is whether it is appropriate to ask judges their position on important policy questions before they are considered suitable for judicial appointment. There is a fear that this kind of public questioning will have the effect of undermining peoples' confidence in the independence of the judiciary in that there may be a tendency for judges to conform to the wishes of the scrutinizing political body. At the very least, however, provincial governments should be given a considerable role in the consultative process, at least with respect to the Supreme Court of Canada and section 96 courts, that is, provincial courts having federally appointed judges.

The Supreme Court of Canada

One of the authors of this work wrote an article in 1966 referring to the Supreme Court of Canada as "the quiet court in an unquiet country."[8] At that time Canada was racked by a spirit of rampaging nationalism in Quebec which reached its zenith with the election in 1976 of the Parti Quebecois. The early sixties, however, saw the beginning of a substantial push for ever-increasing legislative authority, fiscal power and autonomy generally for the province of Quebec. As was pointed out in that article, the Supreme Court of Canada was not a particularly significant focal point in the tensions between Quebec on the one hand and the federal government on the other. In fact, a study of the cases heard before the Supreme Court during the sixties shows that the court usually heard only two or three cases each year on constitutional matters. These cases focussed primarily on the question of the division of legislative powers. Most of these cases did not deal with issues of major importance to Quebec; instead that province sought to press its demands in the political arena, particularly through the process of the federal-provincial conference.

No institution will be more affected by the constitutional events of 1982 than the Supreme Court of Canada. The passage of a Charter of Rights will undoubtedly force the Court more openly and visibly into a policy-making role. There seems little doubt that more and more of the Court's time will be consumed by constitutional questions. A negative aspect of this focus will be the reduced guidance and uniformity coming from the court in the area of what can be called, roughly, private law. The question invariably asked is whether the Supreme Court of Canada will become a replica of the United States Supreme Court, which is almost exclusively concerned with constitutional matters.

The Supreme Court of Canada was created in 1875 by the Parliament of Canada acting under the authority of section 101 of what was then the British North America Act, 1867. This section provided that

> the Parliament of Canada may, notwithstanding anything in this Act, from Time to Time provide for the Constitution, Maintenance, and Organization of a General Court of Appeal for Canada . . .

The Canadian parliament acting in the spirit of this section accordingly provided for a court with as broadly based a jurisdiction as possible, giving it, in essence, appellate authority over all fields of Canadian law. The creation of the Court was a matter of very considerable debate and in fact prior to its establishment in 1875, two bills designed to create a Supreme Court of Canada were introduced and subsequently abandoned before their passage by the Parliament of Canada.[9] We are fortunate in having two monographs dealing with the Supreme Court of Canada, namely Peter H. Russell, *The Supreme Court of Canada as a Bilingual and Bicultural Institution*;[10] and Paul Weiler, *In the Last Resort*.[11] Chapter 1 of the monograph by Russell has some excellent material on the creation and early functioning of the Court.

Some of the early problems with respect to the establishment of the Supreme Court stem from Quebec's hostility to a judicial institution whose members were appointed by the federal government. Canada had had since Confederation in 1867 recourse to a body known as the Judicial Committee of the Privy Council. This body will be described in more detail later, but very briefly it was a committee made up of law lords who could hear appeals on major judicial questions from the overseas dominions and colonies. The report of this committee of law lords was then put into legal form by an order in council of the Imperial Privy Council. Many Quebecers felt more confident in leaving their constitutional destiny in the hands of this body than in those of the Supreme Court of Canada. The Supreme Court of Canada existed under the shadow of the Judicial Committee of the Privy Council right up until the abolition of appeals to that body in 1949. The Supreme Court originally had six members, but in 1927 its numbers were increased to seven until with the abolition of appeals to the Privy Council in 1949 it was expanded to nine.[12] The special role of Quebec has consistently been recognized with respect to the composition of the Court, because until 1949 the Act required that at least two of the judges must come from Quebec and since 1949 that three of the judges must come from that province.[13] French-English dualism thus received statutory recognition but regionalism has been recognized only by usage in that the normal pattern is to have three judges from Ontario, two from the west and one from the Atlantic provinces. There has been only one exception to this tradition, namely from 1979 to 1982 when there were three judges from the west and only two from Ontario.

The judges are appointed by the governor in council, and thus in effect their appointment is under the control of the cabinet. Recommendations to the cabinet with respect to puisne (ordinary) judges are the responsibility of the minister of justice, whereas recommendations as to the appointment of the chief justice rest with the prime minister.

The Court has a very wide jurisdiction by and large, with the cases to be heard determined by the Court itself. Indicative of its sweeping jurisdiction are the words of section 35 of the Supreme Court Act which provide that "the Supreme Court shall have, hold and exercise an appellate, civil and criminal jurisdiction within and throughout Canada." Prior to 1975 there was an appeal as of right where the amount in question exceeded ten thousand dollars. This tended to load the Court with cases which were not of major importance to the nation though of course they were extremely meaningful to the parties involved. In order to give the Court greater control over its jurisdiction, this appeal as of right was abolished in 1975.[14] Now, in order to bring a civil case before the Supreme Court, leave must be obtained from the Supreme Court of Canada, from the appropriate provincial court of appeal or from the Federal Court of Appeal. In practice, however, leave to appeal civil matters is rarely granted by provincial courts of appeal or the Federal Court of Appeal. The key words with respect to jurisdiction which were added to the Supreme Court Act in 1975 are contained in subsection 41(1) which provides that

> . . . where, with respect to the particular case sought to be appealed, the Supreme Court is of the opinion that any question involved therein is, by reason of its public importance, or the importance of any issue of law or any issue of mixed law and fact involved in such question, one that ought to be decided by the Supreme Court or is, for any other reason, of such a nature or significance as to warrant decision by it . . .

The bulk of the Supreme Court's workload is now discretionary, with three members of the Court making the determination required under section 41. There are two areas, however, in which leave to appeal to the court is not required and where appellants may proceed as of right. The first of these is the area of criminal matters and in this regard the appropriate provisions with respect to appeal are contained in the Criminal Code. In three instances the right of appeal is dependent upon a dissenting opinion on a question of law in a provincial court of appeal.[15]

The second area where the court is given no discretion is with respect to reference cases. The reference process is one whereby the federal governor in council or the provincial lieutenant governor in council can direct a question of law to the relevant court. Section 55 of the Supreme Court Act states that the federal governor in council can refer important questions of law or fact to the court ". . . for hearing and consideration. . . ." The governor in council is not restricted to asking constitutional questions but in practice the reference of non-constitutional matters is extremely rare.

Each of the ten provinces has passed a statute permitting the provincial government to direct reference cases to its provincial court of appeal. The provincial laws are broadly drafted so as to allow provincial governments to refer federal laws to their provincial courts of appeal for determination with respect to constitutionality as well as provincial statutes. When the provincial court of appeal has rendered an opinion on a reference case referred to it by the lieutenant governor in council of the province, there is, by virtue of section 37 of the Supreme Court Act, a right of appeal to the Supreme Court of Canada. This means in effect that provincial governments are in the same position as the federal government in ultimately being able to get an opinion from the Supreme Court of Canada on a matter which they believe to be of considerable importance.[16]

Historically, the Supreme Court of Canada has in every sense been a general court of appeal in that it has decided cases in almost every area of law. It is particularly important to note that at least prior to 1982, constitutional matters did not dominate the Court's docket and, in fact, between 1950 and 1974 the Court disposed of only fifty-nine constitutional cases. After 1975 one sees a rise in the number of constitutional cases but not in such numbers as to constitute more than ten to fifteen percent of the cases decided by the Court. With the advent of the Charter of Rights in 1982, observers of the Supreme Court are asking whether the Court will be concentrating increasingly on Charter and other constitutional cases to the exclusion of private law matters. It must be remembered that many of the provisions in the Charter, especially those in sections 7–14, cover issues which would normally be considered matters of criminal procedure and evidence though they are dealt with in a constitutional document. Nevertheless, the number of constitutional matters is bound to rise in view of the important provisions with respect to political and equality rights provided for in the Charter. In addition, the Court will still be faced with its traditional task of determining whether the federal or provincial legislatures are within their appropriate legislative jurisdiction. It is reasonably safe to assume that the advent of the Charter will push the Court more and more in the direction of the United States Supreme Court which concentrates almost exclusively on constitutional matters. It seems unlikely, however, that the Court will want to totally relinquish its role as a court of general jurisdiction, recognizing the useful role it plays in bringing a degree of uniformity to the private law of Canada.

An issue raised by Professor Peter Russell in a recent article[17] is whether the Supreme Court of Canada is effectively entrenched. He refers to the writings of Professor Peter Hogg who feels that the Supreme Court is still under the unilateral control of the Parliament of Canada. He also refers to the writing of one of the authors, who takes the position that most of the provisions of the Supreme Court Act can now be changed only through the use of the amending formula.[18]

The authors still adhere to the view that the specific wording of section 41, referring to the position of the Supreme Court of Canada, and of paragraph 42(d), cannot be ignored; therefore, the Supreme Court Act, although not listed in the schedule of statutes to the Constitution Act, 1982, is largely entrenched. If this matter should come before the Court, the Supreme Court of Canada might be prepared to say, as it did with respect to the Senate, that certain housekeeping matters are still within federal parliamentary control, but that matters of substance, which we feel include the requirement of three judges from Quebec, have passed into the sphere where unanimous approval of the provinces and the federal parliament is required.

Judicial Committee of the Privy Council

It would be remiss to pass on from the subject of the judiciary without brief reference to the Judicial Committee of the Privy Council. This body was composed primarily of law lords in the United Kingdom who listened to appeals from overseas dominions and colonies. They were not technically a court but rather a committee of Her Majesty's Privy Council. They passed on a recommendation, after hearing the case, to the Privy Council. Thus during the days that Canadian appeals were heard by this body, no dissents were permitted. Appeals to the Privy Council were finally abolished in 1949 though matters begun until April of that year could subsequently be appealed to the Judicial Committee of the Privy Council. The final case heard was that of the *Attorney General for Ontario* v. *Winner*.[19]

Although it is impossible to chronicle in depth the impact of the Judicial Committee of the Privy Council, a general description can be given for the benefit of persons who come across their very important decisions. This body played a major role in reshaping Canada into a genuine federal system. Their decisions in the case of *Hodge* v. *The Queen*,[20] which made provincial legislatures supreme within their sphere, and in the case of *The Liquidators of the Maritime Bank of Canada* v. *Receiver General of New Brunswick*,[21] which made the lieutenant governor the representative of the Crown with the attendant prerogative powers, did much to institute the concept of the provincial and federal legislatures and executives as "equal and coordinate" in the phrase of Professor K. C. Wheare.[22]

---

[1] [1957] S.C.R. 285.

[2] R.S.C. 1970, c.J-1.

[3] R.S.C. 1970, c.J-1, s.31.

[4] (1888) 15 O.R. 398 (Q.B. Div.).

[5] See *Seminary of Chicoutimi* v. *Attorney General and Minister of Justice of Quebec*, [1973] S.C.R. 681; *Re Family Relations Act of British Columbia*, [1982] 1 S.C.R. 62; *Reference re an Act Respecting the Jurisdiction of the Magistrate's Court (Que.)*, (1965) 55 D.L.R. (2d) 701 (S.C.C.); *McEvoy* v. *Attorney General for New Brunswick and Attorney General of Canada*, [1983] 1 S.C.R. 704.

[6] See *Reference re an Act Respecting the Jurisdiction of the Magistrate's Court (Que.)*, supra, note 5.

[7] Lysyk, "Reshaping Canadian Federalism," *William Kurelek Memorial Lectures*. Toronto: University of Toronto Press, 1978.

[8] Cheffins, "The Supreme Court of Canada: The Quiet Court in an Unquiet Country" (1966), 4 Osgoode Hall L. J., 259.

[9] For an excellent history of the measures and debates relating to the establishment of the Supreme Court of Canada, see MacKinnon, "The Establishment of the Supreme Court of Canada" (1946), 27 Can. Hist. Rev., 258.

[10] Ottawa: Queen's Printer, 1969.

[11] Toronto: Carswell/Methuen, 1974.

[12] Supreme Court Act, R.S.C. 1970, c.S-19, s.4.

[13] Supreme Court Act, R.S.C. 1970, c.S-19, s.6.

[14] An Act to Amend the Supreme Court Act and to make related amendments to the Federal Court Act, Stats. Can. 1974-75-76, c.18, proc. in force January 27, 1975.

[15] For full details on the right of appeal with respect to criminal matters, see Hogg, "Jurisdiction of the Court: The Supreme Court of Canada" (1980), 3 Can.-U.S. L. J., 39, 48.

[16] Readers interested in a comprehensive discussion of the reference procedure should see Barry L. Strayer, *The Canadian Constitution and the Courts.* Toronto: Butterworth's, 2nd ed., 1983, chapter 9.

[17] "Constitutional Reform of the Judicial Branch: Symbolic v. Operational Considerations" (1984), 17 Can. J. Poli. Sci., 227.

[18] Peter W. Hogg, *Canada Act 1982 Annotated.* Toronto: Carswell, 1982, pp. 92-93; Cheffins, "The Constitution Act, 1982 and the Amending Formula: Political and Legal Implications" (1982), 4 Supreme Court L. R., 43.

[19] [1954] A.C. 543 (P.C.).

[20] *Hodge v. The Queen,* (1883) 9 A.C. 117 (P.C.).

[21] *The Liquidators of the Maritime Bank of Canada* v. *Receiver General of New Brunswick,* [1892] A.C. 437 (P.C.).

[22] For a fuller description of the background and impact of the J.C.P. C. see R. I. Cheffins and R. N. Tucker, *The Constitutional Process in Canada.* Toronto: McGraw-Hill Ryerson, 2nd ed., 1976, pp. 9, 94-95, 123 regarding matters of structure. For brief discussions on the impact of these decisions, see pp. 28, 31-32, 72-74, 88-89, 97, 105-110, 129. See also Strayer, supra, note 16; Peter H. Russell, *Leading Constitutional Decisions.* Ottawa: Carleton University Press, 3rd ed., 1982.

FEDERALISM AND THE DIVISION OF POWERS

The preamble to the statute which created Canada, namely the British North America Act, 1867, reveals that the first principle underlying the formation of Canada was the desire "to be federally united into One Dominion." That statement goes on to indicate that the other unifying principles were the desire "to be under the Crown of the United Kingdom" and to have a constitution "similar in Principle to that of the United Kingdom." This is evidence of the high degree of importance placed upon federalism as a condition of bringing together the three British North American colonies of Canada, New Brunswick and Nova Scotia.

It seems fairly clear in retrospect that the Canadian nation would not have been formed without the recognition and implementation of a federal form of government. New Brunswick and Nova Scotia had in the years prior to Confederation developed distinct political and economic existences which they did not want to see totally merged in a larger union. Federalism is usually adopted as part of a nation's constitution when it is impossible to achieve national status without it. Inevitably tensions exist between those forces favouring unity, for reasons such as common traditions, military security or the economic advantages of a wider marketplace, and those forces opposed to unity. The latter arise from regions which have had a rather lengthy political existence and a degree of separate economic functioning. Language and geographic factors often compound the opposition. K. C. Wheare in his classic work on federalism notes that of the four genuine federal countries, three of them, namely the United States, Canada and Australia, are all large in size with very dispersed populations.[1] Not only were New Brunswick and Nova Scotia relatively remote in geographical terms in 1867, but, in addition, the population of what is now Quebec was largely French-speaking and of Roman Catholic religion as opposed to the rest of North America which was largely English-speaking and Protestant. Thus, except for Ontario, the components of the new nation had strong vested interests in maintaining their economic and political identities. At the same time, however, Ontario and business interests in Quebec had a strong interest in a highly centralized federation. Ontario's interests, in particular, have always coincided with a powerful central government as Ontario is the dominant economic force within Canada. This is probably why, when Canada was formed in 1867 with basically a federal system, the central government was provided with legal weapons to assure ultimate dominance by the central government.

Much of what federalism is about is economic. Federalism is an attempt by regional governments to retain some control over their local economic destinies, which they often feel are in conflict with national policy. In fact, many of the political tensions in Canada since its inception have been struggles between central Canada's economic interests and those of its regional hinterland. Add the fact that Quebec is largely French-speaking, and one can see that the two main threads running through the stream of federal-provincial relations have been those of cultural identity and economic self-interest. But even in the area of cultural identity, much of the argument has revolved around demands by French-speaking Canadians to play a larger role in the ownership and control of their economy.

Probably no other Canadian political subject has been more controversial and more written about than the various aspects of federalism.[2] Although Wheare identifies only four genuinely federal systems of government, one of which is Canada, he is of the view that, in theory at least, it is only a "quasi-federal" state.[3] What is meant by federalism or what Wheare calls the "federal principle"? He defines federalism as ". . . the method of dividing powers so that the general and regional governments are each, within a sphere, coordinate and independent."[4] This means that each general or regional government has an independent sphere of power free from intrusion by the other level of government.

Canada as a Federal State

Wheare is doubtful, however, as to whether in pure theory Canada is a federal system. He describes the situation in this way: ". . . the Canadian Constitution is quasi-federal in law, it is predominantly federal in practice."[5] What Wheare is saying is that in constitutional theory the central government is given sufficient powers to control the autonomy of the provincial governments and thus the principle of "equal and coordinate status" is not sustained in the black letter law of Canada's Constitution. He goes on to make it clear, though, that the centralizing features of the Canadian Constitution which undermine the federal principle have so fallen into disuse that in practice Canada is a genuine federal state. For example, some of the legal features of the Constitution Act, 1867 which in theory render Canada a quasi-federal state include the power of the federal government to disallow any act passed by a provincial legislature. This is essentially a straight veto power which is vested in the federal governor in council. In addition, the federally appointed lieutenant governor of each province can, on instruction from the federal government, reserve provincial bills for the consideration of the governor in council in Ottawa. Furthermore, the lieutenant governor, if he or she so wishes, may refuse assent to provincial bills and thus a considerable constraint can be placed on provincial authority.

In fact, in the early part of Canada's history, lieutenant governors were looked upon as federal officers, almost replicas of the colonial governors sent out from Great Britain prior to 1867. Historically, the use of these powers of reservation and disallowance has been frequent, but it must be remembered that they have now fallen into disuse. For example, although the federal government has disallowed 112 acts of the provincial legislatures, the last of these disallowances took place in 1942. Eleven of them took place between 1937 and 1942, all with respect to Alberta legislation, and were manifestations of the struggle between that province and Canada with respect to the economic tensions produced by the Depression.

The power of the lieutenant governors to reserve bills for the pleasure of the governor in council has been used on seventy occasions. It seemed that with the abatement of the more pressing tensions between Alberta and Canada in the early forties, reservation had also fallen into disuse, but to the surprise of everyone, Lieutenant Governor Bastedo in 1961 reserved a bill passed by the Legislative Assembly of Saskatchewan dealing with the subject of mineral contracts. Prime Minister Diefenbaker quickly tabled in the House of Commons an order in council

> in which His Excellency the Governor General by and with the advice of Her Majesty the Queen's privy council for Canada declares his assent to Bill No. 56 of the legislature of Saskatchewan passed during the present year and which was reserved by the lieutenant governor of Saskatchewan for the signification of the pleasure of the Governor General in accordance with the terms of the British North America Act.

In his statement to the House, the prime minister indicated that he had not been consulted by the lieutenant governor and he further indicated that he certainly would have recommended that the bill not be reserved. It was obvious that he felt this action should not be taken without consultation with the federal government; a logical view since a reservation immediately passes responsibility to the federal governor in council as to whether to give Royal Assent. It should be noted that of the seventy bills reserved for federal consideration, only thirteen were ever given assent by federal order in council. Thus, Wheare's contention is essentially correct: the powers of reservation and disallowance have for all practical purposes fallen into disuse, though as the courts have clearly indicated, this does not mean that they are no longer legally exercisable.[6]

There are other unitary features in the Constitution not mentioned by Professor Wheare, namely the declaratory power in paragraph 92(10)(c) of the Constitution Act, 1867, which allows the Parliament of Canada to declare works to be "for the general advantage of Canada." This power has been exercised on numerous occasions but, since the early 1960s, has fallen into disuse.[7] However, it has been important with respect to matters such as railways, grain elevators, atomic energy and telephone companies, bridges, harbours, wharves and canals. Similarly, another centralizing feature is section 93 of the Constitution Act, 1867, which allows remedial legislation by the federal government in the event that

Roman Catholics and Protestants are deprived of their traditional rights to religious education. This power has never been used.

The Constitution Act, 1867 and the Division of Powers

The starting point for the legal analysis of the distribution of legislative powers in Canada is to be found in the Constitution Act, 1867. Sections 91, 92, 92A, 93, 94, 94A, 95, 101, 109, 117 and 132 of this Act all deal with the division of legislative powers. Furthermore, students of this subject must be aware of the Constitution Act, 1930, which places the three Prairie Provinces in the same position as the original provinces in connection with section 109. This proved to be a fortuitous development because it vested in the Prairie Provinces jurisdiction with respect to ". . . Lands, Mines, Minerals and Royalties . . . and all Sums then due or payable for such Lands, Mines, Minerals or Royalties. . . ." Two other crucial sections dealing with the division of powers, which must be kept in mind, are sections 121 and 125. The first of these sections is a step in the direction of keeping a free flow of trade moving from one province to the other. Section 125 ensures that the central government and provincial governments cannot impose taxes on each other's lands and property. In considering problems of federalism, attention should also be directed towards subsection 6(2) of the Constitution Act, 1982, which was designed to provide for the mobility of persons between provinces in Canada. This was a response to attempts by provinces to give preference to their own residents with respect to employment, at the expense of persons from other provinces. This section along with section 121 of the 1867 statute, attempts to provide fundamental constitutional guarantees with respect to the mobility of goods and people.[8]

Sections 91 and 92 are undoubtedly the key sections with respect to the division of legislative powers. These sections have been used to illustrate the proposition that the Fathers of Confederation assigned economic authority to the central government, while vesting in the provinces jurisdiction with respect to cultural and local matters.[9] Although there is some validity to this viewpoint it does not stand up under close and detailed scrutiny. To be fair to proponents of this view, however, it must be said that it is impossible to develop a comprehensive theory which describes the rationale as to why authority was vested in one legislative jurisdiction rather than the other. Though cultural and linguistic matters are undoubtedly important, there is no question that the underlying tension within a federal system is the allocation of economic resources and economic control. When one begins to look at the specifics of economic control, it becomes increasingly apparent that there is considerable provincial and federal control over economic matters and perhaps even more importantly, a good deal of shared jurisdiction with respect to Canada's economic destiny. Both jurisdictions are given control over direct taxation. Provincial authority in the area of taxation was increased by virtue of the Constitution Act, 1982, whereby an amendment (section 92A) was added to the Constitution Act, 1867, vesting in the provinces the power to impose indirect taxes with respect to certain types of non-renewable natural resources when these resources are part of inter-provincial trade.[10]

One of the most interesting aspects of Canadian federalism is the high degree of concurrent authority vested in both the provincial and federal legislative chambers with respect to certain subjects. As already mentioned, there is a high degree of concurrence with respect to taxation.[11] Similarly, section 94A provides for concurrence with respect to old-age pensions and supplementary benefits, as does section 95 with respect to agriculture and immigration. Even more interesting is the willingness of the courts to allow de facto jurisdiction in a number of areas not specifically mentioned in the written constitution. For example, in the area of highway control the courts have allowed both the federal parliament and the provincial legislatures to exercise penal authority regarding various aspects of highway driving. The high water mark of concurrence as developed by the courts is manifested by the *Multiple Access Ltd.* v. *McCutcheon* case in which the courts were prepared to allow to stand as valid federal and provincial legislation that was virtually identical in terms of content and process but which manifested no "express contradiction." That case involved the Canada Corporations Act and the Ontario Securities Act, both of which dealt with insider trading. The Supreme Court of Canada held that each piece of legislation was based on a valid head of federal or provincial power, each dealt with the subject of insider trading from a valid federal or provincial aspect, and that since there was no express contradiction between them, both pieces of legislation could stand.[12] The Court made it clear that the judiciary should intervene to make certain that the two pieces of legislation, whatever they might be, not be used against the same person. Thus, for example, in the case of the driving laws, the authorities have the choice of selecting prosecution under the Criminal Code or under provincial highway legislation. Generally speaking this has worked to the advantage of the citizen as the authorities generally select prosecution under the less onerous provisions of the latter.

The Judiciary and the Division of Powers

Ultimate decision making with respect to the division of legislative powers has primarily taken place in the courts, although a substantial amount of federal-provincial decision making takes place within the political arena.[13] Quite frequently, however, federal and provincial governments are unable to reach mutually satisfactory agreement with respect to jurisdictional and other contentious federal-provincial issues. In this context it becomes necessary to turn to the courts for a final resolution of the impasse, and it is here that the reference power has proved to be especially valuable in getting before the courts, quickly and effectively, jurisdictional questions with respect to the division of powers.[14]

The majority of cases involving the division of powers, however, have arisen as the result of ordinary litigation. For example, if a person is charged either under the Criminal Code or other federal penal statute, or with an offence under provincial law, it is always open to the accused to raise the question of *ultra vires.* Essentially, this is the proposition that either the entire statute, or the section under which the person has been charged, is beyond the legislative jurisdiction of the enacting legislature. For example, in the case of *Westendorp* v. *The Queen*[15] the accused Westendorp had been charged with the violation of a Calgary bylaw which made it an offence to be on a street or approach another person on a street for the purposes of prostitution. The accused was acquitted at trial on the ground that the Calgary city bylaw was unconstitutional in that it invaded the federal jurisdiction with respect to criminal law. The Court of Appeal of Alberta overturned this decision and found the bylaw to be a valid exercise of delegated authority by the City of Calgary. It found that the bylaw was within the authority delegated by the Municipal Government Act and that this was a valid attempt by the city to control conduct on its own streets. An appeal was taken to the Supreme Court of Canada which unanimously overturned the decision of the Alberta Court of Appeal. The Supreme Court of Canada, in a brief judgment, found the bylaw to be an invasion of the federal jurisdiction with respect to criminal law in that it was designed to control and punish prostitution. The Court found that the subject of prostitution was dealt with by the criminal law and any attempt to enter this domain through provincial law was unconstitutional. The judgment in many ways was an unsatisfactory one in the light of repeated occasions, mentioned earlier, particularly with respect to driving offences, where pieces of legislation which seemingly overlapped were upheld on the basis of the double-aspect doctrine. That is to say, essentially the same subject matter could be dealt with by both the federal parliament and the provincial legislature on the ground that they were dealing with the problem in question from a different legislative aspect. The Court was clear in expressing its concern that to sustain this bylaw would be to open the floodgates for increased invasion of the federal criminal law jurisdiction by municipalities.[16]

It is also interesting to note that this is one of the first cases in which a section of the Charter of Rights had been argued as the basis for striking down a bylaw. Chief Justice Laskin laid down the very sensible proposition that there was no point in looking at the question of the Charter until the question of the division of powers had been first addressed by the Court. Thus, since the bylaw failed in that it was not sustained by a valid head under section 92, there was no need to deal with the second hurdle now faced by all governments, namely the Charter of Rights and Freedoms.

A person charged under the Criminal Code is of course also able to argue that the section under which he or she has been charged is beyond the jurisdiction of the federal parliament's control with respect to criminal law. Defendants have been remarkably unsuccessful in this regard in that only in the case of *Boggs* v. *The Queen* has a defendant successfully argued that the applicable section of the Code went beyond parliament's power over criminal law and encroached on provincial jurisdiction.[17]

In the *Margarine Reference* case, counsel for the Government of Canada tried to argue that a section of the Dairy Industry Act prohibiting the manufacture, importing, selling and possessing of margarine was a valid exercise of the federal criminal law power.[18] The courts struck this down on the ground that it was an attempt to use the criminal law power to interfere in the economic life of Canada in order to benefit one region at the expense of another.

It is of course also possible to raise the question of constitutional validity in civil litigation, that is, in a dispute between private parties. Some of Canada's most important constitutional cases have emanated from such law suits. The law provides, however, that whenever someone intends to raise a constitutional issue, notice must be served on the attorney general of Canada and the attorney general of the appropriate province so that they can intervene to argue the constitutionality of the legislation before the court. Thus one can witness the spectacle of lawyers on each side of a private law dispute arguing contrary positions on contitutionality supported or opposed as the case may be, by representatives of the attorney general of Canada and the attorneys general of the provinces. One author has given us a lengthy list, with case examples, of the different kinds of private law suits in which constitutional issues have been raised.[19]

Though most of the enumerated heads in sections 91 and 92 have been referred to at various times by the courts, the main areas referred to by litigants and the courts include the federal parliament's general power to legislate ". . . for the Peace, Order, and good Government of Canada, in relation to all Matters not coming within the Classes of Subjects by this Act assigned exclusively to the Legislatures of the Provinces." This is generally referred to as the "federal general power" and has been used to sustain federal enactments relating to emergencies and residual matters not outlined in the enumerated heads. A comprehensive theory of when the federal general power can be used was developed by Mr. Justice Betz, who though in dissent, had his views on the use of the federal general power agreed to by four other judges.[20]

The other two key heads of federal authority that have been frequently referred to in litigation are the federal jurisdiction under subsection 91(2), the regulation of trade and commerce, and subsection 91(27), the jurisdiction with respect to criminal law and criminal procedure.

From the provincial perspective, the two provisions that have been most important are subsection 92(13), "Property and Civil Rights in the Province," and subsection 92(16), "Generally all Matters of a merely local or private Nature in the Province." It has been argued in two cases, namely the *Dupond* case and the *Local Prohibition* case, that subsection 92(16) constitutes a second residual source of power operating on behalf of the province as the federal general power does on behalf of the federal parliament. This view has also been argued by prominent constitutional scholars such as Mr. Justice Kenneth Lysyk.[21]

The key to a reasonably balanced distribution of legislative powers between the federal parliament and the provincial legislatures has undoubtedly been the provinces' authority with respect to property and civil rights. Professor Hogg brilliantly synthesizes this point when he states in speaking about the property and civil rights power that *[t]his is by far the most important of the provincial heads of power. Indeed, the previous chapters on the three major federal heads of power, namely, peace, order, and good government, trade and commerce and criminal law, have been as much concerned with property and civil rights in the province as they have been with their ostensible topics. Most of the major constitutional cases have turned on the competition between one or more of the federal heads of power, on the one hand, and property and civil rights, on the other.*[22]

The importance of this provincial jurisdiction with respect to property and civil rights is dramatically illustrated in what is arguably the most important case in the history of litigation with respect to the division of powers: the case of *Citizens Insurance Company of Canada* v. *Parsons.*[23] The issue in this case revolved around the validity of an Ontario statute regulating the insurance industry. This was part of an early battle between the federal parliament and the provincial legislatures to regulate insurance companies. In this case the plaintiff insurance company attempted to argue that the Ontario statute was invalid in that it was an invasion of the federal jurisdiction over trade and commerce. One sees in this case, perhaps more than any other, the motivation of the Judicial Committee of the Privy Council with respect to the division of powers. Sir Montague Smith traces the history of the phrase "property and civil rights" back to the Quebec Act of 1774 and takes the view that these words were used in the Constitution Act, 1867 in their widest sense. By this he means that they were to vest in the provinces control over their private law except to the extent that areas of the private law had been specifically assigned to the federal parliament under the enumerated heads of section 91. As Sir Montague Smith says:

If, however, the narrow construction of the words "civil rights," contended for by the appellants were to prevail, the dominion parliament could, under its general power, legislate in regard to contracts in all and each of the provinces and as a consequence of this the province of Quebec, though now governed by its own Civil Code, founded on the French law, as regards contracts and their incidents, would be subject to have its law on that subject altered by the dominion legislature, and brought into uniformity with the English law prevailing in the other three provinces, notwithstanding that Quebec has been carefully left out of the uniformity section of the Act.[24]

His Lordship goes on to say:

in this statute the words "property" and "civil rights" are plainly used in their largest sense; and there is no reason for holding that in the statute under discussion they are used in a different and narrower one.[25]

He expresses the concern that

> the words "regulation of trade and commerce," in their unlimited sense
> are sufficiently wide, if uncontrolled by the context and other parts of the
> Act, to include every regulation of trade ranging from political arrange-
> ments in regard to trade with foreign governments, requiring the sanc-
> tion of parliament, down to minute rules for regulating particular trades.
> But a consideration of the Act shows that the words were not used in this
> unlimited sense.[26]

His Lordship goes on to say:

> If the words had been intended to have the full scope of which in their
> literal meaning they are susceptible, the specific mention of several of the
> other classes of subjects enumerated in section 91 would have been
> unnecessary; as, 15, banking; 17, weights and measures; 18, bills of
> exchange and promissory notes; 19, interest; and even 21, bankruptcy
> and insolvency.[27]

The court goes on to lay down the famous proposition that the federal parliament's control over trade and commerce is limited to international trade,
interprovincial trade and "it may be that they would include general regulation of
trade affecting the whole dominion."[28] It must be noted however that the last
of these three categories has not been a fruitful source of federal legislative
power and the courts essentially are prepared to give the federal parliament
jurisdiction with respect to trade and commerce only where the matter legislated
upon is international or interprovincial. In summation, the result of the *Parsons*
case was to leave the integrity of the provincial private law intact and ultimately to
give the provincial legislatures control over local trade. Thus much of the
economic struggle between federal and provincial legislatures has been parliament's claim to jurisdiction over interprovincial matters as compared with the
provincial assertion that matters are essentially local in nature. The willingness
of the courts, however, to recognize that the area of contract is essentially a
provincial subject matter has been essential to preserving substantial provincial
control over local economic concerns.[29]

Mr. Justice Lysyk also points out that not only has the property and civil
rights power been carefully balanced with federal control over trade and
commerce, but it has also been used by the courts to contain excessive use of
the federal general power with respect to peace, order and good government.
He states that

> it may be noted that many of the key decisions in which the introductory
> clause of section 91 was advanced unsuccessfully on behalf of federal
> authority were ones in which the legislation in question was directed at
> certain aspects of contracts or contractual relationships: contracts of
> employment, including labour relations and labour welfare legislation,
> commercial contracts associated with local trade, contracts of insurance,

and a public insurance program analogous to private insurance schemes
and touching employment contracts. The pattern is clear. The introductory
clause has not fared well when pitted against the property and civil rights
clause, and particularly when provincial hegemony over contractual mat-
ters, conferred under the rubric of "civil rights," has been challenged.[30]

What has been discussed in the preceding paragraphs is what is referred to
by the courts and lawyers as "characterization," that is, defining who has the
appropriate authority with respect to legislative subject matters. As Hogg points
out in his chapter on the principles of judicial review, one first must identify
the pith and substance of the challenged law and secondly decide the relevant
head of legislative power. The courts often refer to finding the "pith and substance" of the legislation and then proceed to determine whether the legislation is
either supported by an appropriate head of power or is an encroachment on
another legislature's jurisdiction. In a brief work of this kind it is impossible to
begin the extraordinarily lengthy analysis needed to define how the courts have
dealt with and interpreted the various legislative powers assigned to the federal
and provincial legislatures. There has been a welter of articles on this subject
but fortunately it has been reviewed in very considerable depth by Professor
Hogg in his classic work, *The Constitutional Law of Canada.*[31]

It is interesting to note that the role of the courts with respect to the division
of powers has been substantially more important than that of constitutional
amendment. The process of constitutional amendment has brought about only
four changes in the division of powers: subsection 91(2A) dealing with unemployment insurance, which was added to federal jurisdiction in 1940, and section 94A, which was added by two amendments, the British North America
Act, 1951 and the British North America Act, 1964 among them. The cumu-
lative effect of the latter amendments was to give concurrent jurisdiction to the
federal parliament and provincial legislatures with respect to old-age pensions
and supplementary benefits. It is interesting to note, however, that in the event
of conflict the provincial legislative enactments are to prevail. In addition is
the amendment now listed as section 92A, which increased provincial legislative
jurisdiction with respect to non-renewable natural resources. This amendment
not only permitted the provinces to impose indirect taxes with respect to non-
renewable natural resources, but also gave them some authority with respect to
the interprovincial export of non-renewable natural resources in the absence
of federal legislation.[32]

Unquestionably the overwhelming majority of important cases with respect
to the Canadian Constitution until 1982 revolved around the division of legislative
powers. Litigants used the division of legislative powers as a last resort to struggle against legislation which they did not conceive to be in their interest. The
division of legislative powers was often argued in attempts to have declared
unconstitutional regulatory statutes applying to business. Though undoubtedly
there will still continue to be a few cases every year raising questions on the
distribution of legislative power, there is little doubt that most of the consti-

tutional focus will now shift to the utilization, by both accused and ordinary private litigants, of the Charter of Rights and Freedoms. Governments will now have to defend their legislation, both on the ground that it is within the legislative authority assigned to them by the Constitution and at the same time that the legislation does not violate the Charter of Rights and Freedoms.

---

[1] K. C. Wheare, *Federal Government*. London: Oxford University Press, 4th ed., 1963, p. 40.

[2] The leading text on federalism in Canada is that by Donald V. Smiley, *Canada in Question: Federalism in the Eighties*. Toronto: McGraw-Hill Ryerson, 3rd ed., 1980. Among the vast amount of other literature on this subject readers might find especially valuable Richard Simeon, *Federal-Provincial Diplomacy: The Making of Recent Policy in Canada*. Toronto: University of Toronto Press, 1972; Edwin R. Black, *Divided Loyalties*. Montreal: McGill-Queen's University Press, 1975; J. M. Beck, ed., *The Shaping of Canadian Federalism: Central Authority or Provincial Right?* Toronto: Copp Clark, 1971. In fact, so voluminous is the amount of writing on this subject that the Institute of Intergovernmental Relations at Queen's University in 1967 issued a bibliography with respect to federalism in Australia, Canada, the United States and other countries, and a supplementary bibliography in 1975. The institute continues to publish materials focussing on problems of Canadian federalism.

[3] Wheare, supra, note 1, pp. 18-20.

[4] Wheare, supra, note 1, p. 10.

[5] Wheare, supra, note 1, p. 20.

[6] *Reference re Reservation and Disallowance*, [1938] S.C.R. 71. Readers interested in the questions of reservation and disallowance should refer to John T. Saywell, *The Office of Lieutenant Governor*. Toronto: University of Toronto Press, 1957. See also G.V. La Forest, *Disallowance and Reservation of Provincial Legislation*. Ottawa: Department of Justice, 1955. This work is particularly useful because it includes as Appendices A and B lists of all of the acts or bills disallowed or reserved, the reasons for disallowance or reservation and the ultimate disposal of the bills. With reference to the actions of Lieutenant Governor Bastedo, see Mallory, "The Lieutenant Governor's Discretionary Powers: the Reservation of Bill 56 in Saskatchewan" (1961), 27 Can. J. Econ. Poli. Sci., 518.

[7] Professor Peter Hogg notes that this power has been used "no less than 470 times." However, as he points out, with the increasing sensitivity to principles of federalism, the power has not been used since 1961: Peter W. Hogg, *Constitutional Law of Canada*. Toronto: Carswell, 2nd ed., 1985, pp. 491-493. The authors gratefully acknowledge Peter W. Hogg and the Carswell Company Limited for permission to reproduce portions of Constitutional Law of Canada, Second Edition.

[8] For a commentary on and summary of leading cases on sections 121 and 125 of the Constitution Act, 1867, see W. H. McConnell, *Commentary on the British North America Act*. Toronto: Macmillan, 1977. For a commentary on section 6 of the Constitution Act, 1982, see Peter W. Hogg, *Canada Act 1982 Annotated*. Toronto: Carswell, 1982, pp. 21-26.

[9] Penny, Trebilcock and Laskin, "Existing and Proposed Constitutional Restraints on Provincially Induced Barriers to Economic Mobility in Canada," *Federalism and the Canadian Economic Union*. Toronto: University of Toronto Press, Michael J. Trebilcock, J. Robert S. Prichard, Thomas J. Courchene and John Whalley, eds., 1983, pp. 501-502.

[10] See J. Peter Meekison, Roy J. Romanow and William D. Moull, *Origins and Meaning of Section 92A: The Constitutional Amendment on Resources*. Montreal: Institute for Research on Public Policy, 1985.

[11] See G.V. La Forest, *The Allocation of Taxing Power Under the Canadian Constitution*. Toronto: Can. Tax Fdn., 2nd ed., 1981.

[12] *Multiple Access Ltd.* v. *McCutcheon*, [1982] 2 S.C.R. 161, and see case comment by Colvin, "Constitutional Law — Paramountcy — Duplication and Express Contradiction — *Multiple Access Ltd.* v. *McCutcheon*" (1983), 17 U.B.C. L. R., 347.

[13] See Peter H. Russell, *Leading Constitutional Decisions*. Ottawa: Carleton University Press, 3rd ed., 1982; Smiley, supra, note 2, chapter 4; R. I. Cheffins and R. N. Tucker, *The Constitutional*

Process in Canada. Toronto: McGraw-Hill Ryerson, 2nd ed., 1976, chapter 6; Simeon, supra, note 2. Russell's book has a brief but excellent introduction to the role of the courts with respect to the division of powers. For an exceptionally detailed analysis of the principles and cases dealing with the distribution of powers, see Hogg, supra, note 7, chapters 15-27 inclusive.

[14] See Barry L. Strayer, *The Canadian Constitution and the Courts.* Toronto: Butterworths, 2nd ed., 1983, pp. 271-295.

[15] [1983] 1 S.C.R. 43.

[16] For a comment on this case and the unsatisfactory nature of the reasoning, see Whyte, "Prostitution: Municipal Regulation and the Domain of Criminal Law Meet Again" (1983), 32 C. R. (3d), 107.

[17] *Boggs* v. *The Queen*, [1981] 1 S.C.R. 49. Other attempts, such as that made in the case of *Morgentaler* v. *The Queen*, [1976] 1 S.C.R. 616, to assert that a section of the Criminal Code was *ultra vires* on the basis of the division of powers have invariably failed.

[18] *Reference re Validity of Section 5(A) of the Dairy Industry Act*, [1949] S.C.R.1.

[19] See Strayer, supra, note 14. For a further analysis of this subject with illustrations, see John D. Whyte and William R. Lederman, *Canadian Constitutional Law: Cases, Notes and Materials.* Toronto: Butterworths, 2nd ed., 1977, pp. 5-16 and 5-17.

[20] *Reference re Anti-Inflation Act*, [1976] 2 S.C.R. 373.

[21] *Attorney General for Canada* v. *Dupond*, [1978] 2 S.C.R. 770; *Attorney General for Ontario* v. *Attorney General of Canada*,[1896] A.C. 348 (P.C.); Lysyk, "Constitutional Reform and the Introductory Clause of Section 91: Residual and Emergency Law-Making Authority" (1979), 57 Can. B. Rev., 531.

[22] Hogg, supra, note 7, pp. 453-454.

[23] (1882) 7 A.C. 96 (P.C.).

[24] Ibid., p. 111.

[25] Ibid.

[26] Supra, note 23, p. 112.

[27] Ibid.

[28] Supra, note 23, p. 113.

[29] Professor Lederman and others have argued that the interpretation of the property and civil rights power by the Judicial Committee of the Privy Council was accurate in that historically this phrase covered all legal matters with the exception of English criminal law and English public law: W. R. Lederman, "Unity and Diversity in Canadian Federalism: Ideals and Methods of Moderation," chapter 15 in *Continuing Constitutional Dilemmas.* Toronto: Butterworths, 1981. Further support for this position is put forward by Mr. Justice Kenneth Lysyk, supra, note 21, p. 544.

[30] Lysyk, supra, note 21, pp. 545-546.

[31] Supra, note 7.

[32] See Meekison, Romanow and Moull, supra, note 10.

CIVIL LIBERTIES AND THE
CHARTER OF RIGHTS AND FREEDOMS

To state that the Constitution Act, 1982 produced for us a new constitution is, of course, nonsense, as already elucidated in this work. On the other hand, this is not to say that the Constitution Act, 1982 is not a very significant document with far-reaching implications. By and large, it will colour our political culture, moving us significantly in the direction of the United States. A country dedicated in the preamble of its constitution to "peace, order and good government" will give way to a Canadian society much more concerned with the American dream of "life, liberty and the pursuit of happiness." This theme will be more fully developed in the final chapter. We will move away from what Horowitz calls the "Tory touch" into the vortex of American Lockeian liberalism.[1] We will be moving from a nation based on an evolutionary, pragmatic, moderately collectivist approach to one in which the assertion of individual rights will become of paramount concern. We will move from a society in which the overwhelming majority of important decisions are made by politicians and their administrative advisors to a society in which decision-making power will be shared to a much greater extent with the judiciary.

With respect to a great number of areas, the judiciary will end up with the last word because, as subsection 52(1) of the Constitution Act provides, "the Constitution of Canada is the supreme law of Canada and any law that is inconsistent with the provisions of the Constitution is, to the extent of the inconsistency, of no force or effect." This opens up governmental action of various kinds to judicial scrutiny and ultimate judgment. It will mean that matters once resolved in the legislative process will now be resolved through the judicial process. The days of parliamentary and provincial legislative supremacy have clearly come to an end, and the final and determining word with respect to many important Canadian issues will rest with the courts.

Because of the United States judicial experience with its Bill of Rights, the natural tendency will be to look to the United States for guidance in interpreting the loosely worded phrases of the Canadian Charter of Rights. It is suggested that as Canada becomes more and more a part of the American economic structure, its political superstructure will automatically begin to mirror that of the dominant economic presence of the United States.[2] The twilight and demise of the Judicial Committee of the Privy Council will be marked by the intellectual ascendancy in many respects of the United States Supreme Court.

The problem for Canada, however, is that the Canadian Charter of Rights and Freedoms is considerably more sweeping than is the United States Bill of Rights, both in the number of areas covered and in the specificity of its wording. The Charter will raise issues of such significance and scope that not even the American courts will have explored all of their manifestations. In Canada, however, under a most extraordinarily written subsection 24(1), the courts are given a free hand:

> Anyone whose rights or freedoms as guaranteed by this Charter, have been infringed or denied may apply to a court of competent jurisdiction to obtain such remedy as the court considers appropriate and just in the circumstances.

Even experienced American constitutional lawyers and judges might flinch upon reading the wide-ranging power assigned to the Canadian judiciary in the event that governmental action has infringed the Charter of Rights and Freedoms. Never before have judges been handed so much responsibility with so little analysis of the subtleties of what was being done. The Charter was part of the Trudeau package which was introduced into the House of Commons with no warning that the federal government would push ahead on its own to ask that the parliament of the United Kingdom enact the resolution into law. At conferences preceding the actions by the Trudeau government, the provinces had made it quite clear that the majority of them opposed the entrenchment of rights in the Constitution and very few, if any, provincial government officials suspected that Mr. Trudeau would adopt a unilateral path with respect to an entrenched Charter. Drafts of the Charter were presented to provincial officials in the months leading up to the introduction of the October 5, 1980 resolution but their contents were not seriously debated by federal and provincial officials because it was so clear that a majority of the provinces were opposed to the entrenchment of any kind of bill of rights.

The Special Joint Committee of the Senate and the House of Commons on the Constitution, which sat from February 6, 1980 and reported on February 13, 1981, heard many submissions and witnesses but there was a heavy tendency to rely upon spokesmen for special interest groups rather than on legal analysts who could critically review the potential scope of the words and phrases of the Charter. One effect of the enactment of the Charter has been to divert the study of constitutional law away from the study of decisions relating to the division of legislative powers between the federal parliament and the provincial legislatures to case law based on the Charter.

One can already see signs of this diversion in that many Canadian legal academics are extremely excited by the new role of the courts and have already produced a flood of books, pamphlets and articles dealing with the Charter of Rights and Freedoms.[3] In addition there has been a number of conferences discussing the Charter's impact.[4]

The Charter has also proved to be a useful tool for many practising lawyers in that it opens up to legal challenge a plethora of issues that previously could only be challenged on the basis of the division of powers. Let us now turn and look in more detail at the question of civil liberties in general and the Charter of Rights and Freedoms in particular.[5]

Civil Liberties Without Recourse to the Charter

Canada has long recognized a tradition of individual freedom without the necessity of an entrenched Charter of Rights.[6]

First it must be remembered that the starting point of our legal system is that an individual is free except to the extent restrained by law. Due to the plethora of laws and regulations with which we are all surrounded, it is often easy to lose sight of this basic proposition. The reverse of this principle is that a governmental official or governmental agency only has such power as is vested in it or him by law. This was most dramatically illustrated in the case of *Roncarelli* v. *Duplessis*,[7] in which Premier Duplessis of Quebec, without lawful authority, ordered the cancellation of Mr. Roncarelli's liquor licence. After a lengthy judicial struggle, the Supreme Court of Canada awarded damages to Roncarelli on the ground that Duplessis did not have the legal authority vested in him by the legislature of Quebec to exercise this power. Thus in essence, no government, legislature or governmental official has any free-floating authority to act as they may wish; rather, they must trace their authority back to some principle of law deriving from one of the sources of law as outlined in chapter 2 of this book.

In all of the excitement relating to the Charter of Rights it is easy, perhaps, to forget that the cornerstone of all liberty is the democratic system whereby the electorate can choose their political leaders. As noted earlier in this work, parliamentary democracy and responsible government have roots in this country going back long before Confederation.

We must also not lose sight of the important principle of the independence of the judiciary. This independence is guaranteed in that judges are not accountable to legislative bodies for their decisions and their removal from office is very difficult.[8]

The common law has also been a source of protection of civil liberties. In the *Roncarelli* case, the plaintiff Roncarelli requested damages for wrongful action not justified by the law. In cases such as *Chaput* v. *Romain*[9] and *Lamb* v. *Benoit*[10] the Supreme Court of Canada awarded damages against police officers who were acting beyond their lawful authority. Thus the threat of civil suit can be a very real deterrent to governmental officials overreaching their lawful powers.

The Constitution Act, 1867 is an important starting point with respect to certain human rights and the diffusion of and limitation on state power. Federalism itself is by definition a bar to an excessive concentration of power in a single source. As the Tremblay Commission so eloquently put it,

> *[w]hereas, in a unitary system, all powers of the state are concentrated in a single supreme centre of government whose legislative powers are without limit and with all other branches of government subordinated to it; in a*

federative system there is necessarily a distribution of powers and limitation of these powers through the very fact that they are divided between a general authority and regional authorities, each master of its own house but within a well-defined field.[11]

The division of legislative powers has often been used as a method by which litigants have had struck down legislation to which they were opposed. The judges themselves have not shrunk from using the division of powers as a method for declaring *ultra vires* legislation of which they disapproved. The classic illustration of this occurred in the decision of *Switzman v. Elbling* where the Supreme Court of Canada held as being beyond provincial legislative authority, legislation which allowed the attorney general to padlock any premises being used for the distribution of communist propaganda.[12]

Another illustration of this approach is the *Alberta Press Bill* case where the Supreme Court of Canada held invalid a provincial statute requiring that the press in Alberta give the government a right of reply to criticism of provincial policies.[13]

In both the *Switzman v. Elbling* case and the *Alberta Press Bill* case, the Supreme Court of Canada justices in a number of instances made reference to the language of the preamble of the Constitution Act, 1867, which states that Canada was to have a "Constitution similar in Principle to that of the United Kingdom." Many of the judges speculated on what came to be called the theory of "an implied Bill of Rights." This was the suggestion that there were certain fundamental freedoms that were so basic to the functioning of Canadian democracy that they could not be restrained by any level of government. It is absolutely clear that no Canadian court has ever based a decision on the implied bill of rights. For example, in both the *Switzman v. Elbling* case and the *Alberta Press Bill* case, the legislation was held invalid as being an invasion of the federal criminal law power. The highwater mark of this approach was self-admitted *obiter dicta* of Mr. Justice Abbott, who suggested that if the federal parliament attempted to legislate along similar lines to that of Alberta, this might be held unconstitutional on the ground of its violation of civil liberties. He drew this conclusion from the assumption that a constitution similar in principle to that of the United Kingdom by implication encompassed certain basic democratic principles of free speech and debate. This line of analysis was developed at considerable length by judges in the *Alberta Press Bill* case but, as already pointed out, indicated their spirit in approaching the legislation rather than the final legal reasoning, which was that the statute violated the criminal law power of the federal parliament. To put it bluntly, there are probably very few statutes which a court could not strike down on the basis of the division of powers if determined to do so, because of the extremely vague meaning of some of the very general phrases in sections 91 and 92 of the Constitution Act, 1867. It must be remembered, in leaving this subject, that in *Attorney General for Canada v. Dupond*[14] the Supreme Court, in a judgment written by J. Beetz, raised considerable doubt about the theory of an implied bill of rights. Nevertheless, without using this theory, federalism has proved to be a very potent weapon in the hands of the courts, to deal with legislation of which they disapprove.

The Constitution Act, 1867 did provide for certain rights regarded as especially important to Canadians in 1867. Section 93 provides guarantees for denominational schools, and section 133 guarantees the use of the French and English languages in the courts and legislature of Quebec, in the Parliament of Canada and courts created by the federal parliament. It was not that the Fathers of Confederation were not dedicated to a high degree of political freedom, but rather that they looked to Britain as a basic model for governance, with its emphasis on the supremacy of parliament. Furthermore, a venture into whether or not a philosophy of natural rights should be implemented in the Constitution would have exacerbated the already deep tensions with respect to the creation of Canada. Philosophic debate about ultimate values would have delayed and perhaps destroyed the creation of the new nation. In addition, it should be recognized that Canada was in many respects a symbol of North American counter revolution in that its citizens chose deliberately not to be part of the United States. An entrenched bill of rights would have looked suspiciously like the United States model for an ideal constitution. Also, very different political philosophies and heritage were at issue, as exemplified by the fact that in the United States the constitution provides for a separation of church and state, whereas section 93 explicitly recognizes the role and rights of Roman Catholics and Protestants with respect to education.

Another method of protecting civil liberties has been through the passage of statutory bills of rights. For example, Saskatchewan passed the first of these in 1947.[15] This was followed in 1960 by the passage through the federal parliament of the Canadian Bill of Rights.[16] Alberta in 1972 enacted the Alberta Bill of Rights,[17] and in 1975 Quebec passed the Quebec Charter of Human Rights and Freedoms.[18]

The most important of these statutory bills of rights is, of course, the Canadian Bill of Rights. It was inspired by the thoughts and actions of then Prime Minister Diefenbaker who negotiated its passage through the Canadian parliament in 1960. It must be remembered that this statute is still in effect and will undoubtedly be cited from time to time, but it has certainly been overshadowed by the enactment of the Charter of Rights and Freedoms. The Diefenbaker Bill of Rights, as it is often called, is an ordinary statute of the federal parliament and is applicable only in the federal area. This means that the bill can be amended at any time, although this is an unlikely prospect. Professor Hogg adopts the view that where portions of the Bill of Rights are replicated by the Charter, they have ceased to have any meaningful effect. He takes the view that only the non-duplicative portions of the bill will play a leading role in Canada's destiny. In particular, he points out that paragraph 1(a) might be of importance in that it has "due process" provisions with respect to property. Once again it must be reiterated, however, that the Canadian Bill of Rights has no application whatsoever within the provincial sphere.[19]

Another important development has been the enactment first by the provinces and then by the federal parliament of human rights codes. These deal with discrimination by landlords and employers on grounds of race, religion and sex, among other things, rather than dealing with the traditional political liberties such as freedom of association and expression. These codes are usually administered by commissions who often follow conciliatory practices and, if necessary, provide for adjudication by a board of enquiry if other techniques should fail. The general tendency and thrust of these codes was to avoid recourse to the courts, placing an emphasis on conciliation and education rather than on using the judiciary.

The federal Human Rights Commission and its provincial counterparts continue in operation and have not been supplanted by the enactment of the Charter of Rights. In the first place, human rights codes clearly apply to private activity as well as governmental activity, whereas there is real doubt that the Charter of Rights applies to the private sector. In the second place, the human rights commissions allow for a more informal process than resort to the judiciary using the Charter of Rights and Freedoms. This more informal approach, however, has been the subject of considerable criticism in that often persons investigated have to go to considerable expense to defend themselves. The impression is sometimes created that there is a presumption of guilt which the alleged discriminator must disprove. This is often very difficult and has created a good deal of uneasiness about the less judicialized processes of some of the human rights commissions.[20]

The Canadian Charter of Rights and Freedoms

The Canadian Charter of Rights and Freedoms is Part I of the Constitution Act, 1982. It includes a brief preamble and thirty-three substantive sections followed by section 34, which indicates that Part I of the Act may be cited as the Canadian Charter of Rights and Freedoms. This point has been stressed because a number of persons casually refer to the Charter as if it involved the entire Constitution Act, 1982. Some important sections — namely sections 35 and 36 dealing with aboriginal rights and equalization and regional disparity — are not part of the Charter. This does not, however, in any way derogate from their legality. The Charter is a term of art in that its sections are defined as indicated by section 34. The Charter contains a number of subheadings and starts with a brief preamble which states that "Canada is founded upon principles that recognize the supremacy of God and the rule of law." Lengthy discussions were held at the federal-provincial conferences prior to the federal government's unilateral action on the Constitution with respect to a preamble, and a number of proposals were put forward, some several pages in length. Probably, however, due to the controversial nature and effect of material which might be included in a preamble, the decision was made by the federal government to keep it as brief as possible. A preamble can be used as an aid in the interpretation of a statute. However, it is doubtful whether these rather vague references to "the supremacy of God" and "the rule of law" will prove significant in the interpretation of the Charter of Rights and Freedoms.

There is only one section under the subheading of "Guarantee of Rights and Freedoms," namely section 1, which provides that "the *Canadian Charter of Rights and Freedoms* guarantees the rights and freedoms set out in it subject only to such reasonable limits prescribed by law as can be demonstrably justified in a free and democratic society." Lawyers defending government actions and legislative enactments will have to fall back upon this section to argue against allegations that legislation and governmental actions violate the Charter. In the case of *Attorney General of Quebec* v. *Quebec Association of Protestant School Boards,*[21] the Supreme Court of Canada did not pursue the analysis of section 1 done by Chief Justice Deschenes of the Superior Court of Quebec on this subject. The issue in that case was whether the provisions of Quebec's Charter of the French Language (Bill 101) were valid in limiting admission to Protestant schools to children whose parents had had their education in English in Quebec. The allegation was made that this provision of the Act was contrary to paragraph 23(1)(b) of the Charter of Rights. Chief Justice Deschenes took the view that this provision of the Quebec Language Act was not demonstrably necessary in order to protect the French language in that province.[22]

The Supreme Court of Canada did not feel it was necessary to explore the justification provisions under section 1, but rather took the tack that the rights of parents with respect to the education of their children were clearly defined in section 23 of the Charter and that any attempt to change that definition would amount to an amendment of the rights outlined in section 23. In essence, they held that there was a direct collision between the provisions in the French Language Act and those in section 23 and accordingly those rights in the Charter must prevail.[23]

The next subheading, "Fundamental Freedoms," encompasses section 2, which deals with fundamental freedoms including religion, thought, expression, freedom of the press, peaceful assembly and freedom of association. These are normally regarded as the hard-core values of democratic society and will probably produce a certain amount of litigation, but the number of cases will probably fall far short of the amount of litigation involving the legal rights defined in sections 7 through 14. To date the leading case dealing with section 2 is *R.* v. *Big M Drug Mart Ltd.* [24] In that case the Supreme Court of Canada held that the Lord's Day Act, which provided for Sunday closing, was *ultra vires* because it clashed with freedom of religion under section 2 of the Charter. In effect, the court held that the Lord's Day Act gave preference to one religion at the expense of others and, as a consequence, violated freedom of conscience and religion guaranteed to Canadian citizens.

The next subheading, which includes sections 3 to 5, is entitled "Democratic Rights" and provides for certain rights to vote in the election of members of the House of Commons and the legislative assembly of each of the provinces. In addition, it places restraints on the length of time between elections in that no House of Commons or legislative assembly can continue for more than five years except in time of war, where provision is made for continuation of either a House of Commons or legislative assembly if not opposed by more than one third of the members of the applicable legislative body.

Section 5 merely transposes from the Constitution Act, 1867 a provision that parliament and each provincial legislature shall sit at least once every twelve months.

The next subheading is "Mobility Rights" and under that rubric is only section 6. In essence, it provides for the right of citizens to enter and leave Canada and the right of citizens to move from one province to another in order to take up residence and pursue their livelihood. One major case involving this section has already been decided by the Supreme Court of Canada: *Law Society of Upper Canada* v. *Skapinker*.[25] In that case the court held that it was not a violation of section 6 of the Charter for the legal profession in Ontario to require that citizenship be a condition for admission to the profession.

"Legal Rights" is the next subheading. It encompasses sections 7 through 14. It has already precipitated a plethora of legal argument and legal decisions.[26] The main case on these sections to date is *Hunter* v. *Southam Inc.* [27] In this case the Supreme Court of Canada unanimously struck down some very broad search powers vested in the director of the Combines Investigation Branch. It is obvious that in the future, powers of search and seizure are going to be validated only if accompanied by very strict rules and processes laid down by, in this case, parliament.

On a political note it is interesting to read in section 7 that

[e]veryone has the right to life, liberty and security of the person and the right not to be deprived thereof except in accordance with the principles of fundamental justice.

Considerable debate centred around the question of whether "property" should have been included within this section. The legislative assembly of British Columbia has already initiated an amendment to the Constitution to include the word "property" in section 7. To date there does not seem to be sufficient enthusiasm among the provinces and the federal government for the adoption of this particular proposal. Probably the general mood is that government is already considerably restricted in its activities by the Charter without raising the very difficult question of entrenching property rights. It is clear that section 7 was drafted in order to replicate the due process provisions of Article 14 of the American Bill of Rights; the words "due process" were probably deliberately omitted in order to not immediately import on to the Canadian scene the hundreds of American cases on this subject.

Probably no subheading of the Charter of Rights and Freedoms will provoke more debate and litigation than that of "Equality Rights." Only one section is found here. Subsection 15(1) goes far beyond the equal protection provision of the United States Constitution and provides that

[e]very individual is equal before and under the law and has the right to the equal protection and equal benefit of the law without discrimination and, in particular, without discrimination based on race, national or ethnic origin, colour, religion, sex, age or mental or physical disability.

Subsection 15(2) goes on to provide that those types of programs often referred to as "affirmative action programs" are valid and not proscribed by subsection 15(1)if they have as their object

the amelioration of conditions of disadvantaged individuals or groups including those that are disadvantaged because of race, national or ethnic origin, colour, religion, sex, age or mental or physical disability.

Section 15 did not come into effect until April 17, 1985, so at the time of writing no cases on the equality provisions have reached the Supreme Court of Canada. It should be noted, however, that virtually all of the cases decided by reference to the Canadian Bill of Rights by the Supreme Court of Canada arose under paragraph 1(b) which guarantees "equality before the law." It is not unreasonable to suspect that section 15 of the Charter will generate a very high volume of litigation.

The next two subheadings are "Official Languages of Canada," containing sections 16 to 22, and "Minority Language Educational Rights," section 23. Professor Tetley of McGill University and a former cabinet minister in Quebec states that:

> The provisions respecting the official languages of Canada comprise sections 16 to 22 of the Canadian Charter of Rights and Freedoms. These provisions create no new language rights. Several of the sections maintain existing constitutional guarantees, while the others constitutionally entrench existing statutory provisions.

He goes on to state that:

> Section 16 declares French and English to be the official languages of Canada and New Brunswick, and gives each language equality of status in all institutions of both governments. The Act entrenches statutory provisions enacted over a dozen years ago by the federal government and the legislature of New Brunswick.[28]

As Professor Tetley points out, "French and English minority language education supported by public funds up to the university level is now constitutionally guaranteed (where numbers warrant) by section 23 of the Canadian Charter of Rights and Freedoms."[29] It should be noted, however, that paragraph 23(1)(a) only comes into effect upon authorization by the National Assembly or government of Quebec. This provision in section 59 of the Constitution Act, 1982 was included as a concession to Quebec. In response, Quebec passed legislation to the effect that "the Government shall not authorize a proclamation under subsection 1 of section 59 of the Constitution Act, 1982, without obtaining the prior consent of the National Assembly of Quebec."[30]

The Quebec government to date has not issued a proclamation supported by resolution of the National Assembly bringing into effect paragraph 23(1)(a) of the Charter of Rights and Freedoms. Nevertheless, as previously noted, the Supreme Court of Canada in the *Quebec School Board* case[31] gave effect to paragraph (b) of that subsection by guaranteeing the admission to English language schools in Quebec of children of Canadian citizens who had an English language education outside Quebec. Thus, this subsection was held to render invalid the so-called "Quebec clause" of Bill 101. It is impossible to even begin to chronicle the complex and technical analysis of language rights in Canada in a work which is essentially a brief overview of the Canadian Constitution. However, we are fortunate in having a number of excellent works dealing with the issues relating to language and education in Canada.[32]

Section 24, the enforcement section, has been mentioned earlier in this work. As already pointed out, there is no comparable section in the American Bill of Rights, and thus it will not be possible to utilize American decisions as it will be on matters relating to freedom of expression, freedom of the press and other legal rights. The sweeping nature of subsection 24(1) is indeed surprising in that it provides that

> anyone whose rights or freedoms, as guaranteed by this Charter, have been infringed or denied may apply to a court of competent jurisdiction to obtain such remedy as the court considers appropriate and just in the circumstances.

This does not deny recourse to any traditional judicial remedies but with respect to enforcement of Charter rights, a litigant is in a preferred position. A court of competent jurisdiction can provide a remedy which is "appropriate and just in the circumstances." This means that when it comes to enforcing Charter rights the appropriate court is not confined to traditional remedies, but presumably can develop new legal recourses. How far the courts may go in giving effect to the broad meaning of these words is impossible to foresee at the time of writing. Nevertheless, the words of subsection 24(1) certainly underline in most dramatic fashion the frequently expressed theme of this book that the real winner of the events of 1982 were the courts, at the expense of the rest of the governmental system.[33]

It is interesting to note that with respect to the aboriginal peoples of Canada, one of the sections relating to their rights is contained in the Charter, namely section 25, whereas two other sections, 35 and 35.1, are subsumed under Part 2 of the Constitution Act, 1982, headed "Rights of the Aboriginal Peoples of Canada." One of the advantages of having aboriginal rights mentioned in section 25 is that this brings into full force the power of the courts to rely upon the extraordinary remedy section just discussed. No attempt will be made here to go into the excessively lengthy and complex story relating to native rights and native land claims. Professor Hogg has briefly and brilliantly synthesized the impact of the Constitution Act, 1982 on the position of the aboriginal peoples. He states:

> *The Constitution Act, 1982, supplemented by an amendment adopted in 1984, has taken steps to eliminate these three infirmities. Section 35 of*

the Constitution Act, 1982 provides that "the existing aboriginal and treaty rights of the aboriginal peoples of Canada are hereby recognized and affirmed." This gives constitutional recognition (but not definition) to "aboriginal and treaty rights," and protects them from legislative attack. Section 25 of the Constitution Act, 1982, which is part of the Charter of Rights, provides that the Charter of Rights is not to be construed as derogating from "aboriginal, treaty or other rights or freedoms that pertain to the aboriginal peoples of Canada." This makes clear that the equality guarantee in s.15 of the Charter does not invalidate native rights. Finally, s.35.1 declares that constitutional amendments to the native rights provisions of the Constitution Acts, 1867 and 1982 will not be made without a prior constitutional conference involving participation by representatives of the aboriginal peoples of Canada. These three provisions — ss.35, 25 and 35.1 — reinforce s.91(24) in their recognition of special status for the aboriginal peoples.[34]

Sections 25-31, under the subheading "General," are important in clarifying certain basic points. However, they do not really add to the existing collection of rights and freedoms. For example, section 26 is useful in underlining the point that "the guarantee in this Charter of certain rights and freedoms shall not be construed as denying the existence of any other rights and freedoms that exist in Canada"; as is section 28 which provides that "notwithstanding anything in this Charter, the rights and freedoms referred to in it are guaranteed equally to male and female persons."

A great deal of controversy is already swirling about section 32, found under the subheading "Application of Charter," which provides that

> this Charter applies (a) to the Parliament and government of Canada in respect of all matters within the authority of Parliament including all matters relating to the Yukon Territory and Northwest Territories; and (b) to the legislature and government of each province in respect of all matters within the authority of the legislature of each province.

In essence, the debate already developing is whether the Charter goes beyond regulating the relationships between government and private person and also intrudes into relationships between one private person and another. Professor Hogg comes down quite unequivocally with the position that "private action is therefore excluded from the application of the Charter."[35] This certainly was the view espoused by the Minister of Justice before the Special Joint Committee on the Constitution.[36]

Other scholars, for example Professor Katherine Swinton, though not taking sharp issue with the view of Professor Hogg, nevertheless speculate that ". . . some will argue that the Charter should restrict private activity . . ." and Professor Swinton then goes on to examine the line of argument that the Charter can be utilized in situations not involving governments or government agencies.[37]

If in the future the courts sustain the position that the Charter provides for the regulation of legal relationships between private persons, then the already sweeping impact of the Charter with relation to public policy in Canada will be even more dramatic. Surely the courts will be cautious before increasing their already wide degree of responsibility in relation to utilizing the Charter.

After the decision in the *Reference Re Amendment of the Constitution of Canada*,[38] the prime minister of Canada and the premiers gathered together and agreed, with the exception of Quebec, on the package which became the Constitution Act, 1982. The majority of the premiers had been opposed to the entrenchment of a Charter of Rights, but as part of the final compromise which led up to the Constitutional accord, they insisted upon the power to override certain rights contained in the Charter by parliament or the provincial legislatures. They were not completely successful in obtaining a blanket capacity to override sections of the Charter, however, certain important compromises were reached which have the effect of restoring pre-1982 legislative supremacy in some areas. Subsection 33(1) provides that

> Parliament or the legislature of a province may expressly declare in an Act of Parliament or of the legislature, as the case may be, that the Act or a provision thereof shall operate notwithstanding a provision included in section 2 or sections 7 to 15 of this Charter.

Subsection 33(2) goes on to state:

> An Act or a provision of an Act in respect of which a declaration made under this section is in effect shall have such operation as it would have had but for the provision of this Charter referred to in the declaration.

The section further provides for a limitation as to the period of override by stating in subsection (3) that

> a declaration made under subsection (1) shall cease to have effect five years after it comes into force or on such earlier date as may be specified in the declaration.

Subsection (4) provides, however, that

> Parliament or the legislature of a province may re-enact a declaration made under subsection (1).

It is significant that the override power can only be used with respect to section 2 and sections 7 to 15 of the Charter. Accordingly, language rights are beyond the scope of the override provisions. Quebec in its anger at having the Constitution Act, 1982 imposed on it without its consent, passed in 1982 an Act entitled "An Act respecting the Constitution Act, 1982," the effect of which was to add a notwithstanding clause to "each of the Acts adopted by the National Assembly of Quebec before 17 April 1982."[39]

Professor Hogg raises the question of whether this sweeping pronouncement by the Quebec National Assembly is sufficient to meet the legal requirements of section 33. He takes the view that this is probably legally satisfactory but does not reflect the spirit of section 33.[40]

In any event, section 33 is a powerful weapon in the hands of the federal parliament and provincial legislatures in overruling decisions of the courts which they feel are not in the public interest. For example, it is not unlikely that if the courts go too far in guaranteeing rights to the intoxicated driver, the federal parliament would resort to the override provisions in order to give parliament the power to deal adequately with the drunk driver. There are a plethora of other areas whereby the federal parliament or provincial legislatures might be tempted to use the override provisions; one which comes particularly to mind is the question of compulsory retirement. As is well-known, most people are required by their employers to retire at the age of 65, and already a number of actions have been started on the basis that this violates section 15 of the Charter. There may be a movement to use the override provisions in order to sustain employers' power to require compulsory retirement.

All this of course is purely speculative because except for Quebec, no other provincial government or the federal government has, at the time of writing, used the override provisions. There is considerable timidity in this respect because no government wants to be branded as interfering with the working of the Charter. There undoubtedly will be in the future considerable temptation by legislators to use the override if they feel particularly frustrated by judicial decisions which they feel are a serious threat to the public interest.

---

[1] Horowitz, "Conservatism, Liberalism and Socialism in Canada: An Interpretation" (1966), 32 Can. J. Econ. Poli. Sci., 143.

[2] Lord Lloyd of Hampstead, *Introduction to Jurisprudence*. London: Stevens, 4th ed., 1979, p. 724.

[3] Walter S. Tarnopolsky and Gerald-A. Beaudoin, eds., *The Canadian Charter of Rights and Freedoms: Commentary*. Toronto: Carswell, 1982; David C. McDonald, *Legal Rights in the Canadian Charter of Rights and Freedoms: a Manual of Issues and Sources*. Toronto: Carswell, 1982; Lederman, "The Power of the Judges and the New Canadian Charter of Rights and Freedoms" (1982), Charter Edition, U.B.C. L. R. 1; Morris Manning, *Rights, Freedoms and the Courts: a Practical Analysis of the Constitution Act, 1982*. Toronto: Edmond-Montgomery, 1983; Russell, "The Effect of a Charter of Rights on the Policy-Making Role of Canadian Courts" (1982), 25 Can. Pub. Admin., 1; Weiler, "Rights and Judges in a Democracy: A New Canadian Version" (1984), 18 U. Mich. J. L. Ref., 51; *The Canadian Charter of Rights and Freedoms* (1983), 61 Can. B. Rev. The above lists some of the longer works on the Charter, but is only a small sample of the voluminous amount of material already written on the Charter.

[4] These include "Trade Unions and the Charter: Expanded Rights or Straightjacket?" A Pacific Group Conference held in Vancouver, February 15-16, 1985; "The Rights of Minorities," Third International Conference on Constitutional Law held in Quebec City, March 5-8, 1985; "The Canadian Charter of Rights and Freedoms: Litigating the values of a Nation," Pacific Institute of Law and Public Policy held in Vancouver, March 28-29, 1985; "A Conference on the Charter of Rights and Human Rights Legislation: Their Impact on Human Resource Management," Faculty of Commerce, Saint Mary's University held in Halifax, August 23-24, 1985.

[5] For an excellent and detailed analysis of the whole question of civil liberties including the Charter, see Peter W. Hogg, *Constitutional Law of Canada*. Toronto: Carswell, 2nd ed., 1983, Part III.

[6] See Hogg, supra, note 5, chapters 28 and 29. Professor Hogg goes through, in considerable detail, the various methods of protecting human liberty without recourse to the Charter. Included in the foregoing material is an excellent synthesis of the scope and impact of the Canadian Bill of Rights. See in particular pp. 639-647. Readers can also get an excellent overview of the situation prior to the Charter by reading D. A. Schmeiser, *Civil Liberties in Canada*. London: Oxford University Press, 1964. For further material on the Canadian Bill of Rights, see Walter S. Tarnopolsky, *The Canadian Bill of Rights*. Toronto: McClelland and Stewart, 2nd rev. ed., 1975.

[7] [1959] S.C.R. 121.

[8] For further development of the theme of judicial independence, see R. I. Cheffins and R. N. Tucker, *The Constitutional Process in Canada*. Toronto: McGraw-Hill Ryerson, 2nd ed., 1976, pp. 91-92.

[9] [1955] S.C.R. 834.

[10] [1959] S.C.R. 321.

[11] David Kwavnick, ed., *The Tremblay Report: Report of the Royal Commission of Inquiry on Constitutional Problems*. Toronto: McClelland and Stewart, 1973, p. 82. The Tremblay Commission saw in federalism the guarantee of the cultural autonomy of Quebec and the placing of control of the destiny of French Canada, to a considerable extent, in a government mainly composed of French-speaking Canadians. In essence, they saw federalism as supporting a principle of pluralism, and in particular, stopping what was viewed by the commission as the excessively corrosive impact of excessive state power.

[12] [1957] S.C.R. 285.

[13] *Re Alberta Statutes*, [1938] S.C.R. 100. For a fuller analysis of the use of the division of legislative powers as a method of protecting civil liberties, see Schmeiser, supra, note 6, especially chapter 5.

[14] [1978] 2 S.C.R. 770.

[15] The Saskatchewan Bill of Rights, 1947, Stats. Sask. 1947, c.35.

[16] Stats. Can. 1960, c.44, Part I.

[17] Stats. Alta. 1972, c.1.

[18] Stats. Que. 1975, c.6.

[19] Hogg, supra, note 5, p. 640.

[20] For a further discussion of human rights codes and their application, see R. St. J. MacDonald and John P. Humphrey, *The Practice of Freedom*. Toronto: Butterworths, 1979, especially: chapter 3 by Cheffins and Tucker, "Provincial Constitutions and Civil Liberties"; chapter 4 by Leavy, "The Structure of the Law of Human Rights"; chapter 5 by Hunter, "The Origin, Development and Interpretation of Human Rights Legislation"; chapter 15 by Tarnopolsky, "The Control of Racial Discrimination"; and chapter 16 by Fairweather, "The Canadian Human Rights Commissioner."

[21] [1984] 2 S.C.R. 66.

[22] (1982) 140 D.L.R. (3d) 33, 71-90.

[23] For the best summary of the limitation provisions of section 1, see Hogg, supra, note 5, pp. 678-689. See also Conklin, "Interpreting and Applying the Limitations Clause: An Analysis of Section 1" (1982), 4 Supreme Court L. R., 75.

[24] [1985] 3 W.W.R. 481 (S.C.C.).

[25] [1984] 1 S.C.R. 357.

[26] For a comprehensive analysis of these sections and decisions relating to them, see Hogg, supra, note 5, pp. 742-783,

[27] [1984] 2 S.C.R. 145.

[28] Tetley, "Language and Education Rights in Quebec and Canada (A Legislative History and Personal Political Diary)" (1982), 45 No. 4 L. and Contemp. Prob., 178, 208. This paper will form part of a book shortly to be published by Duke University entitled: *Reshaping Confederation: The 1982 Reform of the Canadian Constitution*.

[29] Ibid., p. 209.

[30] An Act Respecting the Constitution Act, 1982, Stats. Que. 1982, c.21, s.4.

[31] Supra, note 21.

[32] See Hogg, supra, note 5, pp. 803-830. See also Tetley, supra, note 28. Another very useful article on this subject is by Magnet, "The Charter's Official Languages Provisions: The Implications of Entrenched Bilingualism" (1982), 4 Supreme Court L. R., 163. For further work on minority language educational rights, see another article by the same author in the same journal: Magnet, "Minority-Language Educational Rights" (1982), 4 Supreme Court L. R., 195.

[33] An especially thoughtful article on section 24 has been written by the Honourable Mr. Justice Kenneth Lysyk of the British Columbia Supreme Court. This article, entitled "Enforcement of Rights and Freedoms Guaranteed by the Charter" (1985), 43 Advocate, 165, examines in considerable depth the existing case law on this subject and provides a detailed analysis of the words of the

section. See also Dale Gibson, "Enforcement of the Canadian Charter of Rights and Freedoms (Section 24)," *The Canadian Charter of Rights and Freedoms: Commentary,* supra, note 3, p. 489; Fairley, "Enforcing the Charter: Some Thoughts on an Appropriate and Just Standard for Judicial Review" (1982), 4 Supreme Court L. R. 217; Hogg, supra, note 5, pp. 694–703.

[34] Hogg, supra, note 5, p. 564. Chapter 24 of this work is entitled "Aboriginal Peoples" and is undoubtedly the best brief overview of the law relating to Canada's native peoples. See also Mr. Justice Kenneth Lysyk, "The Rights and Freedoms of the Aboriginal Peoples of Canada," *The Canadian Charter of Rights and Freedoms: Commentary,* supra, note 3, p. 467; McNeil, "The Constitutional Rights of the Aboriginal Peoples of Canada" (1982), 4 Supreme Court L. R., 255; Sanders, "Prior Claims: An Aboriginal People in the Constitution of Canada," *Canada and the New Constitution: The Unfinished Agenda.* Montreal: Institute for Research on Public Policy, Stanley M. Beck and Ivan Bernier, eds., 1983, p. 225. A classic work on this subject prior to the passage of the Charter was by Lysyk, "The Unique Constitutional Position of the Canadian Indian" (1967), 45 Can. B. Rev., 513.

[35] Hogg, supra, note 5, p. 674.

[36] Government of Canada, *Proceedings of the Special Joint Committee on the Constitution,* Issue 49, January 30, 1981, pp. 49:30–49:31 where the Honourable Jean Chretien stated "What we want to do is cover bodies which. . . have delegated power."

[37] Swinton, "Application of the Canadian Charter of Rights and Freedoms," *The Canadian Charter of Rights and Freedoms: Commentary,* supra, note 3, p. 41, 45.

[38] [1981] 1 S.C.R. 753.

[39] Stats. Que. 1982, c.21, s.1. The complete text of this statute and a commentary on it can be found in an article by Scott, "Entrenchment by Executive Action: A Partial Solution to 'Legislative Override' " (1982), 4 Supreme Court L. R., 301; see also Hogg, supra, note 5, pp. 690–692.

[40] Hogg, supra, note 5, p. 691.

| C | H | A | P | T | E | R | *11* |

FINAL REFLECTIONS

In this work we have attempted to describe the constitutional events of 1982 and to integrate them with the existing constitutional structure. Throughout the previous chapters we have not only described the effects of the events of 1982 on the existing constitutional structure, but have tried to discuss the future implications for Canada of the impact of the Canada Act, 1982 and the Constitution Act, 1982.

Accordingly, some of the thoughts summarized in this chapter will of necessity reflect views put forward earlier, especially those outlined in chapter 1. Nevertheless, a brief final summation of where we stand since the legislative action taken by the United Kingdom in 1982 is necessary in any attempt to provide an overview of the existing situation. The changes of 1982 on the one hand have been radical, in that they shifted power from elected officials to the judiciary, while on the other hand they have reflected the conservative nature of constitutional development in Canada. As Professor Cairns points out,

> [t]he limited nature of the change is readily apparent from several per-
> spectives. The twelve-item constitutional agenda established by the first
> ministers after the Quebec referendum proved to be far too ambitious.
> Of the twelve items, only resource ownership and interprovincial trade,
> equalization and regional disparities, the Charter of Rights, and patriation
> with an amending formula, got past all of the roadblocks to achieve some
> kind of constitutional resolution. Eight other items — communications,
> the Senate, the Supreme Court, family law, fisheries, offshore resources,
> powers over the economy, and statement of principles — were put aside
> for the future.
>
> Not only did this twelve-item agenda experience severe attrition as the
> constitutional process developed, but it was originally said to represent
> only the first of a several package process of constitutional reform. Now,
> with only a limited portion of the first stage achieved, the momentum for
> a further major burst of constitutional renewal seems all but dissipated.[1]

Furthermore, it must be remembered that the items mentioned in the list recited by Professor Cairns were only some of the areas of the Canadian

Constitution which could or should have been reviewed. It was a long-held view of one of the authors of this work, expressed in his book, *The Constitutional Process in Canada*,[2] that it was probably a mistake to begin rewriting the Canadian Constitution. However, having embarked on this hazardous path, it seems as if a fuller review of every aspect of Canadian government should have been undertaken. The relationship between the executive and legislative processes in particular seems to be a fertile ground for further study, in view of the atrophy of the legislative process in Canada in terms of policy formation.

The power of first ministers has increased in recent years. At the federal level, the cabinet ministers until the era of Prime Minister Trudeau had considerable independent initiative and authority, and the cabinet was somewhat of a counterweight to the prime minister. The impression received now is of an ever-increasing centralization of power in the office of the prime minister and in the hands of his advisors in the Prime Minister's Office and the Privy Council Office. This is in line with the position in the provinces where the premiers have historically very much controlled the political process.[3]

The fact that Canadian legislatures at both the federal and provincial levels are merely instruments of cabinet will, with very little independent input, surely should have been the subject of serious constitutional consideration. One of the difficulties, of course, is that constitutional review was carried out at the first ministers' level and none of the first ministers were anxious to change a system which vests incredible powers in their hands. On the other hand, no one was particularly enthusiastic about the notion of a popularly elected constitutional convention representing the citizenry, which might have produced some interesting, but probably a good many bizarre, solutions to constitutional problems.

Furthermore, and probably quite rightly, no one was prepared to involve himself in a sweeping revision of the division of legislative powers in Canada. Various proposals were made for redistributing legislative power, but wisely no serious attempt was made to recast the federal system except with respect to some of the specific items already referred to in the excerpt from the article by Alan Cairns. This limited review of the federal-provincial division of powers in turn produced only limited results.

Among governmental participants, British Columbia led the way in suggesting that Canadian federalism should be reformed, not by redistributing legislative powers as between the federal and provincial legislatures, but rather by utilizing the concept of "intrastate federalism" popularized by a number of political scientists in contradistinction to "interstate federalism." In essence, interstate federalism involves the decentralization of power whereas intrastate federalism is the concept of reforming central institutions so that they become more effective as a means whereby regional viewpoints can be reflected. British Columbia was particularly enthusiastic about an upper house based on the model of the German Bundesrat, which in effect would have converted the Senate into a "House of the Provinces" composed of members appointed by provincial governments.[4]

Despite the lengthy debate that took place from the mid-sixties to 1982, the chances of any dramatic initiatives with respect to reform of the Canadian Constitution being taken now are very remote. As already indicated in the chapter relating to the amending formula, we have put in place such a rigid amending system that the chances of change by amendment are minimal. It was also emphasized in that chapter that not only do we have thirty important legal instruments covered by the amending formula in the Schedule to the Constitution Act, 1982, but also, the authors have argued, other important legal documents are probably entrenched by virtue of the amending formula combined with section 52.

To date we have had only one amendment to the Constitution, namely section 35.1, which in essence provides for consultation with the aboriginal peoples of Canada before any amendment is made with respect to aboriginal rights. The chance of any other dramatic breakthroughs with respect to the amendment of the Constitution is indeed remote. The government of Prime Minister Trudeau made some suggestions with respect to amending section 96, the Legislative Assembly of British Columbia passed a resolution involving the inclusion of property rights in section 7, and a federal Special Joint Committee of the Senate and the House of Commons on Senate Reform has made recommendations.[5] Needless to say, it seems extremely unlikely that any of these initiatives will be pursued to its conclusion and the Constitution of Canada amended accordingly.

The government of Quebec in May of 1985 put forward a series of proposals which it felt were necessary prerequisites to giving Quebec's approval to Canada's constitutional deal of 1982. Proposals contained in this Quebec document included the exemption of Quebec from all of the Charter of Rights and Freedoms with the exception of democratic rights. It proposed a veto or, at the very least, financial compensation for changes in the division of powers and furthermore, a sweeping review of the division of powers. It also proposed a limitation on the federal spending power, especially with respect to grants to individuals and institutions in the area of culture and education. It put forward the notion that Quebec be given primary responsibility with respect to manpower policy, economic development, immigration, communications, marriage, divorce and recognition of the role of the province in the international sphere. It asked for Quebec participation in the appointment of Quebec judges to the Supreme Court of Canada, and that the province of Quebec be able to appoint judges to its own superior courts after consulting with the federal government.[6]

There is very little chance of these proposals by Quebec being implemented. The press seem to have the impression that some kind of bilateral negotiation could take place between Quebec City and Ottawa with a view to satisfying Quebec's demands. It must be remembered, however, that even if Ottawa was sympathetic to those demands, changes along the lines suggested by Quebec would have to be implemented through the use of the amending formula. This means that on some of the foregoing issues, unanimity would be required, and that with respect to the other issues, the approval of at least seven provinces with fifty percent of the population plus the support of the Senate and House of

Commons would be required. The prospects for obtaining this kind of federal-provincial consent are unlikely. The question remains of what can be done to have Quebec accommodate itself to the arrangements of 1982. What is interesting, however, is that the dramatic changes of 1982 were achieved without Quebec's consent, leading to the absolutely unforeseen situation that basic amendment of the Constitution can, in the overwhelming number of instances, be obtained without Quebec's approval. No one could possibly have imagined prior to 1982 that Canada would ever evolve to the state where fundamental constitutional amendment could be achieved without the consent of Quebec. Former Premier Levesque will always be remembered as the man who lost for Quebec its constitutional veto.

Thus, the last entrenched British statute applicable to Canada, namely the Canada Act, 1982 and its accompanying schedule, the Constitution Act, 1982, has left us in a constitutional straight jacket. It has left us with a largely unreformed constitution, and instead has merely added one more piece of legislation to an already extensive list of constitutional documents. We have added further complexity to an already complex system. As one of the authors wrote in an earlier work,

> the tragedy of the constitutional compromise of 1982 is that it did not really address the question of constitutional reform. The heart of what should be reformed, in my opinion, is the system of parliamentary government, and yet far from addressing this subject, the revised Canadian constitution freezes a system which, as already suggested, is unresponsive, inflexible, and non-representative of regional viewpoints. [7]

Readers interested in the notion that a great many of Canada's constitutional problems were left untouched and certainly unresolved will find of particular interest the two-volume collection of articles edited by Stanley M. Beck and Yvon Bernier, *Canada and the New Constitution: The Unfinished Agenda*.[8] In an interesting preface, Gordon Robertson, the former Clerk of the Privy Council in Ottawa states:

> It will be the part of wisdom — and also the part of justice — at some time to return to the discussion of constitutional change and renewal. Apart from the problems of Quebec, there are grievances of the West that could be addressed through the Constitution. We badly need a new second chamber to replace our Senate, where there can be clear, loud, and authoritative voicing of Western views, uninhibited by the party discipline of the House of Commons. Such a House could do much to give our central institutions of government a legitimacy that they do not now have in the West. It would be as dangerous to ignore that need as it would be to ignore our failure thus far to provide the 'renewal' promise to the people of Quebec.[9]

The most important part of the constitutional deal which resulted in the Constitution Act, 1982 was the Charter of Rights and Freedoms. Its importance in terms of Canada's constitutional future is that it is centralizing, legalizing and

Americanizing. Two of Canada's most thoughtful constitutional scholars have eloquently explained the centralizing nature of the Charter of Rights. Professor Hogg states:

> *It is sometimes said that a bill of rights is a centralizing force in a federal state. This is not true in any obvious sense. The Charter of Rights did not confer any additional powers on the federal Parliament. On the contrary, it limited the powers of the federal Parliament as well as the provincial Legislatures. But the Charter is a centralizing force in a subtle sense. It supplies a set of uniform national standards for the protection of civil liberties.*

He goes on to state:

> *It is true that the decisions of the Supreme Court of Canada on Charter issues will not be unifying in the sense of attracting national concurrence. The experience of the United States shows that judicial decisions on matters such as pornography, school prayers, police powers, capital punishment and abortion, are highly controversial and divisive. But the debates engendered by such decisions are national debates on issues that transcend the federal-provincial or regional differences that occupy so much of Canada's public debates.*[10]

The most thorough examination of the centralizing tendencies of the Charter has been done by Professor Peter Russell. As he points out,

> *[t]here is an even more direct sense in which judicial interpretation of the Charter will be a nationalizing process. In interpreting the Charter, the Supreme Court of Canada, at the top of the judicial structure, will set uniform national standards — often in policy areas which otherwise would be subject to diverse provincial standards. Film censorship, school prayers, and discrimination in employment practices are all clear examples. In contrast to the executive and legislative power, the judicial power in Canada is essentially unified. Policy directives flowing from Supreme Court decisions on the Charter are transmitted through a single hierarchy of appeals that binds all the courts in the land, and shapes the rights of all Canadians and the powers of all who govern.*[11]

Many will perhaps applaud this centralizing tendency. However, Quebecers in particular are bound to be suspicious of the homogenizing presence of a court dominated by judges who are not from Quebec and who have been trained in the common law. One of Canada's differences from the United States is its tendency not only to recognize the existence and flourishing of different cultural groups, but also to respect the integrity and variation in viewpoint of different regions.

As Professor Russell goes on to point out:

> *As the Supreme Court's capacity to function as a kind of national Senate reviewing the reasonableness of provincial laws and policies becomes*

evident, the reality of judicial power will overtake the reality of federal politicians. Among other things, this will mean that the federal government's monopoly of the power to appoint judges, not only to the Supreme Court of Canada but to all of the higher provincial courts, will be increasingly questioned . . . it may become necessary to give provincial governments a share of the action in the judicial appointment process.[12]

Not only does the Charter result in a centralizing of power through the judiciary but it also has the effect of legalizing political issues. Professor Russell again puts it most eloquently when he states:

The principal impact of a charter on the process of government can be neatly summarized as a tendency to judicialize politics and politicize the judiciary.

He goes on to say that

[t]he danger here is not so much that non-elected judges will impose their will on a democratic majority, but that questions of social and political justice will be transformed into technical legal questions and the great bulk of the citizenry who are not judges and lawyers will abdicate their responsibility for working out reasonable and mutually acceptable resolutions of the issues which divide them.[13]

There was really not sufficient debate on the long-term implications of entrenching a Charter of Rights as specific and as detailed as the one which we now have as part of our law. Two eminent scholars did attempt to warn us of the implications of entrenching rights and derogating from legislative supremacy, namely Professor Douglas A. Schmeiser and Professor Donald Smiley. Their warnings went largely unheeded.[14]

One of the best pieces of writing critical of the 1982 constitutional package is by Professor Smiley, who as part of his article laments the failure of either the proponents or opponents of the Charter to make a strong case for their position. This is probably due in large measure to the fact that the provinces at least tended to concentrate their debating energies on questions relating to the reform of central institutions and the division of powers. They were undoubtedly caught off guard by the introduction of a package which included a detailed Charter of Rights. This is not to say that they did not know that the federal government strongly favoured an entrenched Charter, but they did not suspect that this would be foisted upon them with very little opportunity for systematic and sustained debate. The result was that, after the introduction into the House of Commons by Prime Minister Trudeau of his constitutional resolution, on October 6, 1980, the focus of argument centred around the unilateral nature of his actions rather than on the scope and meaning of the Charter of Rights and its impact on Canada's political structure and culture.[15]

Perhaps the whole matter is best summarized by Donald Smiley, who states

The debate about the Canadian Charter of Rights and Freedoms has not been very satisfactory and I only wish that such discussions as have been occurring at this late date had taken place when the Charter was 'in the gristle' rather than in its final stages of enactment by the Parliament of the United Kingdom. The debate was, in my mind, superficial and unsophisticated from three points of view. First, even in the higher reaches of academia we have heard almost nothing of the old debates about natural law and natural rights . . . Second, we have not looked very hard at the experience of other nations . . . Third, there has been relatively little discussion of the possible consequence of the Charter for the workings of our political institutions and for the Canadian political culture more broadly.[16]

Though a number of Canada's most creative and experienced constitutional scholars have written about the centralizing and legalizing effect of the Charter of Rights, there does not seem to have been very much comment on the impact of the Charter of Rights on our political culture. One notable exception is the concluding chapter of the work by W. Christian and C. Campbell on political parties and ideologies in Canada.[17]

They stress the view shared by a number of other leading scholars, that Canada has a distinct and different political culture from that of the United States. In essence these thinkers take the view that there is what Horowitz refers to as a "Tory touch" to the Canadian political milieu, which brings to bear on Canadian thinking and acting a different kind of conservatism. These scholars see in Canada a leaning towards values which emphasize tradition, order and historical continuity. This thrust has a much more communitarian and collectivist element in it, in that it tends to stress group interest rather than individual interest. As stated in the chapter on the Charter of Rights, section 91 of the Constitution Act, 1867 speaks of "peace, order and good government" whereas the United States Declaration of Independence speaks of "life, liberty and the pursuit of happiness."[18]

Canada has a much more distinctly European flavour than the United States. Its thinking owes much more to the great philosopher Edmund Burke than to another great English philosopher, John Locke. Locke emphasized the individual, Burke emphasized the community. Canada, in many respects, is a manifestation of counter-revolution. It was founded by a combination of pre-enlightenment, deeply devout, Roman Catholic French Canadians and a dispossessed group of Loyalists leaving the United States in protest against the breakaway of that country from the Crown of Great Britain. As Campbell and Christian state it:

In its North Americanness Canada is like the United States, but the differences between this country and its neighbour are even more striking than the contrast between Canada and Europe. Unlike British immigrants to the United States in the 16th and 17th centuries, those who settled in British North America were not a persecuted and dissenting liberal minority. They reflected more fully the powerful tory or conservative strand in British political culture. Many were Catholic Scots and Irish, bearing a faith that was fundamentally hostile to liberal individualism.

As they point out,

[t]he presence in Canada of this tory element, although weaker than in England, created the conditions out of which an indigenous socialism could arise.

They continue:

Another important difference between Canada and the United States was the existence of French Canada. Many of the immigrants to New France had left France at a time when liberal ideas were virtually non-existent, and hence they brought with them to the new land an attitude to the state and to the society which was more tory/feudal than liberal.[19]

The Charter shifts Canada towards a much more individualist focus: not only will much of the Charter decision making revolve around individual versus group interests, but it will also look to the United States for guidance in the resolution of these disputes. The United States has had over two hundred years of an individualist focussed Lockean liberal tradition. The Charter of Rights and Freedoms will bring an essentially counter-revolutionary, non-rationalist, communitarian society into direct collision with individual-focussed legal rights based upon Charter arguments. Writing back in 1975, Professor Russell urged Canadians to stay with "that approach which is truest to our experience and most in keeping with our capabilities, namely that of Edmund Burke, not John Locke." As he pointed out,

Canadians — neither their judges, nor their politicians — are creatures of the Enlightenment. Their forte is not abstract, rationalist philosophizing. The American Republic may be built on self-evident principles and universal natural rights, but Canadian political and legal thought is far more pragmatic and empirical.[20]

The occasion for these remarks was Professor Russell's view that our excessive concentration on the Bill of Rights was a deviation from our Canadian political tradition. Despite his warning, we have followed the path of John Locke rather than Edmund Burke and our judges, who were until 1982 mirrors of a cautious evolutionary tradition, have now been handed the task of what Russell describes as ". . . abstract, rationalist philosophizing." This task assigned to the judges will naturally, as already indicated, make them ever more conscious of the American judicial experience and judicial precedents. As the Supreme Court of Canada becomes increasingly a constitutional court, it will look across the border to the United States Supreme Court with all of its many years of experience in interpreting a Bill of Rights.

The turn in the American direction with respect to law will parallel our increasing reliance on the United States in a whole host of other areas. This amelioration and redirection of Canadian legal thinking will merely accelerate the Americanization of Canada. This is not to say, however, that Canada will become a complete carbon copy of the United States, as we still retain a number of important traditions such as parliamentary government, and the administrative structure that attaches to that government. Furthermore, until such time as Canada becomes part of a North American common market, it will probably continue to have a much more regulated economy relying in part on state-owned industry. Nevertheless, the Charter of Rights will exacerbate the trend which George Grant so eloquently lamented over twenty-five years ago.[21]

It is difficult not to conclude that we have taken one more step, intellectually and culturally, in the direction of the United States and have increased the distance between us and our British and European heritage.

---

[1] Excerpt from *The Politics of Constitutional Conservatism* by Alan C. Cairns, in *And No One Cheered*, Keith Banting and Richard Simeon, eds. pp. 28, 29. Copyright © 1983 by Methuen Publications, Toronto. Reproduced by permission of the publisher.

[2] R. I. Cheffins and R. N. Tucker, *The Constitutional Process in Canada.* Toronto: McGraw-Hill Ryerson, 2nd ed., 1976.

[3] For a brief summary of the immense powers of the first ministers, see Cheffins and Tucker, supra, note 2, pp. 60, 85.

[4] Government of British Columbia, "Reform of the Canadian Senate," *British Columbia's Constitutional Proposals.* Victoria: 1978, 29. For a fuller discussion of intrastate reforms, see Smiley, "Central Institutions," *Canada and the New Constitution: the Unfinished Agenda.* Montreal: Institute for Research on Public Policy, Stanley M. Beck and Ivan Bernier, eds., 1983, vol. 1, p. 19, especially pp. 54-70. Professor Smiley discusses changes in the electoral system, changes in the House of Commons, a new second chamber, reforms with respect to federal regulatory and executive agencies, and concludes his analysis with a critical comment on intrastate federalism. See also a thoughtful analysis of intrastate federalism and its relationship to central institutions in Hogg, "The Theory and Practice of Constitutional Reform" (1981), 19 Alta. L.R., 335, 339-347. This article is a very useful synthesis of the whole question of constitutional reform. It summarizes in a brief and clear manner a whole plethora of reform proposals relating to the Constitution of Canada.

[5] See a discussion paper, the Honourable Mark McGuigan, Minister of Justice and Attorney General of Canada, *The Constitution of Canada — a suggested amendment related to provincial administrative tribunals.* Ottawa: Dept. of Justice, 1983; Government of Canada, *Report of the Special Joint Committee of the Senate and the House of Commons on Senate Reform.* Ottawa: Queen's Printer, 1984. The legislature of British Columbia, on September 21, 1982, unanimously passed a resolution to the effect that the Constitution of Canada be amended so that section 7 of the Charter of Rights and Freedoms should read "everyone has the right to life, liberty, security of the person and enjoyment of property and the right not to be deprived thereof except in accordance with the principles of fundamental justice," and urged that the legislative assemblies of all other provinces and the Senate and the House of Commons pass similar resolutions.

[6] Graham Fraser, "PQ Wants Sweeping Changes in New Constitutional Stand," *The Globe and Mail,* Saturday, May 18, 1985, pp. 1, 2.

[7] Cheffins, "The Constitution Act, 1982 and the Amending Formula: Political and Legal Implications" (1982), 4 Supreme Court L. R., 43, 54.

[8] Supra, note 4.

[9] Ibid., p.x.

[10] Peter W. Hogg, *Constitutional Law of Canada.* Toronto: Carswell, 2nd ed., 1985, pp. 651-652.

[11] Russell, "The Political Purposes of the Canadian Charter of Rights and Freedoms" (1983), 61

Can. B. Rev., 30, 41. Permission granted by Professor Peter Russell and the Canadian Bar Review.

[12] Russell, supra, note 11, pp. 42-43.

[13] Russell, supra, note 11, pp. 51-52.

[14] The most systematic argument ever expounded in Canada against entrenchment prior to the Constitution Act was by Schmeiser, "The Case Against Entrenchment of a Canadian Bill of Rights" (1973), 1 Dalhousie L. J., 15.

[15] There are still a few prominent scholars who question the desirability of entrenching a Charter of Rights. Readers interested in this analysis should see Smiley, "A Dangerous Deed: The Constitution Act, 1982," *And No one Cheered.* Toronto: Methuen, Keith Banting and Richard Simeon, eds. 1982, p. 74. The entire work is of considerable interest to people who have doubts about the constitutional events of 1982. In particular note the following articles: Cairns, "The Politics of Constitutional Conservatism," p. 28; Latouche, "The Constitutional Misfire of 1982," p. 96; and for a western viewpoint, Gibbins, "Constitutional Politics and the West," p. 119. Gibbins states that "While the Act cannot be said to work against the interests of the West, it does nothing to advance those interests through much overdue institutional reform." He goes on to say, "Instead the Constitution Act takes a troubled political past and casts it in constitutional cement for an uncertain future" (pp. 131-132). Two very wide-ranging critiques of the Charter have been done by the late Professor Robert A. Samek and Dean R. A. Macdonald. They make a number of points, but one interesting theme is that they both deplore the failure to include economic rights as part of the entrenched Charter: Samek, "Untrenching Fundamental Rights" (1982), 27 McGill L. J., 755; Macdonald, "Postscript and Prelude — the Jurisprudence of the Charter: Eight Theses" (1982), 4 Supreme Court L. R., 321.

[16] Quoted by Professor William Christian in a book review of a work entitled, *The U.S. Bill of Rights and the Canadian Charter of Rights and Freedoms* (1984), 17 Can. J. Poli. Sci., 426.

[17] William Christian and Colin Campbell, *Political Parties and Ideologies in Canada.* Toronto: McGraw-Hill Ryerson, 2nd ed., 1983.

[18] There is a great deal of brilliant, creative and incisive writing on the whole question of the difference between Canada's political culture and that of the United States. An especially valuable starting point for this analysis is an article by Horowitz, "Conservatism, Liberalism and Socialism in Canada: An Interpretation" (1966), 32 Can. J. Econ. Poli. Sci., 143. The question of political culture and new societies is very thoughtfully discussed by the father of the fragment theory: Louis Hartz, *The Founding of New Societies.* New York: Harcourt, Brace and World Inc., 1964; in particular see the article on Canada: McGrae, "The Structure of Canadian History," p. 219. Other very valuable works are George Grant, *Lament for a Nation: The Defeat of Canadian Nationalism.* Toronto: McClelland and Stewart, 1965; Charles Taylor, *Radical Tories: The Conservative Tradition in Canada.* Toronto: Anansi, 1982; Pierre Berton, *Why We Act Like Canadians.* Toronto: McClelland and Stewart, 1982; Leslie Armour, *The Idea of Canada and the Crisis of Community.* Ottawa: Steel Rail Publishing, 1981; Christian and Campbell, supra, note 17.

[19] Christian and Campbell, supra, note 17, pp. 227-228.

[20] Russell, "The Political Role of the Supreme Court of Canada in its First Century" (1975), 53 Can. B. Rev., 576, 592.

[21] Grant, supra, note 18.

THE CONSTITUTION ACT, 1867

30 & 31 Victoria, c. 3.

(Consolidated with amendments)

THE CONSTITUTION ACT, 1867

30 & 31 Victoria, c. 3.

(Consolidated with amendments)

An Act for the Union of Canada, Nova Scotia, and New Brunswick, and the Government thereof; and for Purposes connected therewith.

(29th March, 1867.)

WHEREAS the Provinces of Canada, Nova Scotia and New Brunswick have expressed their Desire to be federally united into One Dominion under the Crown of the United Kingdom of Great Britain and Ireland, with a Constitution similar in Principle to that of the United Kingdom:

And whereas such a Union would conduce to the Welfare of the Provinces and promote the Interests of the British Empire:

And whereas on the Establishment of the Union by Authority of Parliament it is expedient, not only that the Constitution of the Legislative Authority in the Dominion be provided for, but also that the Nature of the Executive Government therein be declared:

And whereas it is expedient that Provision be made for the eventual Admission into the Union of other Parts of British North America: (1)

I. - PRELIMINARY.

1. This Act may be cited as the *Constitution Act,* Short title. *1867.*(2)

---

(1) The enacting clause was repealed by the *Statute Law Revision Act, 1893,* 56-57 Vict., c 14 (U.K.). It read as follows:

> Be it therefore enacted and declared by the Queen's Most Excellent Majesty, by and with the Advice and Consent of the Lords Spiritual and Temporal, and Commons, in this present Parliament assembled, and by the Authority of the same, as follows:

(2) As enacted by the *Constitution Act, 1982,* which came into force on April 17, 1982. The section, as originally enacted, read as follows:

> **1.** This Act may be cited as The British North America Act, 1867.

2. Repealed.(3)

II.—UNION.

Declaration of Union.

3. It shall be lawful for the Queen, by and with the Advice of Her Majesty's Most Honourable Privy Council, to declare by Proclamation that, on and after a Day therein appointed, not being more than Six Months after the passing of this Act, the Provinces of Canada, Nova Scotia, and New Brunswick shall form and be One Dominion under the Name of Canada; and on and after that Day those Three Provinces shall form and be One Dominion under that Name accordingly.(4)

Construction of subsequent Provisions of Act.

4. Unless it is otherwise expressed or implied, the Name Canada shall be taken to mean Canada as constituted under this Act.(5)

Four Provinces.

5. Canada shall be divided into Four Provinces, named Ontario, Quebec, Nova Scotia, and New Brunswick.(6)

---

(3) Section 2, repealed by the *Statute Law Revision Act, 1893*, 56-57 Vict., c. 14 (U.K.), read as follows:

> **2.** The Provisions of this Act referring to Her Majesty the Queen extend also to the Heirs and Successors of Her Majesty, Kings and Queens of the United Kingdom of Great Britain and Ireland.

(4) The first day of July, 1867, was fixed by proclamation dated May 22, 1867.

(5) Partially repealed by the *Statute Law Revision Act, 1893*, 56-57 Vict., c. 14 (U.K.). As originally enacted the section read as follows:

> **4.** The subsequent Provisions of this Act, shall, unless it is otherwise expressed or implied, commence and have effect on and after the Union, that is to say, on and after the Day appointed for the Union taking effect in the Queen's Proclamation; and in the same Provisions, unless it is otherwise expressed or implied, the Name Canada shall be taken to mean Canada as constituted under this Act.

(6) Canada now consists of ten provinces (Ontario, Quebec, Nova Scotia, New Brunswick, Manitoba, British Columbia, Prince Edward Island, Alberta, Saskatchewan and Newfoundland) and two territories (the Yukon Territory and the Northwest Territories).

The first territories added to the Union were Rupert's Land and the North-Western Territory, (subsequently designated the Northwest Territories), which were admitted pursuant to section 146 of the *Constitution Act, 1867* and the *Rupert's Land Act*, 1868, 31-32 Vict., c. 105 (U.K.), by the *Rupert's Land and North-Western Territory Order* of June 23, 1870, effective July 15, 1870. Prior to the admission of those territories the Parliament of Canada enacted *An Act for the temporary Government of Rupert's Land and the North-Western Territory when united with Canada* (32-33 Vict., c. 3), and the *Manitoba Act, 1870*, (33 Vict., c. 3), which provided for the formation of the Province of Manitoba.

British Columbia was admitted into the Union pursuant to section 146 of the *Constitution Act, 1867*, by the *British Columbia Terms of Union*, being Order in Council of May 16, 1871, effective July 20, 1871.

Provinces of
Ontario and
Quebec.

6. The Parts of the Province of Canada (as it exists at the passing of this Act) which formerly constituted respectively the Provinces of Upper Canada and Lower Canada shall be deemed to be severed, and shall form Two separate Provinces. The Part which formerly constituted the Province of Upper Canada shall constitute the Province of Ontario; and the Part which formerly constituted the Province of Lower Canada shall constitute the Province of Quebec.

Provinces of
Nova Scotia
and New
Brunswick.

7. The Provinces of Nova Scotia and New Brunswick shall have the same Limits as at the passing of this Act.

Decennial
Census.

8. In the general Census of the Population of Canada which is hereby required to be taken in the Year One thousand eight hundred and seventy-one, and in every Tenth Year thereafter, the respective Populations of the Four Provinces shall be distinguished.

III.—EXECUTIVE POWER.

Declaration of
Executive
Power in the
Queen.

9. The Executive Government and Authority of and over Canada is hereby declared to continue and be vested in the Queen.

Prince Edward Island was admitted pursuant to section 146 of the *Constitution Act, 1867*, by the *Prince Edward Island Terms of Union*, being Order in Council of June 26, 1873, effective July 1, 1873.

On June 29, 1871, the United Kingdom Parliament enacted the *Constitution Act, 1871* (34-35 Vict., c. 28) authorizing the creation of additional provinces out of territories not included in any province. Pursuant to this statute, the Parliament of Canada enacted the *Alberta Act*, (July 20, 1905, 4-5 Edw. VII, c. 3) and the *Saskatchewan Act*, (July 20, 1905, 4-5 Edw.VII, c. 42), providing for the creation of the provinces of Alberta and Saskatchewan, respectively. Both these Acts came into force on Sept. 1, 1905.

Meanwhile, all remaining British possessions and territories in North America and the islands adjacent thereto, except the colony of Newfoundland and its dependencies, were admitted into the Canadian Confederation by the *Adjacent Territories Order*, dated July 31, 1880.

The Parliament of Canada added portions of the Northwest Territories to the adjoining provinces in 1912 by *The Ontario Boundaries Extension Act*, 1912, 2 Geo. V, c. 40, *The Quebec Boundaries Extension Act*, 1912, 2 Geo. V, c. 45 and *The Manitoba Boundaries Extension Act*, 1912, 2 Geo. V, c. 32, and further additions were made to Manitoba by *The Manitoba Boundaries Extension Act*, 1930, 20-21 Geo. V., c. 28.

The Yukon Territory was created out of the Northwest Territories in 1898 by *The Yukon Territory Act*, 61 Vict., c. 6, (Canada).

Newfoundland was added on March 31, 1949, by the *Newfoundland Act*, (U.K.), 12-13 Geo. VI, c. 22, which ratified the Terms of Union between Canada and Newfoundland.

Application of
Provisions
referring to
Governor
General.

10. The Provisions of this Act referring to the Governor General extend and apply to the Governor General for the Time being of Canada, or other the Chief Executive Officer or Administrator for the Time being carrying on the Government of Canada on behalf and in the Name of the Queen, by whatever Title he is designated.

Constitution of
Privy Council
for Canada.

11. There shall be a Council to aid and advise in the Government of Canada, to be styled the Queen's Privy Council for Canada; and the Persons who are to be Members of that Council shall be from Time to Time chosen and summoned by the Governor General and sworn in as Privy Councillors, and Members thereof may be from Time to Time removed by the Governor General.

All Powers
under Acts to
be exercised by
Governor
General with
Advice of Privy
Council, or
alone.

12. All Powers, Authorities, and Functions which under any Act of the Parliament of Great Britain, or of the Parliament of the United Kingdom of Great Britain and Ireland, or of the Legislature of Upper Canada, Lower Canada, Canada, Nova Scotia, or New Brunswick, are at the Union vested in or exerciseable by the respective Governors or Lieutenant Governors of those Provinces, with the Advice, or with the Advice and Consent, of the respective Executive Councils thereof, or in conjunction with those Councils, or with any Number of Members thereof, or by those Governors or Lieutenant Governors individually, shall, as far as the same continue in existence and capable of being exercised after the Union in relation to the Government of Canada, be vested in and exerciseable by the Governor General, with the Advice or with the Advice and Consent of or in conjunction with the Queen's Privy Council for Canada, or any Member thereof, or by the Governor General individually, as the Case requires, subject nevertheless (except with respect to such as exist under Acts of the Parliament of Great Britain or of the Parliament of the United Kingdom of Great Britain and Ireland) to be abolished or altered by the Parliament of Canada.(7)

Application of
Provisions
referring to
Governor
General in
Council.

13. The Provisions of this Act referring to the Governor General in Council shall be construed as referring to the Governor General acting by and with the Advice of the Queen's Privy Council for Canada.

---

(7) See the notes to section 129, *infra.*

14. It shall be lawful for the Queen, if Her Majesty thinks fit, to authorize the Governor General from Time to Time to appoint any Person or any Persons jointly or severally to be his Deputy or Deputies within any Part or Parts of Canada, and in that Capacity to exercise during the Pleasure of the Governor General such of the Powers, Authorities, and Functions of the Governor General as the Governor General deems it necessary or expedient to assign to him or them, subject to any Limitations or Directions expressed or given by the Queen; but the Appointment of such a Deputy or Deputies shall not affect the Exercise by the Governor General himself of any Power, Authority or Function.

Power to Her Majesty to authorize Governor General to appoint Deputies.

15. The Command-in-Chief of the Land and Naval Militia, and of all Naval and Military Forces, of and in Canada, is hereby declared to continue and be vested in the Queen.

Command of armed Forces to continue to be vested in the Queen.

16. Until the Queen otherwise directs, the Seat of Government of Canada shall be Ottawa.

Seat of Government of Canada.

IV.—LEGISLATIVE POWER.

17. There shall be One Parliament for Canada, consisting of the Queen, an Upper House styled the Senate, and the House of Commons.

Constitution of Parliament of Canada.

18. The privileges, immunities, and powers to be held, enjoyed, and exercised by the Senate and by the House of Commons, and by the Members thereof respectively, shall be such as are from time to time defined by Act of the Parliament of Canada, but so that any Act of the Parliament of Canada defining such privileges, immunities, and powers shall not confer any privileges, immunities, or powers exceeding those at the passing of such Act held, enjoyed, and exercised by the Commons House of Parliament of the United Kingdom of Great Britain and Ireland, and by the Members thereof.(8)

Privileges, etc. of Houses.

---

(8) Repealed and re-enacted by the *Parliament of Canada Act, 1875*, 38-39 Vict., c. 38 (U.K.). The original section read as follows:

> **18.** The Privileges, Immunities, and Powers to be held, enjoyed, and exercised by the Senate and by the House of Commons and by the Members thereof respectively shall be such as are from Time to Time defined by Act of the Parliament of Canada, but so that the same shall never exceed those at the passing of this Act held, enjoyed, and exercised by the Commons House of Parliament of the United Kingdom of Great Britain and Ireland and by the Members thereof.

First Session of
the Parliament
of Canada.

19. The Parliament of Canada shall be called together not later than Six Months after the Union.(9)

20. Repealed.(10)

The Senate.

Number of
Senators.

21. The Senate shall, subject to the Provisions of this Act, consist of One Hundred and four Members, who shall be styled Senators.(11)

Representation
of Provinces in
Senate.

22. In relation to the Constitution of the Senate Canada shall be deemed to consist of Four Divisions:–

1. Ontario;
2. Quebec;
3. The Maritime Provinces, Nova Scotia and New Brunswick, and Prince Edward Island;
4. The Western Provinces of Manitoba, British Columbia, Saskatchewan, and Alberta;

which Four Divisions shall (subject to the Provisions of this Act) be equally represented in the Senate as follows: Ontario by twenty-four senators; Quebec by twenty-four senators; the Maritime Provinces and Prince Edward Island by twenty-four senators, ten thereof representing Nova Scotia, ten

---

(9) Spent. The first session of the first Parliament began on November 6, 1867.

(10) Section 20, repealed by the Schedule to the *Constitution Act, 1982*, read as follows:

> **20.** There shall be a Session of the Parliament of Canada once at least in every Year, so that Twelve Months shall not intervene between the last Sitting of the Parliament in one Session and its first Sitting in the next Session.

> Section 20 has been replaced by section 5 of the *Constitution Act, 1982*, which provides that there shall be a sitting of Parliament at least once every twelve months.

(11) As amended by the *Constitution Act, 1915*, 5-6 Geo. V, c. 45 (U.K.) and modified by the *Newfoundland Act*, 12-13 Geo. VI, c. 22 (U.K.), and the *Constitution Act (No. 2), 1975*, S.C. 1974-75-76, c. 53.

The original section read as follows:

> **21.** The Senate shall, subject to the Provisions of this Act, consist of Seventy-two Members, who shall be styled Senators.

The *Manitoba Act, 1870*, added two for Manitoba; the *British Columbia Terms of Union* added three; upon admission of Prince Edward Island four more were provided by section 147 of the *Constitution Act, 1867*; the *Alberta Act* and the *Saskatchewan Act* each added four. The Senate was reconstituted at 96 by the *Constitution Act, 1915*. Six more Senators were added upon union with Newfoundland, and one Senator each was added for the Yukon Territory and the Northwest Territories by the *Constitution Act (No. 2), 1975*.

thereof representing New Brunswick, and four thereof representing Prince Edward Island; the Western Provinces by twenty-four senators, six thereof representing Manitoba, six thereof representing British Columbia, six thereof representing Saskatchewan, and six thereof representing Alberta; Newfoundland shall be entitled to be represented in the Senate by six members; the Yukon Territory and the Northwest Territories shall be entitled to be represented in the Senate by one member each.

In the Case of Quebec each of the Twenty-four Senators representing that Province shall be appointed for One of the Twenty-four Electoral Divisions of Lower Canada specified in Schedule A. to Chapter One of the Consolidated statutes of Canada. (12)

23. The Qualification of a Senator shall be as follows:

(1) He shall be of the full age of Thirty Years:

(2) He shall be either a natural-born Subject of the Queen, or a Subject of the Queen naturalized by an Act of the Parliament of Great Britain, or of the Parliament of the United Kingdom of Great Britain and Ireland, or of the Legislature of One of the Provinces of Upper Canada, Lower Canada; Canada, Nova Scotia, or New Brunswick, before the Union, or of the Parliament of Canada, after the Union:

(3) He shall be legally or equitably seised as of Freehold for his own Use and Benefit of Lands or Tenements held in Free and Common Socage, or seised or possessed for his own Use and Benefit of Lands or Tenements held in Franc-alleu or in Roture, within

Qualifications of Senator.

---

(12) As amended by the *Constitution Act, 1915,* the *Newfoundland Act,* 12-13 Geo. VI, c. 22 (U.K.), and the *Constitution Act (No. 2), 1975,* S.C. 1974-75-76, c. 53. The original section read as follows:

> **22.** In relation to the Constitution of the Senate, Canada shall be deemed to consist of Three Divisions:
>
> 1. Ontario;
>
> 2. Quebec;
>
> 3. The Maritime Provinces, Nova Scotia and New Brunswick;
>
> which Three Divisions shall (subject to the Provisions of this Act) be equally represented in the Senate as follows: Ontario by Twenty-four Senators; Quebec by Twenty-four Senators; and the Maritime Provinces by Twenty-four Senators, Twelve thereof representing Nova Scotia, and Twelve thereof representing New Brunswick.
>
> In the case of Quebec each of the Twenty-four Senators representing that Province shall be appointed for One of the Twenty-four Electoral Divisions of Lower Canada specified in Schedule A. to Chapter One of the Consolidated Statutes of Canada.

the Province for which he is appointed, of the Value of Four thousand Dollars, over and above all Rents, Dues, Debts, Charges, Mortgages, and Incumbrances due or payable out of or charged on or affecting the same:

(4) His Real and Personal Property shall be together worth Four thousand Dollars over and above his Debts and Liabilities:

(5) He shall be resident in the Province for which he is appointed:

(6) In the Case of Quebec he shall have his Real Property Qualification in the Electoral Division for which he is appointed, or shall be resident in that Division. (13)

Summons of Senator.

24. The Governor General shall from Time to Time, in the Queen's Name, by Instrument under the Great Seal of Canada, summon qualified Persons to the Senate; and, subject to the Provisions of this Act, every Person so summoned shall become and be a Member of the Senate and a Senator.

25. Repealed. (14)

Addition of Senators in certain cases.

26. If at any Time on the Recommendation of the Governor General the Queen thinks fit to direct that Four or Eight Members be added to the Senate, the Governor General may by Summons to Four or Eight qualified Persons (as the Case may be), representing equally the Four Divisions of Canada, add to the Senate accordingly.(15)

---

(13) Section 2 of the *Constitution Act (No. 2), 1975*, S.C. 1974-75-76, c. 53 provided that for the purposes of that Act (which added one Senator each for the Yukon Territory and the Northwest Territories) the term "Province" in section 23 of the *Constitution Act, 1867*, has the same meaning as is assigned to the term "province" by section 28 of the *Interpretation Act*, R.S.C. 1970, c. I-23, which provides that the term "province" means "a province of Canada, and includes the Yukon Territory and the Northwest Territories."

(14) Repealed by the *Statute Law Revision Act, 1893*, 56-57 Vict., 14 (U.K.). The section read as follows:

> **25.** Such Persons shall be first summoned to the Senate as the Queen by Warrant under Her Majesty's Royal Sign Manual thinks fit to approve, and their Names shall be inserted in the Queen's Proclamation of Union.

(15) As amended by the *Constitution Act, 1915*, 5-6 Geo. V, c. 45 (U.K.). The original section read as follows:

> **26.** If at any Time on the Recommendation of the Governor General the Queen thinks fit to direct that Three or Six Members be added to the Senate, the Governor General may by Summons to Three or Six qualified Persons (as the Case may be), representing equally the Three Divisions of Canada, add to the Senate accordingly.

27. In case of such Addition being at any Time made, the Governor General shall not summon any Person to the Senate, except upon a further like Direction by the Queen on the like Recommendation, to represent one of the Four Divisions until such Division is represented by Twenty-four Senators and no more.(16)

Reduction of Senate to normal Number.

28. The Number of Senators shall not at any Time exceed One Hundred and twelve. (17)

Maximum Number of Senators.

29. (1) Subject to subsection (2), a Senator shall, subject to the provisions of this Act, hold his place in the Senate for life.

Tenure of Place in Senate.

(2) A Senator who is summoned to the Senate after the coming into force of this subsection shall, subject to this Act, hold his place in the Senate until he attains the age of seventy-five years. (18)

Retirement upon attaining age of seventy-five years.

30. A Senator may by Writing under his Hand addressed to the Governor General resign his Place in the Senate, and thereupon the same shall be vacant.

Resignation of Place in Senate.

31. The Place of a Senator shall become vacant in any of the following Cases:

Disqualification of Senators.

(1) If for Two consecutive Sessions of the Parliament he fails to give his Attendance in the Senate:

(2) If he takes an Oath or makes a Declaration or Acknowledgement of Allegiance, Obedience, or Adherence to a Foreign Power, or does an Act whereby he becomes a Subject or Citizen, or entitled to the

---

(16) As amended by the *Constitution Act, 1915*, 5-6 Geo. V, c. 45 (U.K.). The original section read as follows:

> **27.** In case of such Addition being at any Time made the Governor General shall not summon any Person to the Senate except on a further like Direction by the Queen on the like Recommendation, until each of the Three Divisions of Canada is represented by Twenty-four Senators and no more.

(17) As amended by the *Constitution Act, 1915*, 5-6 Geo. V, c. 45 (U.K.), and the *Constitution Act (No. 2), 1975*, S.C. 1974-75-76, c. 53. The original section read as follows:

> **28.** The Number of Senators shall not at any Time exceed Seventy-eight.

(18) As enacted by the *Constitution Act, 1965*, Statutes of Canada, 1965, c. 4 which came into force on the 1st of June 1965. The original section read as follows:

> **29.** A Senator shall, subject to the Provisions of this Act, hold his Place in the Senate for Life.

Rights or Privileges of a Subject or Citizen, of a Foreign Power.

(3) If he is adjudged Bankrupt or Insolvent, or applies for the Benefit of any Law relating to Insolvent Debtors, or becomes a public Defaulter:

(4) If he is attainted of Treason or convicted of Felony or of any infamous Crime:

(5) If he ceases to be qualified in respect of Property or of Residence; provided, that a Senator shall not be deemed to have ceased to be qualified in respect of Residence by reason only of his residing at the Seat of the Government of Canada while holding an Office under that Government requiring his Presence there.

Summons on Vacancy in Senate.

32. When a Vacancy happens in the Senate by Resignation, Death or otherwise, the Governor General shall by Summons to a fit and qualified Person fill the Vacancy.

Questions as to Qualifications and Vacancies in Senate.

33. If any Question arises respecting the Qualification of a Senator or a Vacancy in the Senate the same shall be heard and determined by the Senate.

Appointment of Speaker of Senate.

34. The Governor General may from Time to Time, by Instrument under the Great Seal of Canada, appoint a Senator to be Speaker of the Senate, and may remove him and appoint another in his Stead. (19)

Quorum of Senate.

35. Until the Parliament of Canada otherwise provides, the Presence of at least Fifteen Senators, including the Speaker, shall be necessary to constitute a Meeting of the Senate for the Exercise of its Powers.

Voting in Senate.

36. Questions arising in the Senate shall be decided by a Majority of Voices, and the Speaker shall in all Cases have a Vote, and when the Voices are equal the Decision shall be deemed to be in the Negative.

---

(19) Provision for exercising the functions of Speaker during his absence is made by the *Speaker of the Senate Act*, R.S.C. 1970, c. S-14. Doubts as to the power of Parliament to enact such an Act were removed by the *Canadian Speaker (Appointment of Deputy) Act, 1895*, 59 Vict., c. 3 (U.K.) which was repealed by the *Constitution Act, 1982*.

The House of Commons.

37. The House of Commons shall, subject to the Provisions of this Act, consist of two hundred and eighty-two members of whom ninety-five shall be elected for Ontario, seventy-five for Quebec, eleven for Nova Scotia, ten for New Brunswick, fourteen for Manitoba, twenty-eight for British Columbia, four for Prince Edward Island, twenty-one for Alberta, fourteen for Saskatchewan, seven for Newfoundland, one for the Yukon Territory and two for the Northwest Territories.(20)

Constitution of House of Commons in Canada.

38. The Governor General shall from Time to Time, in the Queen's Name, by Instrument under the Great Seal of Canada, summon and call together the House of Commons.

Summoning of House of Commons.

39. A Senator shall not be capable of being elected or of sitting or voting as a Member of the House of Commons.

Senators not to sit in House of Commons.

40. Until the Parliament of Canada otherwise provides, Ontario, Quebec, Nova Scotia and New Brunswick shall, for the Purposes of the Election of Members to serve in the House of Commons, be divided into Electoral districts as follows:

Electoral districts of the four Provinces

1.—ONTARIO.

Ontario shall be divided into the Counties, Ridings of Counties, Cities, Parts of Cities, and Towns enumerated in the First Schedule to this Act, each whereof shall be an Electoral District, each such District as numbered in that Schedule being entitled to return One Member.

2.—QUEBEC.

Quebec shall be divided into Sixty-five Electoral Districts, composed of the Sixty-five Electoral Divisions into which Lower Canada is at the passing of this Act divided under

---

(20) The figures given here result from the application of section 51, as enacted by the *Constitution Act, 1974*, S.C. 1974-75-76, c. 13, amended by the *Constitution Act (No. 1), 1975*, S.C. 1974-75-76, c. 28 and readjusted pursuant to the *Electoral Boundaries Readjustment Act*, R.S.C., 1970, c. E-2. The original section (which was altered from time to time as the result of the addition of new provinces and changes in population) read as follows:

> **37.** The House of Commons shall, subject to the Provisions of this Act, consist of one hundred and eighty-one members, of whom Eighty-two shall be elected for Ontario, Sixty-five for Quebec, Nineteen for Nova Scotia, and Fifteen for New Brunswick.

Chapter Two of the Consolidated Statutes of Canada, Chapter Seventy-five of the Consolidated Statutes for Lower Canada, and the Act of the Province of Canada of the Twenty-third Year of the Queen, Chapter One, or any other Act amending the same in force at the Union, so that each such Electoral Division shall be for the Purposes of this Act an Electoral District entitled to return One Member.

3.—NOVA SCOTIA.

Each of the Eighteen Counties of Nova Scotia shall be an Electoral District. The County of Halifax shall be entitled to return Two Members, and each of the other Counties One Member.

4.—NEW BRUNSWICK.

Each of the Fourteen Counties into which New Brunswick is divided, including the City and County of St. John, shall be an Electoral District. The City of St. John shall also be a separate Electoral District. Each of those Fifteen Electoral Districts shall be entitled to return One Member.(21)

Continuance of existing Election Laws until Parliament of Canada otherwise provides

41. Until the Parliament of Canada otherwise provides, all Laws in force in the several Provinces at the Union relative to the following Matters or any of them, namely,— the Qualifications and Disqualifications of Persons to be elected or to sit or vote as Members of the House of Assembly or Legislative Assembly in the several Provinces, the Voters at Elections of such Members, the Oaths to be taken by Voters, the Returning Officers, their Powers and Duties, the Proceedings at Elections, the Periods during which Elections may be continued, the Trial of controverted Elections, and Proceedings incident thereto, the vacating of Seats of Members, and the Execution of new Writs in case of Seats vacated otherwise than by Dissolution,—shall respectively apply to Elections of Members to serve in the House of Commons for the same several Provinces.

Provided that, until the Parliament of Canada otherwise provides, at any Election for a Member of the House of

(21) Spent. The electoral districts are now established by Proclamations issued from time to time under the *Electoral Boundaries Readjustment Act*, R.S.C., 1970, c. E-2, as amended for particular districts by Acts of Parliament, for which see the most recent Table of Public Statutes.

Commons for the District of Algoma, in addition to Persons qualified by the Law of the Province of Canada to vote, every Male British Subject, aged Twenty-one Years or upwards, being a Householder, shall have a Vote.(22)

42. Repealed.(23)

43. Repealed.(24)

44. The House of Commons on its first assembling after a General Election shall proceed with all practicable Speed to elect One of its Members to be Speaker.

As to Election of Speaker of House of Commons.

45. In case of a Vacancy happening in the Office of Speaker by Death, Resignation, or otherwise, the House of Commons shall with all practicable Speed proceed to elect another of its Members to be Speaker.

As to filling up Vacancy in Office of Speaker.

46. The Speaker shall preside at all Meetings of the House of Commons.

Speaker to preside.

47. Until the Parliament of Canada otherwise provides, in case of the Absence for any Reason of the Speaker from the Chair of the House of Commons for a Period of Forty-eight consecutive Hours, the House may elect another of its Mem-

Provision in case of Absence of Speaker.

---

(22) Spent. Elections are now provided for by the *Canada Elections Act*, R.S.C. 1970 (1st Supp.), c. 14; controverted elections by the *Dominion Controverted Elections Act*, R.S.C. 1970, c. C-28; qualifications and disqualifications of members by the *House of Commons Act*, R.S.C. 1970, c. H-9 and the *Senate and House of Commons Act*, R.S.C. 1970, c. S-8. The right of citizens to vote and hold office is provided for in section 3 of the *Constitution Act, 1982*.

(23) Repealed by the *Statute Law Revision Act, 1893*, 56-57 Vict., c. 14 (U.K.). The section read as follows:

> **42.** For the First Election of Members to serve in the House of Commons the Governor General shall cause Writs to be issued by such Person, in such Form, and addressed to such Returning Officers as he thinks fit.
>
> The Person issuing Writs under this Section shall have the like Powers as are possessed at the Union by the Officers charged with the issuing of Writs for the Election of Members to serve in the respective House of Assembly or Legislative Assembly of the Province of Canada, Nova Scotia, or New Brunswick; and the Returning Officers to whom Writs are directed under this Section shall have the like Powers as are possessed at the Union by the Officers charged with the returning of Writs for the Election of Members to serve in the same respective House of Assembly or Legislative Assembly.

(24) Repealed by the *Statute Law Revision Act, 1893*, 56-57 Vict., c. 14 (U.K.). The section read as follows:

> **43.** In case a Vacancy in the Representation in the House of Commons of any Electoral District happens before the Meeting of the Parliament, or after the Meeting of the Parliament before Provision is made by the Parliament in this Behalf, the Provisions of the last foregoing Section of this Act shall extend and apply to the issuing and returning of a Writ in respect of such vacant District.

bers to act as Speaker, and the Member so elected shall during the Continuance of such Absence of the Speaker have and execute all the Powers, Privileges, and Duties of Speaker.(25)

Quorum of House of Commons.

48. The Presence of at least Twenty Members of the House of Commons shall be necessary to constitute a Meeting of the House for the Exercise of its Powers, and for that Purpose the Speaker shall be reckoned as a Member.

Voting in House of Commons.

49. Questions arising in the House of Commons shall be decided by a Majority of Voices other than that of the Speaker, and when the Voices are equal, but not otherwise, the Speaker shall have a Vote.

Duration of House of Commons.

50. Every House of Commons shall continue for Five Years from the Day of the Return of the Writs for choosing the House (subject to be sooner dissolved by the Governor General), and no longer.(26)

Readjustment of representation in Commons.

51. (1) The number of members of the House of Commons and the representation of the provinces therein shall upon the coming into force of this subsection and thereafter on the completion of each decennial census be readjusted by such authority, in such manner, and from such time as the Parliament of Canada from time to time provides, subject and according to the following Rules:

Rules.

1. There shall be assigned to Quebec seventy-five members in the readjustment following the completion of the decennial census taken in the year 1971, and thereafter four additional members in each subsequent readjustment.

2. Subject to Rules 5(2) and (3), there shall be assigned to a large province a number of members equal to the number obtained by dividing the population of the large province by the electoral quotient of Quebec.

---

(25) Provision for exercising the functions of Speaker during his absence is now made by the *Speaker of the House of Commons Act*, R.S.C. 1970, c. S-13.

(26) The term of the twelfth Parliament was extended by the *British North America Act, 1916*, 6-7 Geo. V, c. 19 (U.K.), which Act was repealed by the *Statute Law Revision Act, 1927*, 17-18 Geo. V, c. 42 (U.K.). See also subsection 4(1) of the *Constitution Act, 1982*, which provides that no House of Commons shall continue for longer than five years from the date fixed for the return of the writs at a general election of its members, and subsecion 4(2) thereof, which provides for continuation of the House of Commons in special circumstances.

3. Subject to Rules 5(2) and (3), there shall be assigned to a small province a number of members equal to the number obtained by dividing

(*a*) the sum of the populations, determined according to the results of the penultimate decennial census, of the provinces (other than Quebec) having populations of less than one and a half million, determined according to the results of that census, by the sum of the numbers of members assigned to those provinces in the readjustment following the completion of that census; and

(*b*) the population of the small province by the quotient obtained under paragraph (*a*).

4. Subject to Rules 5(1)(*a*), (2) and (3), there shall be assigned to an intermediate province a number of members equal to the number obtained

(*a*) by dividing the sum of the populations of the provinces (other than Quebec) having populations of less than one and a half million by the sum of the number of members assigned to those provinces under any of Rules 3, 5(1)(*b*), (2) and (3);

(*b*) by dividing the population of the intermediate province by the quotient obtained under paragraph (*a*); and

(*c*) by adding to the number of members assigned to the intermediate province in the readjustment following the completion of the penultimate decennial census one-half of the difference resulting from the subtraction of that number from the quotient obtained under paragraph (*b*).

5. (1) On any readjustment,

(*a*) if no province (other than Quebec) has a population of less than one and a half million, Rule 4 shall not be applied and, subject to Rules 5(2) and (3), there shall be assigned to an intermediate province a number of members equal to the number obtained by dividing

(i) the sum of the populations, determined according to the results of the penultimate decennial census, of the provinces (other than Quebec) having populations of not less than one and a half million and not more than two and a half million, determined according to the results of that census, by the sum of the numbers of members assigned to those provinces in the readjustment following the completion of that census, and

(ii) the population of the intermediate province by the quotient obtained under subparagraph (i);

(*b*) if a province (other than Quebec) having a population of

(i) less than one and a half million, or

(ii) not less than one and a half million and not more than two and a half million

does not have a population greater than its population determined according to the results of the penultimate decennial census, it shall, subject to Rules 5(2) and (3), be assigned the number of members assigned to it in the readjustment following the completion of that census.

(2) On any readjustment,

(*a*) if, under any of Rules 2 to 5(1), the number of members to be assigned to a province (in this paragraph referred to as "the first province") is smaller than the number of members to be assigned to any other province not having a population greater than that of the first province, those Rules shall not be applied to the first province and it shall be assigned a number of members equal to the largest number of members to be assigned to any other province not having a population greater than that of the first province;

(*b*) if, under any of Rules 2 to 5(1)(*a*), the number of members to be assigned to a province is smaller than the number of members assigned to it in the readjustment following the completion of the penultimate decennial census, those Rules shall not be applied to it and it shall be assigned the latter number of members;

(*c*) if both paragraphs (*a*) and (*b*) apply to a province, it shall be assigned a number of members equal to the greater of the numbers produced under those paragraphs.

(3) On any readjustment,

(*a*) if the electoral quotient of a province (in this paragraph referred to as "the first province") obtained by dividing its population by the number of members to be assigned to it under any of Rules 2 to 5(2) is greater than the electoral quotient of Quebec, those Rules shall not be applied to the first province and it shall be assigned a number of members equal to the number obtained by dividing its population by the electoral quotient of Quebec;

(*b*) if, as a result of the application of Rule 6(2)(*a*), the number of members assigned to a province under paragraph (*a*) equals the number of members to be assigned to it under any of Rules 2 to 5(2), it shall be assigned that number of members and paragraph (*a*) shall cease to apply to that province.

6. (1) In these Rules,

"electoral quotient" means, in respect of a province, the quotient obtained by dividing its population, determined according to the results of the then most recent decennial census, by the number of members to be assigned to it under any of Rules 1 to 5(3) in the readjustment following the completion of that census;

"intermediate province" means a province (other than Quebec) having a population greater than its population determined according to the results of the penultimate decennial census but not more than two and a half million and not less than one and a half million;

"large province" means a province (other than Quebec) having a population greater than two and a half million;

"penultimate decennial census" means the decennial census that preceded the then most recent decennial census;

"population" means, except where otherwise specified, the population determined according to the results of the then most recent decennial census;

"small province" means a province (other than Quebec) having a population greater than its population determined according to the results of the penultimate decennial census and less than one and a half million.

(2) For the purposes of these Rules,

(*a*) if any fraction less than one remains upon completion of the final calculation that produces the number of members to be assigned to a province, that number of members shall equal the number so produced disregarding the fraction;

(*b*) if more than one readjustment follows the completion of a decennial census, the most recent of those readjustments shall, upon taking effect, be deemed to be the only readjustment following the completion of that census;

(*c*) a readjustment shall not take effect until the termination of the then existing Parliament.(27)

---

(27) As enacted by the *Constitution Act, 1974*, S.C. 1974-75-76, c. 13, which came into force on December 31, 1974. The section, as originally enacted, read as follows:

51. On the Completion of the Census in the Year One Thousand eight hundred and seventy-one, and of each subsequent decennial Census, the Representation of the Four Provinces shall be readjusted by such Authority, in such Manner, and from such Time, as the Parliament of Canada from Time to Time provides, subject and according to the following Rules:

(1) Quebec shall have the fixed Number of Sixty-five Members:

(2) There shall be assigned to each of the other Provinces such a Number of Members as will bear the same Proportion to the Number of its Population (ascertained at such Census) as the Number Sixty-five bears to the Number of the Population of Quebec (so ascertained):

(3) In the Computation of the Number of Members for a Province a fractional Part not exceeding One Half of the whole Number requisite for entitling the Province to a Member shall be disregarded; but a fractional Part exceeding One Half of that Number shall be equivalent to the whole Number:

(4) On any such Re-adjustment the Number of Members for a Province shall not be reduced unless the Proportion which the Number of the Population of the Province bore to the Number of the aggregate Population of Canada at the then last preceding Re-adjustment of the Number of Members for the Province is ascertained at the then latest Census to be diminished by One Twentieth Part or upwards:

(5) Such Re-adjustment shall not take effect until the Termination of the then existing Parliament.

The section was amended by the *Statute Law Revision Act, 1893*, 56-57 Vict., c. 14 (U.K.) by repealing the words from "of the census" to "seventy-one and" and the word "subsequent".

By the *British North America Act, 1943*, 6-7 Geo. VI, c. 30 (U.K.), which Act was repealed by the *Constitution Act, 1982*, redistribution of seats following the 1941 census was postponed until the first session of Parliament after the war. The section was re-enacted by the *British North America Act, 1946*, 9-10 Geo. VI, c. 63 (U.K.), which Act was also repealed by the *Constitution Act, 1982*, to read as follows:

51. (1) The number of members of the House of Commons shall be two hundred and fifty-five and the representation of the provinces therein shall forthwith upon the coming into force of this section and thereafter on the completion of each decennial census be readjusted by such authority, in such manner, and from such time as the

Parliament of Canada from time to time provides, subject and according to the following rules:

(1) Subject as hereinafter provided, there shall be assigned to each of the provinces a number of members computed by dividing the total population of the provinces by two hundred and fifty-four and by dividing the population of each province by the quotient so obtained, disregarding, except as hereinafter in this section provided, the remainder, if any, after the said process of division.

(2) If the total number of members assigned to all the provinces pursuant to rule one is less than two hundred and fifty-four, additional members shall be assigned to the provinces (one to a province) having remainders in the computation under rule one commencing with the province having the largest remainder and continuing with the other provinces in the order of the magnitude of their respective remainders until the total number of members assigned is two hundred and fifty-four.

(3) Notwithstanding anything in this section, if upon completion of a computation under rules one and two, the number of members to be assigned to a province is less than the number of senators representing the said province, rules one and two shall cease to apply in respect of the said province, and there shall be assigned to the said province a number of members equal to the said number of senators.

(4) In the event that rules one and two cease to apply in respect of a province then, for the purpose of computing the number of members to be assigned to the provinces in respect of which rules one and two continue to apply, the total population of the provinces shall be reduced by the number of the population of the province in respect of which rules one and two have ceased to apply and the number two hundred and fifty-four shall be reduced by the number of members assigned to such province pursuant to rule three.

(5) Such readjustment shall not take effect until the termination of the then existing Parliament.

(2) The Yukon Territory as constituted by Chapter forty-one of the Statutes of Canada, 1901, together with any Part of Canada not comprised within a province which may from time to time be included therein by the Parliament of Canada for the purposes of representation in Parliament, shall be entitled to one member.

The section was re-enacted by the *British North America Act, 1952*, S.C. 1952, c. 15, which Act was also repealed by the *Constitution Act, 1982*, as follows:

51. (1) Subject as hereinafter provided, the number of members of the House of Commons shall be two hundred and sixty-three and the representation of the provinces therein shall forthwith upon the coming into force of this section and thereafter on the completion of each decennial census be readjusted by such authority, in such manner, and from such time as the Parliament of Canada from time to time provides, subject and according to the following rules:

1. There shall be assigned to each of the provinces a number of members computed by dividing the total population of the provinces by two hundred and sixty-one and by dividing the population of each province by the quotient so obtained, disregarding, except as hereinafter in this section provided, the remainder, if any, after the said process of division.

2. If the total number of members assigned to all the provinces pursuant to rule one is less than two hundred and sixty-one, additional members shall be assigned to the provinces (one to a province) having remainders in the computation under rule one commencing with the province having the largest remainder and continuing with the other provinces in the order of the magnitude of their respective remainders until the total number of members assigned is two hundred and sixty-one.

3. Notwithstanding anything in this section, if upon completion of a computation under rules one and two the number of members to be assigned to a province is less than the number of senators representing the said province, rules one and two shall cease to apply in respect of the said province, and there shall be assigned to the said province a number of members equal to the said number of senators.

4. In the event that rules one and two cease to apply in respect of a province then, for the purposes of computing the number of members to be assigned to the provinces in respect of which rules one and two continue to apply, the total population of the provinces shall be reduced by the number of the population of the province in respect of which rules one and two have ceased

Yukon Territory and Northwest Territories.

(2) The Yukon Territory as bounded and described in the schedule to chapter Y-2 of the Revised Statutes of Canada, 1970, shall be entitled to one member, and the Northwest Territories as bounded and described in section 2 of chapter N-22 of the Revised Statutes of Canada, 1970, shall be entitled to two members.(28)

Constitution of House of Commons.

51A. Notwithstanding anything in this Act a province shall always be entitled to a number of members in the House of Commons not less than the number of senators representing such province.(29)

Increase of Number of House of Commons.

52. The Number of Members of the House of Commons may be from Time to Time increased by the Parliament of Canada, provided the proportionate Representation of the Provinces prescribed by this Act is not thereby disturbed.

Money Votes; Royal Assent

Appropriation and Tax Bills.

53. Bills for appropriating any Part of the Public Revenue, or for imposing any Tax or Impost, shall originate in the House of Commons.

Recommendation of Money Votes.

54. It shall not be lawful for the House of Commons to adopt or pass any Vote, Resolution, Address, or Bill for the

---

to apply and the number two hundred and sixty-one shall be reduced by the number of members assigned to such province pursuant to rule three.

5. On any such readjustment the number of members for any province shall not be reduced by more than fifteen per cent below the representation to which such province was entitled under rules one to four of this subsection at the last preceding readjustment of the representation of that province, and there shall be no reduction in the representation of any province as a result of which that province would have a smaller number of members than any other province that according to the results of the then last decennial census did not have a larger population; but for the purposes of any subsequent readjustment of representation under this section any increase in the number of members of the House of Commons resulting from the application of this rule shall not be included in the divisor mentioned in rules one to four of this subsection.

readjustment of representation under this section any increase in the number of members of the House of Commons resulting from the application of this rule shall not be included in the divisor mentioned in rules one to four of this subsection.

6. Such readjustment shall not take effect until the termination of the then existing Parliament.

(2) The Yukon Territory as constituted by chapter forty-one of the statutes of Canada, 1901, shall be entitled to one member, and such other part of Canada not comprised within a province as may from time to time be defined by the Parliament of Canada shall be entitled to one member.

(28) As enacted by the *Constitution Act (No. 1), 1975*, S.C. 1974-75-76, c. 28.

(29) As enacted by the *Constitution Act, 1915*, 5-6 Geo. V, c. 45 (U.K.)

Appropriation of any Part of the Public Revenue, or of any Tax or Impost, to any Purpose that has not been first recommended to that House by Message of the Governor General in the Session in which such Vote, Resolution, Address, or Bill is proposed.

55. Where a Bill passed by the Houses of the Parliament is presented to the Governor General for the Queen's Assent, he shall declare, according to his Discretion, but subject to the Provisions of this Act and to Her Majesty's Instructions, either that he assents thereto in the Queen's Name, or that he withholds the Queen's Assent, or that he reserves the Bill for the Signification of the Queen's Pleasure.

Royal Assent to Bills, etc.

56. Where the Governor General assents to a Bill in the Queen's Name, he shall by the first convenient Opportunity send an authentic Copy of the Act to one of Her Majesty's Principal Secretaries of State, and if the Queen in Council within Two Years after Receipt thereof by the Secretary of State thinks fit to disallow the Act, such Disallowance (with a Certificate of the Secretary of State of the Day on which the Act was received by him) being signified by the Governor General, by Speech or Message to each of the Houses of the Parliament or by Proclamation, shall annul the Act from and after the Day of such Signification.

Disallowance by Order in Council of Act assented to by Governor General.

57. A Bill reserved for the Signification of the Queen's Pleasure shall not have any Force unless and until, within Two Years from the Day on which it was presented to the Governor General for the Queen's Assent, the Governor General signifies, by Speech or Message to each of the Houses of the Parliament or by Proclamation, that it has received the Assent of the Queen in Council.

Signification of Queen's Pleasure on Bill reserved.

An Entry of every such Speech, Message, or Proclamation shall be made in the Journal of each House, and a Duplicate thereof duly attested shall be delivered to the proper Officer to be kept among the Records of Canada.

V.—Provincial Constitutions.

Executive Power.

58. For each Province there shall be an Officer, styled the Lieutenant Governor, appointed by the Governor General in Council by Instrument under the Great Seal of Canada.

Appointment of Lieutenant Governors of Provinces.

Tenure of
Office of
Lieutenant
Governor.

59. A Lieutenant Governor shall hold Office during the Pleasure of the Governor General; but any Lieutenant Governor appointed after the Commencement of the First Session of the Parliament of Canada shall not be removeable within Five Years from his Appointment, except for Cause assigned, which shall be communicated to him in Writing within One Month after the Order for his Removal is made, and shall be communicated by Message to the Senate and to the House of Commons within One Week thereafter if the Parliament is then sitting, and if not then within One Week after the Commencement of the next Session of the Parliament.

Salaries of
Lieutenant
Governors.

60. The Salaries of the Lieutenant Governors shall be fixed and provided by the Parliament of Canada. (30)

Oaths, etc., of
Lieutenant
Governor.

61. Every Lieutenant Governor shall, before assuming the Duties of his Office, make and subscribe before the Governor General or some Person authorized by him Oaths of Allegiance and Office similar to those taken by the Governor General.

Application of
provisions
referring to
Lieutenant
Governor.

62. The Provisions of this Act referring to the Lieutenant Governor extend and apply to the Lieutenant Governor for the Time being of each Province, or other the Chief Executive Officer or Administrator for the Time being carrying on the Government of the Province, by whatever Title he is designated.

Appointment of
Executive
Officers for
Ontario and
Quebec.

63. The Executive Council of Ontario and of Quebec shall be composed of such Persons as the Lieutenant Governor from Time to Time thinks fit, and in the first instance of the following Officers, namely, — the Attorney General, the Secretary and Registrar of the Province, the Treasurer of the Province, the Commissioner of Crown Lands, and the Commissioner of Agriculture and Public Works, with in Quebec, the Speaker of the Legislative Council and the Solicitor General. (31)

Executive
Government of
Nova Scotia
and New
Brunswick.

64. The Constitution of the Executive Authority in each of the Provinces of Nova Scotia and New Brunswick shall,

---

(30) Provided for by the *Salaries Act*, R.S.C. 1970, c. S-2.

(31) Now provided for in Ontario by the *Executive Council Act*, R.S.O. 1980, c. 147, and in Quebec by the *Executive Power Act*, R.S.Q. 1977, c. E-18.

subject to the Provisions of this Act, continue as it exists at the Union until altered under the Authority of this Act. (32)

65. All Powers, Authorities, and Functions which under any Act of the Parliament of Great Britain, or of the Parliament of the United Kingdom of Great Britain and Ireland, or of the Legislature of Upper Canada, Lower Canada, or Canada, were or are before or at the Union vested in or exerciseable by the respective Governors or Lieutenant Governors of those Provinces, with the Advice or with the Advice and Consent of the respective Executive Councils thereof, or in conjunction with those Councils, or with any Number of Members thereof, or by those Governors or Lieutenant Governors individually, shall, as far as the same are capable of being exercised after the Union in relation to the Government of Ontario and Quebec respectively, be vested in and shall or may be exercised by the Lieutenant Governor of Ontario and Quebec respectively, with the Advice or with the Advice and consent of or in conjunction with the respective Executive Councils, or any Members thereof, or by the Lieutenant Governor individually, as the Case requires, subject nevertheless (except with respect to such as exist under Acts of the Parliament of Great Britain, or of the Parliament of the United Kingdom of Great Britain and Ireland,) to be abolished or altered by the respective Legislatures of Ontario and Quebec. (33)

Powers to be exercised by Lieutenant Governor of Ontario or Quebec with Advice, or alone.

66. The Provisions of this Act referring to the Lieutenant Governor in Council shall be construed as referring to the Lieutenant Governor of the Province acting by and with the Advice of the Executive Council thereof.

Application of Provisions referring to Lieutenant Governor in Council.

67. The Governor General in Council may from Time to Time appoint an Administrator to execute the office and Functions of Lieutenant Governor during his Absence, Illness, or other Inability.

Administration in Absence, etc., of Lieutenant Governor.

68. Unless and until the Executive Government of any Province otherwise directs with respect to that Province, the

Seats of Provincial Governments.

---

(32) A similar provision was included in each of the instruments admitting British Columbia, Prince Edward Island, and Newfoundland. The Executive Authorities for Manitoba, Alberta and Saskatchewan were established by the statutes creating those provinces. See the notes to section 5, *supra.*

(33) See the notes to section 129, *infra.*

Seats of Government of the Provinces shall be as follows, namely, — of Ontario, the City of Toronto; of Quebec, the City of Quebec; of Nova Scotia, the City of Halifax; and of New Brunswick, the City of Fredericton.

Legislative Power.

1.—ONTARIO.

Legislature for Ontario.

69. There shall be a Legislature for Ontario consisting of the Lieutenant Governor and of One House, styled the Legislative Assembly of Ontario.

Electoral districts.

70. The Legislative Assembly of Ontario shall be composed of Eighty-two Members, to be elected to represent the Eighty-two Electoral Districts set forth in the First Schedule to this Act. (34)

2.—QUEBEC

Legislature for Quebec.

71. There shall· be a Legislature for Quebec consisting of the Lieutenant Governor and of Two Houses, styled the Legislative Council of Quebec and the Legislative Assembly of Quebec. (35)

Constitution of Legislative Council.

72. The Legislative Council of Quebec shall be composed of Twenty-four Members, to be appointed by the Lieutenant Governor, in the Queen's Name, by Instrument under the Great Seal of Quebec, One being appointed to represent each of the Twenty-four Electoral Divisions of Lower Canada in this Act referred to, and each holding Office for the Term of his Life, unless the Legislature of Quebec otherwise provides under the Provisions of this Act.

Qualification of Legislative Councillors.

73. The Qualifications of the Legislative Councillors of Quebec shall be the same as those of the Senators for Quebec.

Resignation, Disqualification etc.

74. The Place of a Legislative Councillor of Quebec shall become vacant in the Cases, *mutatis mutandis*, in which the Place of Senator becomes vacant.

---

(34) Spent. Now covered by the *Representation Act*, R.S.O. 1980, c. 450.

(35) The Act respecting the Legislative Council of Quebec, S.Q. 1968, c. 9, provided that the Legislature for Quebec shall consist of the Lieutenant Governor and the National Assembly of Quebec, and repealed the provisions of the *Legislature Act*, R.S.Q. 1964, c. 6, relating to the Legislative Council of Quebec. Sections 72 to 79 following are therefore completely spent.

75. When a Vacancy happens in the Legislative Council of Quebec by Resignation, Death, or otherwise, the Lieutenant Governor, in the Queen's Name, by Instrument under the Great Seal of Quebec, shall appoint a fit and qualified Person to fill the Vacancy.

Vacancies.

76. If any Question arises respecting the Qualification of a Legislative Councillor of Quebec, or a Vacancy in the Legislative Council of Quebec, the same shall be heard and determined by the Legislative Council.

Questions as to Vacancies, etc.

77. The Lieutenant Governor may from Time to Time, by Instrument under the Great Seal of Quebec, appoint a Member of the Legislative Council of Quebec to be Speaker thereof, and may remove him and appoint another in his Stead.

Speaker of Legislative Council.

78. Until the Legislature of Quebec otherwise provides, the Presence of at least Ten Members of the Legislative Council, including the Speaker, shall be necessary to constitute a Meeting for the Exercise of its Powers.

Quorum of Legislative Council.

79. Questions arising in the Legislative Council of Quebec shall be decided by a Majority of Voices, and the Speaker shall in all Cases have a Vote, and when the Voices are equal the Decision shall be deemed to be in the Negative.

Voting in Legislative Council.

80. The Legislative Assembly of Quebec shall be composed of Sixty-five 'Members, to be elected to represent the Sixty-five Electoral Divisions or Districts of Lower Canada in this Act referred to, subject to Alteration thereof by the Legislature of Quebec: Provided that it shall not be lawful to present to the Lieutenant Governor of Quebec for Assent any Bill for altering the Limits of any of the Electoral Divisions or Districts mentioned in the Second Schedule to this Act, unless the Second and Third Readings of such Bill have been passed in the Legislative Assembly with the Concurrence of the Majority of the Members representing all those Electoral Divisions or Districts, and the Assent shall not be given to such Bill unless an Address has been presented by the Legislative Assembly to the Lieutenant Governor stating that it has been so passed. (36)

Constitution of Legislative Assembly of Quebec.

---

(36) The Act respecting electoral districts, S.Q. 1970, c. 7, s. 1, provides that this section no longer has effect.

3.—ONTARIO AND QUEBEC

81. Repealed. (37)

Summoning of Legislative Assemblies.

82. The Lieutenant Governor of Ontario and of Quebec shall from Time to Time, in the Queen's Name, by Instrument under the Great Seal of the Province, summon and call together the Legislative Assembly of the Province.

Restriction on election of Holders of offices.

83. Until the Legislature of Ontario or of Quebec otherwise provides, a Person accepting or holding in Ontario or in Quebec any Office, Commission, or Employment, permanent or temporary, at the Nomination of the Lieutenant Governor, to which an annual Salary, or any Fee, Allowance, Emolument, or Profit of any Kind or Amount whatever from the Province is attached, shall not be eligible as a Member of the Legislative Assembly of the respective Province, nor shall he sit or vote as such; but nothing in this Section shall make ineligible any Person being a member of the Executive Council of the respective Province, or holding any of the following Offices, that is to say, the Offices of Attorney General, Secretary and Registrar of the Province, Treasurer of the Province, Commissioner of Crown Lands, and Commissioner of Agriculture and Public Works, and in Quebec Solicitor General, or shall disqualify him to sit or vote in the House for which he is elected, provided he is elected while holding such Office. (38)

Continuance of existing Election Laws.

84. Until the legislatures of Ontario and Quebec respectively otherwise provide, all Laws which at the Union are in force in those Provinces respectively, relative to the following Matters, or any of them, namely, — the Qualifications and Disqualifications of Persons to be elected or to sit or vote as Members of the Assembly of Canada, the Qualifications or Disqualifications of Voters, the Oaths to be taken by Voters, the Returning Officers, their Powers and Duties, the Proceedings at Elections, the Periods during which such Elections may be continued, and the Trial of controverted Elections

---

(37) Repealed by the *Statute Law Revision Act, 1893,* 56-57 Vict., c. 14 (U.K.). The section read as follows:

81. The Legislatures of Ontario and Quebec respectively shall be called together not later than Six Months after the Union.

(38) Probably spent. The subject-matter of this section is now covered in Ontario by the *Legislative Assembly Act,* R.S.O. 1980, c. 235, and in Quebec by the *Legislature Act,* R.S.Q. 1977, c. L-1.

and the Proceedings incident thereto, the vacating of the Seats of Members and the issuing and execution of new Writs in case of Seats vacated otherwise than by Dissolution, — shall respectively apply to Elections of Members to serve in the respective Legislative Assemblies of Ontario and Quebec.

Provided that, until the Legislature of Ontario otherwise provides, at any Election for a Member of the Legislative Assembly of Ontario for the District of Algoma, in addition to Persons qualified by the Law of the Province of Canada to vote, every male British Subject, aged Twenty-one Years or upwards, being a Householder, shall have a vote. (39)

85. Every Legislative Assembly of Ontario and every Legislative Assembly of Quebec shall continue for Four Years from the Day of the Return of the Writs for choosing the same (subject nevertheless to either the Legislative Assembly of Ontario or the Legislative Assembly of Quebec being sooner dissolved by the Lieutenant Governor of the Province), and no longer. (40)

Duration of Legislative Assemblies.

86. There shall be a Session of the Legislature of Ontario and of that of Quebec once at least in every Year, so that Twelve Months shall not intervene between the last Sitting of the Legislature in each Province in one Session and its first Sitting in the next Session. (41)

Yearly Session of Legislature.

87. The following Provisions of this Act respecting the House of Commons of Canada shall extend and apply to the Legislative Assemblies of Ontario and Quebec, that is to say, — the Provisions relating to the Election of a Speaker originally and on Vacancies, the Duties of the Speaker, the Absence of the Speaker, the Quorum, and the Mode of voting, as if those Provisions were here re-enacted and made applicable in Terms to each such Legislative Assembly.

Speaker, Quorum, etc.

---

(39) Probably spent. The subject-matter of this section is now covered in Ontario by the *Election Act*, R.S.O. 1980, c. 133, and the *Legislative Assembly Act*, R.S.O. 1980, c. 235, in Quebec by the *Elections Act*, R.S.Q. 1977, c. E-3, the *Provincial Controverted Elections Act*, R.S.Q. 1977, c. C-65, and the *Legislature Act*, R.S.Q. 1977, c. L-1.

(40) The maximum duration of the Legislative Assemblies of Ontario and Quebec has been changed to five years. See the *Legislative Assembly Act*, R.S.O. 1980, c. 235, and the *Legislature Act*, R.S.Q. 1977, c. L-1, respectively. See also section 4 of the *Constitution Act, 1982*, which provides a maximum duration for a legislative assembly of five years but also authorizes continuation in special circumstances.

(41) See also section 5 of the *Constitution Act, 1982*, which provides that there shall be a sitting of each legislature at least once every twelve months.

4.—NOVA SCOTIA AND NEW BRUNSWICK.

Constitutions of
Legislatures of
Nova Scotia
and New
Brunswick.

88. The Constitution of the Legislature of each of the Provinces of Nova Scotia and New Brunswick shall, subject to the Provisions of this Act, continue as it exists at the Union until altered under the Authority of this Act. (42)

89. Repealed. (43)

6.—THE FOUR PROVINCES.

Application to
Legislatures of
Provinces
respecting
Money Votes,
etc.

90. The following Provisions of this Act respecting the Parliament of Canada, namely,— the Provisions relating to Appropriation and Tax Bills, the Recommendation of Money Votes, the Assent to Bills, the Disallowance of Acts, and the Signification of Pleasure on Bills reserved, — shall extend and apply to the Legislatures of the several Provinces as if those Provisions were here re-enacted and made applicable in Terms to the respective Provinces and the Legislatures thereof, with the Substitution of the Lieutenant Governor of the Province for the Governor General, of the Governor General for the Queen and for a Secretary of State, of One Year for Two Years, and of the Province for Canada.

---

(42) Partially repealed by the *Statute Law Revision Act, 1893*, 56-57 Vict., c. 14 (U.K.), which deleted the following concluding words of the original enactment:

> and the House of Assembly of New Brunswick existing at the passing of this Act shall, unless sooner dissolved, continue for the Period for which it was elected.

A similar provision was included in each of the instruments admitting British Columbia, Prince Edward Island and Newfoundland. The Legislatures of Manitoba, Alberta and Saskatchewan were established by the statutes creating those provinces. See the footnotes to section 5, *supra*.

See also sections 3 to 5 of the *Constitution Act, 1982*, which prescribe democratic rights applicable to all provinces, and subitem 2(2) of the Schedule to that Act, which sets out the repeal of section 20 of the *Manitoba Act, 1870*. Section 20 of the *Manitoba Act, 1870*, has been replaced by section 5 of the *Constitution Act, 1982*.

Section 20 reads as follows:

> **20.** There shall be a Session of the Legislature once at least in every year, so that twelve months shall not intervene between the last sitting of the Legislature in one Session and its first sitting in the next Session.

(43) Repealed by the *Statute Law Revision Act, 1893*, 56-57 Vict., c. 14 (U.K.). The section read as follows:

> 5.—Ontario, Quebec, and Nova Scotia.
>
> **89.** Each of the Lieutenant Governors of Ontario, Quebec and Nova Scotia shall cause Writs to be issued for the First Election of Members of the Legislative Assembly thereof in such Form and by such Person as he thinks fit, and at such Time and addressed to such Returning Officer as the Governor General directs, and so that the First Election of Member of Assembly for any Electoral District or any Subdivision thereof shall be held at the same Time and at the same Places as the Election for a Member to serve in the House of Commons of Canada for the Electoral District.

VI.—DISTRIBUTION OF LEGISLATIVE POWERS.

Powers of the Parliament.

91. It shall be lawful for the Queen, by and with the Advice and Consent of the Senate and House of Commons, to make Laws for the Peace, Order, and good Government of Canada, in relation to all Matters not coming within the Classes of Subjects by this Act assigned exclusively to the Legislatures of the Provinces; and for greater Certainty, but not so as to restrict the Generality of the foregoing Terms of this Section, it is hereby declared that (notwithstanding anything in this Act) the exclusive Legislative Authority of the Parliament of Canada extends to all Matters coming within the Classes of Subjects next hereinafter enumerated; that is to say,— {Legislative Authority of Parliament of Canada.}

1. Repealed. (44)

1A. The Public Debt and Property. (45)

2. The Regulation of Trade and Commerce.

2A. Unemployment insurance. (46)

3. The raising of Money by any Mode or System of Taxation.

4. The borrowing of Money on the Public Credit.

5. Postal Service.

6. The Census and Statistics.

7. Militia, Military and Naval Service, and Defence.

8. The fixing of and providing for the Salaries and Allowances of Civil and other Officers of the Government of Canada.

---

(44) Class 1 was added by the *British North America (No. 2) Act, 1949,* 13 Geo. VI, c. 8 (U.K.). That Act and class 1 were repealed by the *Constitution Act, 1982.* The matters referred to in class 1 are provided for in subsection 4(2) and Part V of the *Constitution Act, 1982.* As enacted, class 1 read as follows:

> 1. The amendment from time to time of the Constitution of Canada, except as regards matters coming within the classes of subjects by this Act assigned exclusively to the Legislatures of the provinces, or as regards rights or privileges by this or any other Constitutional Act granted or secured to the Legislature or the Government of a province, or to any class of persons with respect to schools or as regards the use of the English or the French language or as regards the requirements that there shall be a session of the Parliament of Canada at least once each year, and that no House of Commons shall continue for more than five years from the day of the return of the Writs for choosing the House: provided, however, that a House of Commons may in time of real or apprehended war, invasion or insurrection be continued by the Parliament of Canada if such continuation is not opposed by the votes of more than one-third of the members of such House.

(45) Re-numbered by the *British North America (No. 2) Act, 1949.*

(46) Added by the *Constitution Act, 1940,* 3-4 Geo. VI, c. 36 (U.K.).

9. Beacons, Buoys, Lighthouses, and Sable Island.
10. Navigation and Shipping.
11. Quarantine and the Establishment and Maintenance of Marine Hospitals.
12. Sea Coast and Inland Fisheries.
13. Ferries between a Province and any British or Foreign Country or between Two Provinces.
14. Currency and Coinage.
15. Banking, Incorporation of Banks, and the Issue of Paper Money.
16. Savings Banks.
17. Weights and Measures.
18. Bills of Exchange and Promissory Notes.
19. Interest.
20. Legal Tender.
21. Bankruptcy and Insolvency.
22. Patents of Invention and Discovery.
23. Copyrights.
24. Indians, and Lands reserved for the Indians.
25. Naturalization and Aliens.
26. Marriage and Divorce.
27. The Criminal Law, except the Constitution of Courts of Criminal Jurisdiction, but including the Procedure in Criminal Matters.
28. The Establishment, Maintenance, and Management of Penitentiaries.
29. Such Classes of Subjects as are expressly excepted in the Enumeration of the Classes of Subjects by this Act assigned exclusively to the Legislatures of the Provinces.

And any Matter coming within any of the Classes of Subjects enumerated in this Section shall not be deemed to come within the Class of Matters of a local or private Nature comprised in the Enumeration of the Classes of Subjects by this Act assigned exclusively to the Legislatures of the Provinces. (47)

---

(47) Legislative authority has been conferred on Parliament by other Acts as follows:

1. The *Constitution Act, 1871*, 34-35 Vict., c. 28 (U.K.).

Exclusive Powers of Provincial Legislatures.

92. In each Province the Legislature may exclusively make Laws in relation to Matters coming within the Classes of Subject next hereinafter enumerated; that is to say,—

Subjects of exclusive Provincial Legislation.

1. Repealed. (48)

---

2. The Parliament of Canada, may from time to time establish new Provinces in any territories forming for the time being part of the Dominion of Canada, but not included in any Province thereof, and may, at the time of such establishment, make provision for the constitution and administration of any such Province, and for the passing of laws for the peace, order, and good government of such Province, and for its representation in the said Parliament.

3. The Parliament of Canada may from time to time, with the consent of the Legislature of any province of the said Dominion, increase, diminish, or otherwise alter the limits of such Province, upon such terms and conditions as may be agreed to by the said Legislature, and may, with the like consent, make provision respecting the effect and operation of any such increase or diminution or alteration of territory in relation to any Province affected thereby.

4. The Parliament of Canada may from time to time make provision for the administration, peace, order, and good government of any territory not for the time being included in any Province.

5. The following Acts passed by the said Parliament of Canada, and intituled respectively, —"An Act for the temporary government of Rupert's Land and the North Western Territory when united with Canada"; and "An Act to amend and continue the Act thirty-two and thirty-three Victoria, chapter three, and to establish and provide for the government of "the Province of Manitoba", shall be and be deemed to have been valid and effectual for all purposes whatsoever from the date at which they respectively received the assent, in the Queen's name, of the Governor General of the said Dominion of Canada.

6. Except as provided by the third section of this Act, it shall not be competent for the Parliament of Canada to alter the provisions of-the last-mentioned Act of the said Parliament in so far as it relates to the Province of Manitoba, or of any other Act hereafter establishing new Provinces in the said Dominion, subject always to the right of the Legislature of the Province of Manitoba to alter from time to time the provisions of any law respecting the qualification of electors and members of the Legislative Assembly, and to make laws respecting elections in the said Province.

The *Rupert's Land Act 1868*, 31-32 Vict., c. 105 (U.K.) (repealed by the *Statute Law Revision Act, 1893*, 56-57 Vict., c. 14 (U.K.)) had previously conferred similar authority in relation to Rupert's Land and the North Western Territory upon admission of those areas.

2. The *Constitution Act, 1886*, 49-50 Vict., c. 35, (U.K.).

1. The Parliament of Canada may from time to time make provision for the representation in the Senate and House of Commons of Canada, or in either of them, of any territories which for the time being form part of the Dominion of Canada, but are not included in any province thereof.

3. The *Statute of Westminster, 1931*, 22 Geo. V, c. 4 (U.K.).

3. It is hereby declared and enacted that the Parliament of a Dominion has full power to make laws having extra-territorial operation.

4. Section 44 of the *Constitution Act, 1982*, authorizes Parliament to amend the Constitution of Canada in relation to the executive government of Canada or the Senate and House of Commons. Sections 38, 41, 42, and 43 of that Act authorize the Senate and House of Commons to give their approval to certain other constitutional amendments by resolution.

(48) Class 1 was repealed by the *Constitution Act, 1982*. As enacted, it read as follows:

1. The Amendment from Time to Time, notwithstanding anything in this Act, of the Constitution of the province, except as regards the Office of Lieutenant Governor.

2. Direct Taxation within the Province in order to the raising of a Revenue for Provincial Purposes.

3. The borrowing of Money on the sole Credit of the Province.

4. The Establishment and Tenure of Provincial Offices and the Appointment and Payment of Provincial Officers.

5. The Management and Sale of the Public Lands belonging to the Province and of the Timber and Wood thereon.

6. The Establishment, Maintenance, and Management of Public and Reformatory Prisons in and for the Province.

7. The Establishment, Maintenance, and Management of Hospitals, Asylums, Charities, and Eleemosynary Institutions in and for the Province, other than Marine Hospitals.

8. Municipal Institutions in the Province.

9. Shop, Saloon, Tavern, Auctioneer, and other Licences in order to the raising of a Revenue for Provincial, Local, or Municipal Purposes.

10. Local Works and Undertakings other than such as are of the following Classes:—

(*a*) Lines of Steam or other Ships, Railways, Canals, Telegraphs, and other Works and Undertakings connecting the Province with any other or others of the Provinces, or extending beyond the Limits of the Province;

(*b*) Lines of Steam Ships between the Province and any British or Foreign Country;

(*c*) Such Works as, although wholly situate within the Province, are before or after their Execution declared by the Parliament of Canada to be for the general Advantage of Canada or for the Advantage of Two or more of the Provinces.

11. The Incorporation of Companies with Provincial Objects.

12. The Solemnization of Marriage in the Province.

13. Property and Civil Rights in the Province.

Section 45 of the *Constitution Act, 1982*, now authorizes legislatures to make laws amending the constitution of the province. Sections 38, 41, 42, and 43 of that Act authorize legislative assemblies to give their approval by resolution to certain other amendments to the Constitution of Canada.

14. The Administration of Justice in the Province, including the Constitution, Maintenance, and Organization of Provincial Courts, both of Civil and of Criminal Jurisdiction, and including Procedure in Civil Matters in those Courts.

15. The Imposition of Punishment by Fine, Penalty, or Imprisonment for enforcing any Law of the Province made in relation to any Matter coming within any of the Classes of Subjects enumerated in this Section.

16. Generally all Matters of a merely local or private Nature in the Province.

Non-Renewable Natural Resources, Forestry Resources and Electrical Energy

92A. (1) In each province, the legislature may exclusively make laws in relation to

> (*a*) exploration for non-renewable natural resources in the province;
>
> (*b*) development, conservation and management of non-renewable natural resources and forestry resources in the province, including laws in relation to the rate of primary production therefrom; and
>
> (*c*) development, conservation and management of sites and facilities in the province for the generation and production of electrical energy.

Laws respecting non-renewable natural resources, forestry resources and electrical energy

(2) In each province, the legislature may make laws in relation to the export from the province to another part of Canada of the primary production from non-renewable natural resources and forestry resources in the province and the production from facilities in the province for the generation of electrical energy, but such laws may not authorize or provide for discrimination in prices or in supplies exported to another part of Canada.

Export from provinces of resources

(3) Nothing in subsection (2) derogates from the authority of Parliament to enact laws in relation to the matters referred to in that subsection and, where such a law of Parliament and a law of a province conflict, the law of Parliament prevails to the extent of the conflict.

Authority of Parliament

(4) In each province, the legislature may make laws in relation to the raising of money by any mode or system of taxation in respect of

Taxation of resources

(*a*) non-renewable natural resources and forestry resources in the province and the primary production therefrom, and

(*b*) sites and facilities in the province for the generation of electrical energy and the production therefrom,

whether or not such production is exported in whole or in part from the province, but such laws may not authorize or provide for taxation that differentiates between production exported to another part of Canada and production not exported from the province.

"Primary
production"

(5) The expression "primary production" has the meaning assigned by the Sixth Schedule.

Existing powers
or rights

(6) Nothing in subsections (1) to (5) derogates from any powers or rights that a legislature or government of a province had immediately before the coming into force of this section. (49)

Education.

Legislation
respecting
Education.

93. In and for each Province the Legislature may exclusively make Laws in relation to Education, subject and according to the following Provisions:—

(1) Nothing in any such Law shall prejudicially affect any Right or Privilege with respect to Denominational Schools which any Class of Persons have by Law in the Province at the Union:

(2) All the Powers, Privileges, and Duties at the Union by Law conferred and imposed in Upper Canada on the Separate Schools and School Trustees of the Queen's Roman Catholic Subjects shall be and the same are hereby extended to the Dissentient Schools of the Queen's Protestant and Roman Catholic Subjects in Quebec:

(3) Where in any Province a System of Separate or Dissentient Schools exists by Law at the Union or is thereafter established by the Legislature of the Province, an Appeal shall lie to the Governor General in Council from any Act or Decision of any Provincial

---

(49) Added by the *Constitution Act, 1982.*

Authority affecting any Right or Privilege of the Protestant or Roman Catholic Minority of the Queen's Subjects in relation to Education:

(4) In case any such Provincial Law as from Time to Time seems to the Governor General in Council requisite for the due Execution of the Provisions of this Section is not made, or in case any Decision of the Governor General in Council on any Appeal under this Section is not duly executed by the proper Provincial Authority in that Behalf, then and in every such Case, and as far only as the Circumstances of each Case require, the Parliament of Canada may make remedial Laws for the due Execution of the Provisions of this Section and of any Decision of the Governor General in Council under this Section. (50)

---

(50) Altered for Manitoba by section 22 of the *Manitoba Act, 1870*, 33 Vict., c. 3 (Canada), (confirmed by the *Constitution Act, 1871*), which reads as follows:

> **22.** In and for the Próvince, the said Legislature may exclusively make Laws in relation to Education, subject and according to the following provisions:—

> (1) Nothing in any such Law shall prejudicially affect any right or privilege with respect to Denominational Schools which any class of persons have by Law or practice in the Province at the Union:

> (2) An appeal shall lie to the Governor General in Council from any Act or decision of the Legislature of the Province, or of any Provincial Authority, affecting any right or privilege, of the Protestant or Roman Catholic minority of the Queen's subjects in relation to Education:

> (3) In case any such Provincial Law, as from time to time seems to the Governor General in Council requisite for the due execution of the provisions of this section, is not made, or in case any decision of the Governor General in Council on any appeal under this section is not duly executed by the proper Provincial Authority in that behalf, then, and in every such case, and as far only as the circumstances of each case require, the Parliament of Canada may make remedial Laws for the due execution of the provisions of this section, and of any decision of the Governor General in Council under this section.

Altered for Alberta by section 17 of the *Alberta Act*, 4-5 Edw. VII, c. 3, 1905 (Canada), which reads as follows:

> **17.** Section 93 of the *Constitution Act, 1867*, shall apply to the said province, with the substitution for paragraph (1) of the said section 93 of the following paragraph:—

> (1) Nothing in any such law shall prejudicially affect any right or privilege with respect to separate schools which any class of persons have at the date of the passing of this Act, under the terms of chapters 29 and 30 of the Ordinances of the Northwest Territories, passed in the year 1901, or with respect to religious instruction in any public or separate school as provided for in the said ordinances.

> **2.** In the appropriation by the Legislature or distribution by the Government of the province of any moneys for the support of schools organized and carried on in accordance with the said chapter 29 or any Act passed in amendment thereof, or in substitution therefor, there shall be no discrimination against schools of any class described in the said chapter 29.

Uniformity of Laws in Ontario, Nova Scotia and New Brunswick.

Legislation for
Uniformity of
Laws in Three
Provinces.

94. Notwithstanding anything in this Act, the Parliament of Canada may make Provision for the Uniformity of all or any of the Laws relative to Property and Civil Rights in Ontario, Nova Scotia, and New Brunswick, and of the Proce-

---

> **3.** Where the expression "by law" is employed in paragraph 3 of the said section 93, it shall be held to mean the law as set out in the said chapters 29 and 30, and where the expression "at the Union" is employed, in the said paragraph 3, it shall be held to mean the date at which this Act comes into force.

Altered for Saskatchewan by section 17 of the *Saskatchewan Act*, 4-5 Edw. VII, c. 42, 1905 (Canada), which reads as follows:

> **17.** Section 93 of the *Constitution Act, 1867*, shall apply to the said province, with the substitution for paragraph (1) of the said section 93, of the following paragraph:—
>
> (1) Nothing in any such law shall prejudicially affect any right or privilege with respect to separate schools which any class of persons have at the date of the passing of this Act, under the terms of chapters 29 and 30 of the Ordinances of the Northwest Territories, passed in the year 1901, or with respect to religious instruction in any public or separate school as provided for in the said ordinances.
>
> **2.** In the appropriation by the Legislature or distribution by the Government of the province of any moneys for the support of schools organized and carried on in accordance with the said chapter 29, or any Act passed in amendment thereof or in substitution therefor, there shall be no discrimination against schools of any class described in the said chapter 29.
>
> **3.** Where the expression "by law" is employed in paragraph (3) of the said section 93, it shall be held to mean the law as set out in the said chapters 29 and 30; and where the expression "at the Union" is employed in the said paragraph (3), it shall be held to mean the date at which this Act comes into force.

Altered by Term 17 of the Terms of Union of Newfoundland with Canada (confirmed by the *Newfoundland Act*, 12-13 Geo. VI, c. 22 (UK.)), which reads as follows:

> **17.** In lieu of section ninety-three of the *Constitution Act, 1867*, the following term shall apply in respect of the Province of Newfoundland:
>
> In and for the Province of Newfoundland the Legislature shall have exclusive authority to make laws in relation to education, but the Legislature will not have authority to make laws prejudicially affecting any right or privilege with respect to denominational schools, common (amalgamated) schools, or denominational colleges, that any class or classes of persons have by law in Newfoundland at the date of Union, and out of public funds of the Province of Newfoundland, provided for education,
>
> (a) all such schools shall receive their share of such funds in accordance with scales determined on a non-discriminatory basis from time to time by the Legislature for all schools then being conducted under authority of the Legislature; and
>
> (b) all such colleges shall receive their share of any grant from time to time voted for all colleges then being conducted under authority of the Legislature, such grant being distributed on a non-discriminatory basis.

See also sections 23, 29, and 59 of the *Constitution Act, 1982*. Section 23 provides for new minority language educational rights and section 59 permits a delay in respect of the coming into force in Quebec of one aspect of those rights. Section 29 provides that nothing in the *Canadian Charter of Rights and Freedoms* abrogates or derogates from any rights or privileges guaranteed by or under the Constitution of Canada in respect of denominational, separate or dissentient schools.

dure of all or any of the Courts in Those Three Provinces, and from and after the passing of any Act in that Behalf the Power of the Parliament of Canada to make Laws in relation to any Matter comprised in any such Act shall, notwithstanding anything in this Act, be unrestricted; but any Act of the Parliament of Canada making Provision for such Uniformity shall not have effect in any Province unless and until it is adopted and enacted as Law by the Legislature thereof.

Old Age Pensions.

94A. The Parliament of Canada may make laws in relation to old age pensions and supplementary benefits, including survivors, and disability benefits irrespective of age, but no such law shall affect the operation of any law present or future of a provincial legislature in relation to any such matter. (51)

Legislation respecting old age pensions and supplementary benefits.

Agriculture and Immigration.

95. In each Province the Legislature may make Laws in relation to Agriculture in the Province, and to Immigration into the Province; and it is hereby declared that the Parliament of Canada may from Time to Time make Laws in relation to Agriculture in all or any of the Provinces, and to Immigration into all or any of the Provinces; and any Law of the Legislature of a Province relative to Agriculture or to Immigration shall have effect in and for the Province as long and as far only as it is not repugnant to any Act of the Parliament of Canada.

Concurrent Powers of Legislation respecting Agriculture, etc.

VII.—JUDICATURE.

96. The Governor General shall appoint the Judges of the Superior, District, and County Courts in each Province, except those of the Courts of Probate in Nova Scotia and New Brunswick.

Appointment of Judges.

---

(51) Added by the *Constitution Act, 1964*, 12-13 Eliz. II, c. 73 (U.K.). As originally enacted by the *British North America Act, 1951*, 14-15 Geo. VI, c. 32 (U.K.), which was repealed by the *Constitution Act, 1982*, section 94A read as follows:

> **94A.** It is hereby declared that the Parliament of Canada may from time to time make laws in relation to old age pensions in Canada, but no law made by the Parliament of Canada in relation to old age pensions shall affect the operation of any law present or future of a Provincial Legislature in relation to old age pensions.

Selection of
Judges in
Ontario, etc.

97. Until the laws relative to Property and Civil Rights in Ontario, Nova Scotia, and New Brunswick, and the Procedure of the Courts in those Provinces, are made uniform, the Judges of the Courts of those Provinces appointed by the Governor General shall be selected from the respective Bars of those Provinces.

Selection of
Judges in
Quebec.

98. The Judges of the Courts of Quebec shall be selected from the Bar of that Province.

Tenure of office
of Judges.

99. (1) Subject to subsection two of this section, the Judges of the Superior Courts shall hold office during good behaviour, but shall be removable by the Governor General on Address of the Senate and House of Commons.

Termination at
age 75.

(2) A Judge of a Superior Court, whether appointed before or after the coming into force of this section, shall cease to hold office upon attaining the age of seventy-five years, or upon the coming into force of this section if at that time he has already attained that age. (52)

Salaries etc., of
Judges.

100. The Salaries, Allowances, and Pensions of the Judges of the Superior, District, and County Courts (except the Courts of Probate in Nova Scotia and New Brunswick), and of the Admiralty Courts in Cases where the Judges thereof are for the Time being paid by Salary, shall be fixed and provided by the Parliament of Canada. (53)

General Court
of Appeal, etc.

101. The Parliament of Canada may, notwithstanding anything in this Act, from Time to Time provide for the Constitution, Maintenance, and Organization of a General Court of Appeal for Canada, and for the Establishment of any additional Courts for the better Administration of the Laws of Canada. (54)

---

(52) Repealed and re-enacted by the *Constitution Act, 1960*, 9 Eliz. II, c. 2 (U.K.), which came into force on the 1st day of March, 1961. The original section read as follows:

> **99.** The Judges of the Superior Courts shall hold Office during good Behaviour, but shall be removable by the Governor General on Address of the Senate and House of Commons.

(53) Now provided for in the *Judges Act*, R.S.C. 1970, c. J-1.

(54) See the *Supreme Court Act*, R.S.C. 1970, c. S-19, and the *Federal Court Act*, R.S.C. 1970, (2nd Supp.) c. 10.

VIII.—REVENUES; DEBTS; ASSETS; TAXATION.

102. All Duties and Revenues over which the respective Legislatures of Canada, Nova Scotia, and New Brunswick before and at the Union had and have Power of Appropriation, except such Portions thereof as are by this Act reserved to the respective Legislatures of the Provinces, or are raised by them in accordance with the special Powers conferred on them by this Act, shall form One Consolidated Revenue Fund, to be appropriated for the Public Service of Canada in the Manner and subject to the Charges of this Act provided.

<small>Creation of Consolidated Revenue Fund.</small>

103. The Consolidated Revenue Fund of Canada shall be permanently charged with the Costs, Charges, and Expenses incident to the Collection, Management, and Receipt thereof, and the same shall form the First Charge thereon, subject to be reviewed and audited in such Manner as shall be ordered by the Governor General in Council until the Parliament otherwise provides.

<small>Expenses of Collection, etc.</small>

104. The annual Interest of the Public Debts of the several Provinces of Canada, Nova Scotia, and New Brunswick at the Union shall form the Second Charge on the Consolidated Revenue Fund of Canada.

<small>Interest of Provincial Public Debts.</small>

105. Unless altered by the Parliament of Canada, the Salary of the Governor General shall be Ten thousand Pounds Sterling Money of the United Kingdom of Great Britain and Ireland, payable out of the Consolidated Revenue Fund of Canada, and the same shall form the Third Charge thereon. (55)

<small>Salary of Governor General.</small>

106. Subject to the several Payments by this Act charged on the Consolidated Revenue Fund of Canada, the same shall be appropriated by the Parliament of Canada for the Public Service.

<small>Appropriation from Time to Time.</small>

107. All Stocks, Cash, Banker's Balances, and Securities for Money belonging to each Province at the Time of the Union, except as in this Act mentioned, shall be the Property of Canada, and shall be taken in Reduction of the Amount of the respective Debts of the Provinces at the Union.

<small>Transfer of Stocks, etc.</small>

---

(55) Now covered by the *Governor General's Act*, R.S.C. 1970, c. G-14.

Tansfer of
Property in
Schedule.

108. The Public Works and Property of each Province, enumerated in the Third Schedule to this Act, shall be the Property of Canada.

Property in
Lands, Mines,
etc.

109. All Lands, Mines, Minerals, and Royalties belonging to the several Provinces of Canada, Nova Scotia, and New Brunswick at the Union, and all Sums then due or payable for such Lands, Mines, Minerals, or Royalties, shall belong to the several Provinces of Ontario, Quebec, Nova Scotia, and New Brunswick in which the same are situate or arise, subject to any Trusts existing in respect thereof, and to any Interest other than that of the Province in the same. (56)

Assets
connected with
Provincial
Debts.

110. All Assets connected with such Portions of the Public Debt of each Province as are assumed by that Province shall belong to that Province.

Canada to be
liable for
Provincial
Debts.

111. Canada shall be liable for the Debts and Liabilities of each Province existing at the Union.

Debts of
Ontario and
Quebec.

112. Ontario and Quebec conjointly shall be liable to Canada for the Amount (if any) by which the Debt of the Province of Canada exceeds at the Union Sixty-two million five hundred thousand Dollars, and shall be charged with Interest at the Rate of Five Per Centum per Annum thereon.

Assets of
Ontario and
Quebec.

113. The Assets enumerated in the Fourth Schedule to this Act belonging at the Union to the Province of Canada shall be the Property of Ontario and Quebec conjointly.

Debt of Nova
Scotia.

114. Nova Scotia shall be liable to Canada for the Amount (if any) by which its Public Debt exceeds at the Union Eight million Dollars, and shall be charged with Interest at the Rate of Five per Centum per Annum thereon. (57)

Debt of New
Brunswick.

115. New Brunswick shall be liable to Canada for the Amount (if any) by which its Public Debt exceeds at the

---

(56) The three prairie provinces were placed in the same position as the original provinces by the *Constitution Act, 1930,* 21 Geo. V, c. 26 (U.K.).

(57) The obligations imposed by this section, sections 115 and 116, and similar obligations under the instruments creating or admitting other provinces, have been carried into legislation of the Parliament of Canada and are now to be found in the *Provincial Subsidies Act,* R.S.C. 1970, c. P-26.

Union Seven million Dollars, and shall be charged with Interest at the Rate of Five per Centum per Annum thereon.

116. In case the Public Debts of Nova Scotia and New Brunswick do not at the Union amount to Eight million and Seven million Dollars respectively, they shall respectively receive by half-yearly Payments in advance from the Government of Canada Interest at Five per Centum per Annum on the Difference between the actual Amounts of their respective Debts and such stipulated Amounts.

Payment of Interest to Nova Scotia and New Brunswick.

117. The several Provinces shall retain all their respective Public Property not otherwise disposed of in this Act, subject to the Right of Canada to assume any Lands or Public Property required for Fortifications or for the Defence of the Country.

Provincial Public Property.

118. Repealed. (58)

---

(58) Repealed by the *Statute Law Revision Act, 1950,* 14 Geo. VI, c. 6 (U.K.). As originally enacted the section read as follows:

> **118.** The following Sums shall be paid yearly by Canada to the several Provinces for the Support of their Governments and Legislatures:
>
> Dollars
>
> | | |
> |---|---|
> | Ontario | Eighty thousand. |
> | Quebec | Seventy thousand. |
> | Nova Scotia | Sixty thousand. |
> | New Brunswick | Fifty thousand. |
>
> Two hundred and sixty thousand;
>
> and an annual Grant in aid of each Province shall be made, equal to Eighty Cents per Head of the Population as ascertained by the Census of One thousand eight hundred and sixty-one, and in the Case of Nova Scotia and New Brunswick, by each subsequent Decennial Census until the Population of each of those two Provinces amounts to Four hundred thousand Souls, at which Rate such Grant shall thereafter remain. Such Grants shall be in full Settlement of all future Demands on Canada, and shall be paid half-yearly in advance to each Province; but the Government of Canada shall deduct from such Grants, as against any Province, all Sums chargeable as Interest on the Public Debt of that Province in excess of the several Amounts stipulated in this Act.

The section was made obsolete by the *Constitution Act, 1907,* 7 Edw. VII, c. 11 (U.K.) which provided:

> **1.** (1) The following grants shall be made yearly by Canada to every province, which at the commencement of this Act is a province of the Dominion, for its local purposes and the support of its Government and Legislature: —
>
> (a) A fixed grant —
>
> where the population of the province is under one hundred and fifty thousand, of one hundred thousand dollars;
>
> where the population of the province is one hundred and fifty thousand, but does not exceed two hundred thousand, of one hundred and fifty thousand dollars;

Further Grant
to New
Brunswick.

119. New Brunswick shall receive by half-yearly Payments in advance from Canada for the period of Ten years from the Union an additional Allowance of Sixty-three thou-

---

where the population of the province is two hundred thousand, but does not exceed four hundred thousand, of one hundred and eighty thousand dollars;

where the population of the province is four hundred thousand, but does not exceed eight hundred thousand, of one hundred and ninety thousand dollars;

where the population of the province is eight hundred thousand, but does not exceed one million five hundred thousand, of two hundred and twenty thousand dollars;

where the population of the province exceeds one million five hundred thousand, of two hundred and forty thousand dollars; and

(*b*) Subject to the special provisions of this Act as to the provinces of British Columbia and Prince Edward Island, a grant at the rate of eighty cents per head of the population of the province up to the number of two million five hundred thousand, and at the rate of sixty cents per head of so much of the population as exceeds that number.

(2) An additional grant of one hundred thousand dollars shall be made yearly to the province of British Columbia for a period of ten years from the commencement of this Act.

(3) The population of a province shall be ascertained from time to time in the case of the provinces of Manitoba, Saskatchewan, and Alberta respectively by the last quinquennial census or statutory estimate of population made under the Acts establishing those provinces or any other Act of the Parliament of Canada making provision for the purpose, and in the case of any other province by the last decennial census for the time being.

(4) The grants payable under this Act shall be paid half-yearly in advance to each province.

(5) The grants payable under this Act shall be substituted for the grants or subsidies (in this Act referred to as existing grants) payable for the like purposes at the commencement of this Act to the several provinces of the Dominion under the provisions of section one hundred and eighteen of the *Constitution Act, 1867*, or of any Order in Council establishing a province, or of any Act of the Parliament of Canada containing directions for the payment of any such grant or subsidy, and those provisions shall cease to have effect.

(6) The Government of Canada shall have the same power of deducting sums charged against a province on account of the interest on public debt in the case of the grant payable under this Act to the province as they have in the case of the existing grant.

(7) Nothing in this Act shall affect the obligation of the Government of Canada to pay to any province any grant which is payable to that province, other than the existing grant for which the grant under this Act is substituted.

(8) In the case of the provinces of British Columbia and Prince Edward Island, the amount paid on account of the grant payable per head of the population to the provinces under this Act shall not at any time be less than the amount of the corresponding grant payable at the commencement of this Act, and if it is found on any decennial census that the population of the province has decreased since the last decennial census, the amount paid on account of the grant shall not be decreased below the amount then payable, notwithstanding the decrease of the population.

See the *Provincial Subsidies Act*, R.S.C. 1970, c. P-26, *The Maritime Provinces Additional Subsidies Act*, 1942-43, c. 14, and the Terms of Union of Newfoundland with Canada, appended to the *Newfoundland Act*, and also to *An Act to approve the Terms of Union of Newfoundland with Canada*, chapter 1 of the Statutes of Canada, 1949.

See also Part III of the *Constitution Act, 1982*, which sets out commitments by Parliament and the provincial legislatures respecting equal opportunities, economic development and the provision of essential public services and a commitment by Parliament and the government of Canada to the principle of making equalization payments.

sand Dollars per Annum; but as long as the Public Debt of that Province remains under Seven million Dollars, a Deduction equal to the Interest at Five per Centum per Annum on such Deficiency shall be made from that Allowance of Sixty-three thousand Dollars. (59)

120. All Payments to be made under this Act, or in discharge of Liabilities created under any Act of the Provinces of Canada, Nova Scotia, and New Brunswick respectively, and assumed by Canada, shall, until the Parliament of Canada otherwise directs, be made in such Form and Manner as may from Time to Time be ordered by the Governor General in Council. *Form of Payments.*

121. All Articles of the Growth, Produce, or Manufacture of any one of the Provinces shall, from and after the Union, be admitted free into each of the other Provinces. *Canadian Manufactures, etc.*

122. The Customs and Excise Laws of each Province shall, subject to the Provisions of this Act, continue in force until altered by the Parliament of Canada. (60) *Continuance of Customs and Excise Laws.*

123. Where Customs Duties are, at the Union, leviable on any Goods, Wares, or Merchandises in any Two Provinces, those Goods, Wares, and Merchandises may, from and after the Union, be imported from one of those Provinces into the other of them on Proof of Payment of the Customs Duty leviable thereon in the Province of Exportation, and on Payment of such further Amount (if any) of Customs Duty as is leviable thereon in the Province of Importation. (61) *Exportation and Importation as between Two Provinces.*

124. Nothing in this Act shall affect the Right of New Brunswick to levy the Lumber Dues provided in Chapter Fifteen of Title Three of the Revised Statutes of New Brunswick, or in any Act amending that Act before or after the Union, and not increasing the Amount of such Dues; but the Lumber of any of the Provinces other than New Brunswick shall not be subject to such Dues. (62) *Lumber Dues in New Brunswick.*

---

(59) Spent.

(60) Spent. Now covered by the *Customs Act*, R.S.C. 1970, c. C-40, the *Customs Tariff*, R.S.C. 1970, c. C-41, the *Excise Act*, R.S.C. 1970, c. E-12 and the *Excise Tax Act*, R.S.C. 1970, c. E-13.

(61) Spent.

(62) These dues were repealed in 1873 by 36 Vict., c. 16 (N.B.). And see *An Act respecting the Export Duties imposed on Lumber*, etc. (1873) 36 Vict., c. 41 (Canada), and section 2 of the *Provincial Subsidies Act*, R.S.C. 1970, c. P-26.

Exemption of
Public Lands,
etc.

125. No Lands or Property belonging to Canada or any Province shall be liable to Taxation.

Provincial
Consolidated
Revenue Fund.

126. Such Portions of the Duties and Revenues over which the respective Legislatures of Canada, Nova Scotia, and New Brunswick had before the Union Power of Appropriation as are by this Act reserved to the respective Governments or Legislatures of the Provinces, and all Duties and Revenues raised by them in accordance with the special Powers conferred upon them by this Act, shall in each Province form One Consolidated Revenue Fund to be appropriated for the Public Service of the Province.

IX. — MISCELLANEOUS PROVISIONS.

General.

127. Repealed. (63)

Oath of
Allegiance, etc.

128. Every Member of the Senate or House of Commons of Canada shall before taking his Seat therein take and subscribe before the ´ Governor General or some Person authorized by him, and every Member of a Legislative Council or Legislative Assembly of any Province shall before taking his Seat therein take and subscribe before the Lieutenant Governor of the Province or some Person authorized by him, the Oath of Allegiance contained in the Fifth Schedule to this Act; and every Member of the Senate of Canada and every Member of the Legislative Council of Quebec shall also, before taking his Seat therein, take and subscribe before the Governor General, or some Person authorized by him, the Declaration of Qualification contained in the same Schedule.

Continuance of
existing Laws,
Courts,
Officers, etc.

129. Except as otherwise provided by this Act, all Laws in force in Canada, Nova Scotia, or New Brunswick at the Union, and all Courts of Civil and Criminal Jurisdiction, and

---

(63) Repealed by the *Statute Law Revision Act, 1893*, 56-57 Vict., c. 14 (U.K.). The section read as follows:

> **127.** If any Person being at the passing of this Act a Member of the Legislative Council of Canada, Nova Scotia, or New Brunswick to whom a Place in the Senate is offered, does not within Thirty Days thereafter, by Writing under his Hand addressed to the Governor General of the Province of Canada or to the Lieutenant Governor of Nova Scotia or New Brunswick (as the Case may be), accept the same, he shall be deemed to have declined the same; and any Person who, being at the passing of this Act a Member of the Legislative Council of Nova Scotia or New Brunswick, accepts a Place in the Senate, shall thereby vacate his Seat in such Legislative Council.

all legal Commissions, Powers, and Authorities, and all Officers, Judicial, Administrative, and Ministerial, existing therein at the Union, shall continue in Ontario, Quebec, Nova Scotia, and New Brunswick respectively, as if the Union had not been made; subject nevertheless (except with respect to such as are enacted by or exist under Acts of the Parliament of Great Britain or of the Parliament of the United Kingdom of Great Britain and Ireland), to be repealed, abolished, or altered by the Parliament of Canada, or by the Legislature of the respective Province, according to the Authority of the Parliament or of that Legislature under this Act. (64)

130. Until the Parliament of Canada otherwise provides, all Officers of the several Provinces having Duties to discharge in relation to Matters other than those coming within the Classes of Subjects by this Act assigned exclusively to the Legislatures of the Provinces shall be Officers of Canada, and shall continue to discharge the Duties of their respective Offices under the same Liabilities, Responsibilities, and Penalties as if the Union had not been made. (65)

Transfer of Officers to Canada.

131. Until the Parliament of Canada otherwise provides, the Governor General in Council may from Time to Time appoint such Officers as the Governor General in Council deems necessary or proper for the effectual Execution of this Act.

Appointment of new Officers.

132. The Parliament and Government of Canada shall have all Powers necessary or proper for performing the Obligations of Canada or of any Province thereof, as Part of the British Empire, towards Foreign Countries, arising under Treaties between the Empire and such Foreign Countries.

Treaty Obligations.

133. Either the English or the French Language may be used by any Person in the Debates of the Houses of the Parliament of Canada and of the Houses of the Legislature of Quebec; and both those Languages shall be used in the respective Records and Journals of those Houses; and either of those Languages may be used by any Person or in any

Use of English and French Languages.

---

(64) The restriction against altering or repealing laws enacted by or existing under statutes of the United Kingdom was removed by the *Statute of Westminster, 1931*, 22 Geo. V, c. 4 (U.K.) except in respect of certain constitutional documents. Comprehensive procedures for amending enactments forming part of the Constitution of Canada were provided by Part V of the *Constitution Act, 1982*, (U.K.) 1982, c. 11.

(65) Spent.

Pleading or Process in or issuing from any Court of Canada established under this Act, and in or from all or any of the Courts of Quebec.

The Acts of the Parliament of Canada and of the Legislature of Quebec shall be printed and published in both those Languages. (66)

Ontario and Quebec.

Appointment of Executive Officers for Ontario and Quebec.

134. Until the Legislature of Ontario or of Quebec otherwise provides, the Lieutenant Governors of Ontario and Quebec may each appoint under the Great Seal of the Province the following Officers, to hold Office during Pleasure, that is to say, — the Attorney General, the Secretary and Registrar of the Province, the Treasurer of the Province, the Commissioner of Crown Lands, and the Commissioner of Agriculture and Public Works, and in the Case of Quebec the Solicitor General, and may, by Order of the Lieutenant Governor in Council, from Time to Time prescribe the Duties of those Officers, and of the several Departments over which they shall preside or to which they shall belong, and of the Officers and Clerks thereof, and may also appoint other and additional Officers to hold Office during Pleasure, and may from Time to Time prescribe the Duties of those Officers, and of the several Departments over which they shall preside or to which they shall belong, and of the Officers and Clerks thereof. (67)

---

(66) A similar provision was enacted for Manitoba by Section 23 of the *Manitoba Act, 1870*, 33 Vict., c. 3 (Canada), (confirmed by the *Constitution Act, 1871*. Section 23 read as follows:

> **23.** Either the English or the French language may be used by any person in the debates of the Houses of the Legislature, and both those languages shall be used in the respective Records and Journals of those Houses; and either of those languages may be used by any person, or in any Pleading or Process, in or issuing from any Court of Canada established under the British North America Act, 1867, or in or from all or any of the Courts of the Province. The Acts of the Legislature shall be printed and published in both those languages.

Sections 17 to 19 of the *Constitution Act, 1982*, restate the language rights set out in section 133 in respect of Parliament and the courts established under the *Constitution Act, 1867*, and also guarantees those rights in respect of the legislature of New Brunswick and the courts of that province.

Section 16 and sections 20, 21 and 23 of the *Constitution Act, 1982*, recognize additional language rights in respect of the English and French languages. Section 22 preserves language rights and privileges of languages other than English and French.

(67) Spent. Now covered in Ontario by the *Executive Council Act*, R.S.O. 1980, c. 147 and in Quebec by the *Executive Power Act*, R.S.Q. 1977, c. E-18.

135. Until the Legislature of Ontario or Quebec other- Powers, Duties, etc. of Executive Officers.
wise provides, all Rights, Powers, Duties, Functions, Respon-
sibilities, or Authorities at the passing of this Act vested in or
imposed on the Attorney General, Solicitor General, Secretary and Registrar of the Province of Canada, Minister of
Finance, Commissioner of Crown Lands, Commissioner of
Public Works, and Minister of Agriculture and Receiver
General, by any Law, Statute, or Ordinance of Upper
Canada, Lower Canada, or Canada, and not repugnant to
this Act, shall be vested in or imposed on any Officer to be
appointed by the Lieutenant Governor for the discharge of
the same or any of them; and the Commissioner of Agriculture and Public Works shall perform the Duties and Functions of the Office of Minister of Agriculture at the passing
of this Act imposed by the Law of the Province of Canada, as
well as those of the Commissioner of Public Works. (68)

136. Until altered by the Lieutenant Governor in Coun- Great Seals.
cil, the Great Seals of Ontario and Quebec respectively shall
be the same, or of the same Design, as those used in the
Provinces of Upper Canada and Lower Canada respectively
before their Union as the Province of Canada.

137. The words "and from thence to the End of the then Construction of temporary Acts.
next ensuing Session of the Legislature," or Words to the
same Effect, used in any temporary Act of the Province of
Canada not expired before the Union, shall be construed to
extend and apply to the next Session of the Parliament of
Canada if the Subject Matter of the Act is within the Powers
of the same as defined by this Act, or to the next Sessions of
the Legislatures of Ontario and Quebec respectively if the
Subject Matter of the Act is within the Powers of the same as
defined by this Act.

138. From and after the Union the Use of the Words As to Errors in Names.
"Upper Canada", instead of "Ontario," or "Lower Canada"
instead of "Quebec," in any Deed, Writ, Process, Pleading,
Document, Matter, or Thing shall not invalidate the same.

139. Any Proclamation under the Great Seal of the Prov- As to issue of Proclamations before Union, to commence after Union.
ince of Canada issued before the Union to take effect at a
Time which is subsequent to the Union, whether relating to

---

(68) Probably spent.

that Province, or to Upper Canada, or to Lower Canada, and the several Matters and Things therein proclaimed, shall be and continue of like Force and Effect as if the Union had not been made. (69)

As to issue of Proclamations after Union.

140. Any Proclamation which is authorized by any Act of the Legislature of the Province of Canada to be issued under the Great Seal of the Province of Canada, whether relating to that Province, or to Upper Canada, or to Lower Canada, and which is not issued before the Union, may be issued by the Lieutenant Governor of Ontario or Quebec, as its Subject Matter requires, under the Great Seal thereof; and from and after the Issue of such Proclamation the same and the several Matters and Things therein proclaimed shall be and continue of the like Force and Effect in Ontario or Quebec as if the Union had not been made. (70)

Penitentiary.

141. The Penitentiary of the Province of Canada shall, until the Parliament of Canada otherwise provides, be and continue the Penitentiary of Ontario and of Quebec. (71)

Arbitration respecting Debts, etc.

142. The Division and Adjustment of the Debts, Credits, Liabilities, Properties, and Assets of Upper Canada and Lower Canada shall be referred to the Arbitrament of Three Arbitrators, One chosen by the Government of Ontario, One by the Government of Quebec, and One by the Government of Canada; and the Selection of the Arbitrators shall not be made until the Parliament of Canada and the Legislatures of Ontario and Quebec have met; and the Arbitrator chosen by the Government of Canada shall not be a Resident either in Ontario or in Quebec. (72)

Division of Records.

143. The Governor General in Council may from Time to Time order that such and so many of the Records, Books, and Documents of the Province of Canada as he thinks fit shall be appropriated and delivered either to Ontario or to Quebec, and the same shall thenceforth be the Property of that Province; and any Copy thereof or Extract therefrom, duly

---

(69) Probably spent.

(70) Probably spent.

(71) Spent. Penitentiaries are now provided for by the *Penitentiary Act*, R.S.C. 1970, c. P-6.

(72) Spent. See pages (xi) and (xii) of the Public Accounts, 1902-03.

certified by the Officer having charge of the Original thereof, shall be admitted as Evidence. (73)

144. The Lieutenant Governor of Quebec may from Time to Time, by Proclamation under the Great Seal of the Province, to take effect from a Day to be appointed therein, constitute Townships in those Parts of the Province of Quebec in which Townships are not then already constituted, and fix the Metes and Bounds thereof.

Constitution of Townships in Quebec.

145. Repealed. (74)

XI.—ADMISSION OF OTHER COLONIES

146. It shall be lawful for the Queen, by and with the Advice of Her Majesty's Most Honourable Privy Council, on Addresses from the Houses of the Parliament of Canada, and from the Houses of the respective Legislatures of the Colonies or Provinces of Newfoundland, Prince Edward Island, and British Columbia, to admit those Colonies or Provinces, or any of them, into the Union, and on Address from the Houses of the Parliament of Canada to admit Rupert's Land and the North-western Territory, or either of them, into the Union, on such Terms and Conditions in each Case as are in the Addresses expressed and as the Queen thinks fit to approve, subject to the Provisions of this Act; and the Provisions of any Order in Council in that Behalf shall have effect as if they had been enacted by the Parliament of the United Kingdom of Great Britain and Ireland. (75)

Power to admit Newfoundland etc., into the Union.

---

(73) Probably spent. Two orders were made under this section on the 24th of January, 1868.

(74) Repealed by the *Statute Law Revision Act, 1893*, 56-57 Vict., c. 14, (U.K.). The section read as follows:

X.—Intercolonial Railway.

145. Inasmuch as the Provinces of Canada, Nova Scotia, and New Brunswick have joined in a Declaration that the Construction of the Intercolonial Railway is essential to the Consolidation of the Union of British North America, and to the Assent thereto of Nova Scotia and New Brunswick, and have consequently agreed that Provision should be made for its immediate Construction by the Government of Canada; Therefore, in order to give effect to that Agreement, it shall be the Duty of the Government and Parliment of Canada to provide for the Commencement, within Six Months after the Union, of a Railway connecting the River St. Lawrence with the City of Halifax in Nova Scotia, and for the Construction thereof without Intermission, and the Completion thereof with all practicable Speed.

(75) All territories mentioned in this section are now part of Canada. See the notes to section 5, *supra*.

As to Represen-
tation of
Newfoundland
and Prince
Edward Island
in Senate.

147. In case of the Admission of Newfoundland and Prince Edward Island, or either of them, each shall be entitled to a Representation in the Senate of Canada of Four Members, and (notwithstanding anything in this Act) in case of the Admission of Newfoundland the normal Number of Senators shall be Seventy-six and their maximum Number shall be Eighty-two; but Prince Edward Island when admitted shall be deemed to be comprised in the Third of Three Divisions into which Canada is, in relation to the Constitution of the Senate, divided by this Act, and accordingly, after the Admission of Prince Edward Island, whether Newfoundland is admitted or not, the Representation of Nova Scotia and New Brunswick in the Senate shall, as Vacancies occur, be reduced from Twelve to Ten Members respectively, and the Representation of each of those Provinces shall not be increased at any Time beyond Ten, except under the Provisions of this Act for the Appointment of Three or Six additional Senators under the Direction of the Queen. (76)

---

(76) Spent. See the notes to sections 21, 22, 26, 27 and 28, *supra*.

SCHEDULES

THE FIRST SCHEDULE. (77)

Electoral Districts of Ontario.

A.

EXISTING ELECTORAL DIVISIONS.

COUNTIES

1. Prescott.
2. Glengarry.
3. Stormont.
4. Dundas.
5. Russell.

6. Carleton.
7. Prince Edward.
8. Halton.
9. Essex.

RIDINGS OF COUNTIES.

10. North Riding of Lanark.
11. South Riding of Lanark.
12. North Riding of Leeds and North Riding of Grenville.
13. South Riding of Leeds.
14. South Riding of Grenville.
15. East Riding of Northumberland.
16. West Riding of Northumberland (excepting therefrom the Township of South Monaghan).
17. East Riding of Durham.
18. West Riding of Durham.
19. North Riding of Ontario.
20. South Riding of Ontario.
21. East Riding of York.
22. West Riding of York.
23. North Riding of York.
24. North Riding of Wentworth.
25. South Riding of Wentworth.
26. East Riding of Elgin.
27. West Riding of Elgin.
28. North Riding of Waterloo.

---

(77) Spent. *Representation Act*, R.S.O. 1970, c. 413.

29. South Riding of Waterloo.
30. North Riding of Brant.
31. South Riding of Brant.
32. North Riding of Oxford.
33. South Riding of Oxford. .
34. East Riding of Middlesex.

CITIES, PARTS OF CITIES, AND TOWNS.

35. West Toronto.
36. East Toronto.
37. Hamilton.
38. Ottawa.
39. Kingston.
40. London.
41. Town of Brockville, with the Township of Elizabethtown thereto attached.
42. Town of Niagara, with the Township of Niagara, thereto attached.
43. Town of Cornwall, with the Township of Cornwall thereto attached.

B.

NEW ELECTORAL DISTRICTS.

44. The Provisional Judicial District of ALGOMA.

The County of ·BRUCE, divided into Two Ridings, to be called respectively the North and South Ridings: —

45. The North Riding of Bruce to consist of the Townships of Bury, Lindsay, Eastnor, Albermarle, Amable, Arran, Bruce, Elderslie, and Saugeen, and the Village of Southampton.

46. The South Riding of Bruce to consist of the Townships of Kincardine (including the Village of Kincardine), Greenock, Brant, Huron, Kinloss, Culross, and Carrick.

The County of HURON, divided into Two Ridings, to be called respectively the North and South Ridings: —

47. The North Riding to consist of the Townships of Ashfield, Wawanosh, Turnberry, Howick, Morris, Grey, Col-

borne, Hullett, including the Village of Clinton, and McKillop.

48. The South Riding to consist of the Town of Goderich and the Townships of Goderich, Tuckersmith, Stanley, Hay, Usborne, and Stephen.

The County of MIDDLESEX, divided into Three Ridings, to be called respectively the North, West, and East Ridings: —

49. The North Riding to consist of the Townships of McGillivray and Biddulph (taken from the County of Huron), and Williams East, Williams West, Adelaide, and Lobo.

50. The West Riding to consist of the Townships of Delaware, Carradoc, Metcalfe, Mosa and Ekfrid, and the Village of Strathroy.

[The East Riding to consist of the Townships now embraced therein, and be bounded as it is at present.]

51. The County of LAMBTON to consist of the Townships of Bosanquet, Warwick, Plympton, Sarnia, Moore, Enniskillen, and Brooke, and the Town of Sarnia.

52. The County of KENT to consist of the Townships of Chatham, Dover, East Tilbury, Romney, Raleigh, and Harwich, and the town of Chatham.

53. The County of BOTHWELL to consist of the Townships of Sombra, Dawn, and Euphemia (taken from the County of Lambton), and the Townships of Zone, Camden with the Gore thereof, Orford, and Howard (taken from the County of Kent).

The County of GREY divided into Two Ridings to be called respectively the South and North Ridings: —

54. The South Riding to consist of the Townships of Bentinck, Glenelg, Artemesia, Osprey, Normanby, Egremont, Proton, and Melancthon.

55. The North Riding to consist of the Townships of Collingwood, Euphrasia, Holland, Saint-Vincent, Sydenham, Sullivan, Derby, and Keppel, Sarawak and Brooke, and the Town of Owen Sound.

The County of PERTH divided into Two Ridings, to be called respectively the South and North Ridings: —

56. The North Riding to consist of the Townships of Wallace, Elma, Logan, Ellice, Mornington, and North Easthope, and the Town of Strathford.

57. The South Riding to consist of the Townships of Blanchard, Downie, South Easthope, Fullarton, Hibbert, and the Villages of Mitchell and Ste. Mary's.

The County of WELLINGTON divided into Three Ridings to be called respectively North, South and Centre Ridings: —

58. The North Riding to consist of the Townships of Amaranth, Arthur, Luther, Minto, Maryborough, Peel, and the Village of Mount Forest.

59. The Centre Riding to consist of the Townships of Garafraxa, Erin, Eramosa, Nichol, and Pilkington, and the Villages of Fergus and Elora.

60. The South Riding to consist of the Town of Guelph, and the Townships of Guelph and Puslinch.

The County of NORFOLK, divided into Two Ridings, to be called respectively the South and North Ridings:—

61. The South Riding to consist of the Townships of Charlotteville, Houghton, Walsingham, and Woodhouse, and with the Gore thereof.

62. The North Riding to consist of the Townships of Middleton, Townsend, and Windham, and the Town of Simcoe.

63. The County of HALDIMAND to consist of the Townships of Oneida, Seneca, Cayuga North, Cayuga South, Rainham, Walpole, and Dunn.

64. The County of MONCK to consist of the Townships of Canborough and Moulton, and Sherbrooke, and the Village of Dunnville (taken from the County of Haldimand), the Townships of Caister and Gainsborough (taken from the County of Lincoln), and the Townships of Pelham and Wainfleet (taken from the County of Welland).

65. The County of LINCOLN to consist of the Townships of Clinton, Grantham, Grimsby, and Louth, and the Town of St. Catherines.

66. The County of WELLAND to consist of the Townships of Bertie, Crowland, Humberstone, Stamford, Thorold, and Willoughby, and the Villages of Chippewa, Clifton, Fort Erie, Thorold, and Welland.

67. The County of PEEL to consist of the Townships of Chinguacousy, Toronto, and the Gore of Toronto, and the Villages of Brampton and Streetsville.

68. The County of CARDWELL to consist of the Townships of Albion and Caledon (taken from the County of Peel), and the Townships of Adjala and Mono (taken from the County of Simcoe).

The County of SIMCOE, divided into Two Ridings, to be called respectively the South and North Ridings:—

69. The South Riding to consist of the Townships of West Gwillimbury, Tecumseth, Innisfil, Essa, Tossorontio, Mulmur, and the Village of Bradford.

70. The North Riding to consist of the Townships of Nottawasaga, Sunnidale, Vespra, Flos, Oro, Medonte, Orillia and Matchedash, Tiny and Tay, Balaklava and Robinson, and the Towns of Barrie and Collingwood.

The County of VICTORIA, divided into Two Ridings, to be called respectively the South and North Ridings:—

71. The South Riding to consist of the Townships of Ops, Mariposa, Emily, Verulam, and the Town of Lindsay.

72. The North Riding to consist of the Townships of Anson, Bexley, Carden, Dalton, Digby, Eldon, Fenelon, Hindon, Laxton, Lutterworth, Macaulay and Draper, Sommerville, and Morrison, Muskoka, Monck and Watt (taken from the County of Simcoe), and any other surveyed Townships lying to the North of the said North Riding.

The County of PETERBOROUGH, divided into Two Ridings, to be called respectively the West and East Ridings:—

73. The West Riding to consist of the Townships of South Monaghan (taken from the County of Northumberland), North Monaghan, Smith, and Ennismore, and the Town of Peterborough.

74. The East Riding to consist of the Townships of Asphodel, Belmont and Methuen, Douro, Dummer, Galway, Harvey, Minden, Stanhope and Dysart, Otonabee, and Snowden, and the Village of Ashburnham, and any other surveyed Townships lying to the North of the said East Riding.

The County of HASTINGS, divided into Three Ridings, to be called respectively the West, East, and North Ridings:—

75. The West Riding to consist of the Town of Belleville, the Township of Sydney, and the Village of Trenton.

76. The East Riding to consist of the Townships of Thurlow, Tyendinaga, and Hungerford.

77. The North Riding to consist of the Townships of Rawdon, Huntingdon, Madoc, Elzevir, Tudor, Marmora, and Lake, and the Village of Stirling, and any other surveyed Townships lying to the North of the said North Riding.

78. The County of LENNOX, to consist of the Townships of Richmond, Adolphustown, North Fredericksburgh, South Fredericksburgh, Ernest Town, and Amherst Island, and the Village of Napanee.

79. The County of ADDINGTON to consist of the Townships of Camden, Portland, Sheffield, Hinchinbrooke, Kaladar, Kennebec, Olden, Oso, Anglesea, Barrie, Clarendon, Palmerston, Effingham, Abinger, Miller, Canonto, Denbigh, Loughborough, and Bedford.

80. The County of FRONTENAC to consist of the Townships of Kingston, Wolfe Island, Pittsburgh and Howe Island, and Storrington.

The County of RENFREW, divided into Two Ridings, to be called respectively the South and North Ridings:—

81. The South Riding to consist of the Townships of McNab, Bagot, Blithfield, Brougham, Horton, Admaston, Grattan, Matawatchan, Griffith, Lyndoch, Raglan, Radcliffe, Brudenell, Sebastopol, and the Villages of Arnprior and Renfrew.

82. The North Riding to consist of the Townships of Ross, Bromley, Westmeath, Stafford, Pembroke, Wilberforce, Alice, Petawawa, Buchanan, South Algoma, North Algoma, Fraser, McKay, Wylie, Rolph, Head, Maria, Clara, Haggerty, Sherwood, Burns, and Richards, and any other surveyed Townships lying Northwesterly of the said North Riding.

Every Town and incorporated Village existing at the Union, not specially mentioned in this Schedule, is to be taken as Part of the County or Riding within which it is locally situate.

THE SECOND SCHEDULE.

Electoral Districts of Quebec specially fixed.

COUNTIES OF—

Pontiac.	Missisquoi.	Compton.
Ottawa.	Brome.	Wolfe and
Argenteuil.	Shefford.	Richmond.
Huntingdon.	Stanstead.	Megantic.

Town of Sherbrooke.

THE THIRD SCHEDULE.

Provincial Public Works and Property to be the Property of Canada.

1. Canals, with Lands and Water Power connected therewith.

2. Public Harbours.
3. Lighthouses and Piers, and Sable Island.
4. Steamboats, Dredges, and public Vessels.
5. Rivers and Lake Improvements.
6. Railways and Railway Stocks, Mortgages, and other Debts due by Railway Companies.
7. Military Roads.
8. Custom Houses, Post Offices, and all other Public Buildings, except such as the Government of Canada appropriate for the Use of the Provincial Legislature and Governments.
9. Property transferred by the Imperial Government, and known as Ordinance Property.
10. Armouries, Drill Sheds, Military Clothing, and Munitions of War, and Lands set apart for general Public Purposes.

THE FOURTH SCHEDULE.

Assets to be the Property of Ontario and Quebec conjointly.

Upper Canada Building Fund.
Lunatic Asylums.
Normal School.
Court Houses, ⎫
    in   ⎪
Aylmer.   ⎬ Lower Canada
Montreal.   ⎪
Kamouraska. ⎭
Law Society, Upper Canada.
Montreal Turnpike Trust.
University Permanent Fund.
Royal Institution.
Consolidated Municipal Loan Fund, Upper Canada.
Consolidated Municipal Loan Fund, Lower Canada.
Agricultural Society, Upper Canada.
Lower Canada Legislative Grant.
Quebec Fire Loan.
Temiscouata Advance Account.
Quebec Turnpike Trust.
Education—East.
Building and Jury Fund, Lower Canada.

Municipalities Fund.
Lower Canada Superior Education Income Fund.

THE FIFTH SCHEDULE.

OATH OF ALLEGIANCE.

I, *A.B.* do swear, That I will be faithful and bear true Allegiance to Her Majesty Queen Victoria.

Note.—The Name of the King or Queen of the United Kingdom of Great Britain and Ireland for the Time being is to be substituted from Time to Time, with Proper Terms of Reference thereto.

DECLARATION OF QUALIFICATION.

I, *A.B.* do declare and testify, That I am by Law duly qualified to be appointed a Member of the Senate of Canada [*or as the Case may be*]; and that I am legally or equitably seised as of Freehold for my own Use and Benefit of Lands or Tenements held in Free and Common Socage [*or* seised or possessed for my own Use and Benefit of Lands or Tenements held in Franc-alleu or in Roture (*as the Case may be*),] in the Province of Nova Scotia [*or as the Case may be*] of the Value of Four thousand Dollars over and above all Rents, Dues, Debts, Mortgages, Charges, and Incumbrances due or payable out of or charged on or affecting the same, and that I have not collusively or colourably obtained a Title to or become possessed of the said Lands and Tenements or any Part thereof for the Purpose of enabling me to become a Member of the Senate of Canada [*or as the Case may be*,] and that my Real and Personal Property are together worth Four thousand Dollars over and above my Debts and Liabilities.

THE SIXTH SCHEDULE. (78)

Primary Production from Non-Renewable Natural Resources and Forestry Resources

1. For the purposes of section 92A of this Act,

(*a*) production from a non-renewable natural resource is primary production therefrom if

---

(78) As enacted by the *Constitution Act, 1982.*

(i) it is in the form in which it exists upon its recovery or severance from its natural state, or

(ii) it is a product resulting from processing or refining the resource, and is not a manufactured product or a product resulting from refining crude oil, refining upgraded heavy crude oil, refining gases or liquids derived from coal or refining a synthetic equivalent or crude oil; and

(b) production from a forestry resource is primary production therefrom if it consists of sawlogs, poles, lumber, wood chips, sawdust or any other primary wood product, or wood pulp, and is not a product manufactured from wood.

CONSTITUTION ACT, 1982 (79)

SCHEDULE B

CONSTITUTION ACT, 1982

PART I

CANADIAN CHARTER OF RIGHTS AND FREEDOMS

Whereas Canada is founded upon principles that recognize the supremacy of God and the rule of law:

Guarantee of Rights and Freedoms

1. The *Canadian Charter of Rights and Freedoms* guarantees the rights and freedoms set out in it subject only to such reasonable limits prescribed by law as can be demonstrably justified in a free and democratic society.

Rights and freedoms in Canada

Fundamental Freedoms

2. Everyone has the following fundamental freedoms:
(*a*) freedom of conscience and religion;
(*b*) freedom of thought, belief, opinion and expression, including freedom of the press and other media of communication;

Fundamental freedoms

---

(79) Enacted as Schedule B to the *Canada Act 1982*, (U.K.) 1982, c. 11, which came into force on April 17, 1982. The *Canada Act 1982*, other than Schedules A and B thereto, reads as follows:

An Act to give effect to a request by the Senate and House of Commons of Canada

Whereas Canada has requested and consented to the enactment of an Act of the Parliament of the United Kingdom to give effect to the provisions hereinafter set forth and the Senate and the House of Commons of Canada in Parliament assembled have submitted an address to Her Majesty requesting that Her Majesty may graciously be pleased to cause a Bill to be laid before the Parliament of the United Kingdom for that purpose.

Be it therefore enacted by the Queen's Most Excellent Majesty, by and with the advice and consent of the Lords Spiritual and Temporal, and Commons, in this present Parliament assembled, and by the authority of the same, as follows:

1. The *Constitution Act, 1982* set out in Schedule B to this Act is hereby enacted for and shall have the force of law in Canada and shall come into force as provided in that Act.

2. No Act of the Parliament of the United Kingdom passed after the *Constitution Act, 1982* comes into force shall extend to Canada as part of its law.

3. So far as it is not contained in Schedule B, the French version of this Act is set out in Schedule A to this Act and has the same authority in Canada as the English version thereof.

4. This Act may be cited as the *Canada Act 1982*.

(*c*) freedom of peaceful assembly; and

(*d*) freedom of association.

Democratic Rights

Democratic rights of citizens

3. Every citizen of Canada has the right to vote in an election of members of the House of Commons or of a legislative assembly and to be qualified for membership therein.

Maximum duration of legislative bodies

4. (1) No House of Commons and no legislative assembly shall continue for longer than five years from the date fixed for the return of the writs of a general election of its members.(80)

Continuation in special circumstances

(2) In time of real or apprehended war, invasion or insurrection, a House of Commons may be continued by Parliament and a legislative assembly may be continued by the legislature beyond five years if such continuation is not opposed by the votes of more than one-third of the members of the House of Commons or the legislative assembly, as the case may be.(81)

Annual sitting of legislative bodies

5. There shall be a sitting of Parliament and of each legislature at least once every twelve months.(82)

Mobility Rights

Mobility of citizens

6. (1) Every citizen of Canada has the right to enter, remain in and leave Canada.

Rights to move and gain livelihood

(2) Every citizen of Canada and every person who has the status of a permanent resident of Canada has the right

(*a*) to move to and take up residence in any province; and

(*b*) to pursue the gaining of a livelihood in any province.

Limitation

(3) The rights specified in subsection (2) are subject to

(*a*) any laws or practices of general application in force in a province other than those that discriminate among

---

(80) See section 50 and the footnotes to sections 85 and 88 of the *Constitution Act, 1867.*

(81) Replaces part of Class 1 of section 91 of the *Constitution Act, 1867,* which was repealed as set out in subitem 1(3) of the Schedule to this Act.

(82) See the footnotes to sections 20, 86 and 88 of the *Constitution Act, 1867.*

persons primarily on the basis of province of present or previous residence; and

(*b*) any laws providing for reasonable residency requirements as a qualification for the receipt of publicly provided social services.

(4) Subsections (2) and (3) do not preclude any law, program or activity that has as its object the amelioration in a province of conditions of individuals in that province who are socially or economically disadvantaged if the rate of employment in that province is below the rate of employment in Canada.

Affirmative action programs

Legal Rights

7. Everyone has the right to life, liberty and security of the person and the right not to be deprived thereof except in accordance with the principles of fundamental justice.

Life, liberty and security of person

8. Everyone has the right to be secure against unreasonable search or seizure.

Search or seizure

9. Everyone has the right not to be arbitrarily detained or imprisoned.

Detention or imprisonment

10. Everyone has the right on arrest or detention
(*a*) to be informed promptly of the reasons therefor;
(*b*) to retain and instruct counsel without delay and to be informed of that right; and
(*c*) to have the validity of the detention determined by way of *habeas corpus* and to be released if the detention is not lawful.

Arrest or detention

11. Any person charged with an offence has the right
(*a*) to be informed without unreasonable delay of the specific offence;
(*b*) to be tried within a reasonable time;
(*c*) not to be compelled to be a witness in proceedings against that person in respect of the offence;
(*d*) to be presumed innocent until proven guilty according to law in a fair and public hearing by an independent and impartial tribunal;

Proceedings in criminal and penal matters

(*e*) not to be denied reasonable bail without just cause;

(*f*) except in the case of an offence under military law tried before a military tribunal, to the benefit of trial by jury where the maximum punishment for the offence is imprisonment for five years or a more severe punishment;

(*g*) not to be found guilty on account of any act or omission unless, at the time of the act or omission, it constituted an offence under Canadian or international law or was criminal according to the general principles of law recognized by the community of nations;

(*h*) if finally acquitted of the offence, not to be tried for it again and, if finally found guilty and punished for the offence, not to be tried or punished for it again; and

(*i*) if found guilty of the offence and if the punishment for the offence has been varied between the time of commission and the time of sentencing, to the benefit of the lesser punishment.

Treatment or punishment

12. Everyone has the right not to be subjected to any cruel and unusual treatment or punishment.

Self-crimina-tion

13. A witness who testifies in any proceedings has the right not to have any incriminating evidence so given used to incriminate that witness in any other proceedings, except in a prosecution for perjury or for the giving of contradictory evidence.

Interpreter

14. A party or witness in any proceedings who does not understand or speak the language in which the proceedings are conducted or who is deaf has the right to the assistance of an interpreter.

Equality Rights

Equality before and under law and equal protection and benefit of law

15. (1) Every individual is equal before and under the law and has the right to the equal protection and equal benefit of the law without discrimination and, in particular, without discrimination based on race, national or ethnic origin, colour, religion, sex, age or mental or physical disability.

Affirmative action programs

(2) Subsection (1) does not preclude any law, program or activity that has as its object the amelioration of conditions of disadvantaged individuals or groups including those that are

disadvantaged because of race, national or ethnic origin, colour, religion, sex, age or mental or physical disability.

Official Languages of Canada

16. (1) English and French are the official languages of Canada and have equality of status and equal rights and privileges as to their use in all institutions of the Parliament and government of Canada.

Official languages of Canada

(2) English and French are the official languages of New Brunswick and have equality of status and equal rights and privileges as to their use in all institutions of the legislature and government of New Brunswick.

Official languages of New Brunswick

(3) Nothing in this Charter limits the authority of Parliament or a legislature to advance the equality of status or use of English and French.

Advancement of status and use

17. (1) Everyone has the right to use English or French in any debates and other proceedings of Parliament.(83)

Proceedings of Parliament

(2) Everyone has the right to use English or French in any debates and other proceedings of the legislature of New Brunswick.(84)

Proceedings of New Brunswick legislature

18. (1) The statutes, records and journals of Parliament shall be printed and published in English and French and both language versions are equally authoritative.(85)

Parliamentary statutes and records

(2) The statutes, records and journals of the legislature of New Brunswick shall be printed and published in English and French and both language versions are equally authoritative.(86)

New Brunswick statutes and records

19. (1) Either English or French may be used by any person in, or in any pleading in or process issuing from, any court established by Parliament.(87)

Proceedings in courts established by Parliament

(83) See section 133 of the *Constitution Act, 1867*, and the footnote thereto.

(84) *Id.*

(85) *Id.*

(86) *Id.*

(87) *Id.*

Proceedings in
New Brunswick
courts

(2) Either English or French may be used by any person in, or in any pleading in or process issuing from, any court of New Brunswick.(88)

Communica-
tions by public
with federal
institutions

20. (1) Any member of the public in Canada has the right to communicate with, and to receive available services from, any head or central office of an institution of the Parliament or government of Canada in English or French, and has the same right with respect to any other office of any such institution where

(*a*) there is a significant demand for communications with and services from that office in such language; or

(*b*) due to the nature of the office, it is reasonable that communications with and services from that office be available in both English and French.

Communica-
tions by public
with New
Brunswick
institutions

(2) Any member of the public in New Brunswick has the right to communicate with, and to receive available services from, any office of an institution of the legislature or government of New Brunswick in English or French.

Continuation of
existing
constitutional
provisions

21. Nothing in sections 16 to 20 abrogates or derogates from any right, privilege or obligation with respect to the English and French languages, or either of them, that exists or is continued by virtue of any other provision of the Constitution of Canada.(89)

Rights and
privileges
preserved

22. Nothing in sections 16 to 20 abrogates or derogates from any legal or customary right or privilege acquired or enjoyed either before or after the coming into force of this Charter with respect to any language that is not English or French.

Minority Language Educational Rights

Language of
instruction

23. (1) Citizens of Canada

(*a*) whose first language learned and still understood is that of the English or French linguistic minority population of the province in which they reside, or

---

(88) *Id.*

(89) See, for example, section 133 of the *Constitution Act, 1867*, and the reference to the *Manitoba Act, 1870*, in the footnote thereto.

(*b*) who have received their primary school instruction in Canada in English or French and reside in a province where the language in which they received that instruction is the language of the English or French linguistic minority population of the province,

have the right to have their children receive primary and secondary school instruction in that language in that province.(90)

(2) Citizens of Canada of whom any child has received or is receiving primary or secondary school instruction in English or French in Canada, have the right to have all their children receive primary and secondary school instruction in the same language. Continuity of language instruction

(3) The right of citizens of Canada under subsections (1) and (2) to have their children receive primary and secondary school instruction in the language of the English or French linguistic minority population of a province Application where numbers warrant

(*a*) applies wherever in the province the number of children of citizens who have such a right is sufficient to warrant the provision to them out of public funds of minority language instruction; and

(*b*) includes, where the number of those children so warrants, the right to have them receive that instruction in minority language educational facilities provided out of public funds.

Enforcement

24. (1) Anyone whose rights or freedoms, as guaranteed by this Charter, have been infringed or denied may apply to a court of competent jurisdiction to obtain such remedy as the court considers appropriate and just in the circumstances. Enforcement of guaranteed rights and freedoms

(2) Where, in proceedings under subsection (1), a court concludes that evidence was obtained in a manner that infringed or denied any rights or freedoms guaranteed by this Charter, the evidence shall be excluded if it is established that, having regard to all the circumstances, the admission of it in the proceedings would bring the administration of justice into disrepute. Exclusion of evidence bringing administration of justice into disrepute

---

(90) Paragraph 23(1)(*a*) is not in force in respect of Quebec. See section 59 *infra*.

General

Aboriginal rights and freedoms not affected by Charter

25. The guarantee in this Charter of certain rights and freedoms shall not be construed so as to abrogate or derogate from any aboriginal, treaty or other rights or freedoms that pertain to the aboriginal peoples of Canada including

(*a*) any rights or freedoms that have been recognized by the Royal Proclamation of October 7, 1763; and

(*b*) any rights or freedoms that may be acquired by the aboriginal peoples of Canada by way of land claims settlement.

Other rights and freedoms not affected by Charter

26. The guarantee in this Charter of certain rights and freedoms shall not be construed as denying the existence of any other rights or freedoms that exist in Canada.

Multicultural heritage

27. This Charter shall be interpreted in a manner consistent with the preservation and enhancement of the multicultural heritage of Canadians.

Rights guaranteed equally to both sexes

28. Notwithstanding anything in this Charter, the rights and freedoms referred to in it are guaranteed equally to male and female persons.

Rights respecting certain schools preserved

29. Nothing in this Charter abrogates or derogates from any rights or privileges guaranteed by or under the Constitution of Canada in respect of denominational, separate or dissentient schools.(91)

Application to territories and territorial authorities

30. A reference in this Charter to a Province or to the legislative assembly or legislature of a province shall be deemed to include a reference to the Yukon Territory and the Northwest Territories, or to the appropriate legislative authority thereof, as the case may be.

Legislative powers not extended

31. Nothing in this Charter extends the legislative powers of any body or authority.

Application of Charter

Application of Charter

32. (1) This Charter applies

(*a*) to the Parliament and government of Canada in respect of all matters within the authority of Parliament

---

(91) See section 93 of the *Constitution Act, 1867*, and the footnote thereto.

including all matters relating to the Yukon Territory and Northwest Territories; and

(*b*) to the legislature and government of each province in respect of all matters within the authority of the legislature of each province.

(2) Notwithstanding subsection (1), section 15 shall not have effect until three years after this section comes into force. *Exception*

33. (1) Parliament or the legislature of a province may expressly declare in an Act of Parliament or of the legislature, as the case may be, that the Act or a provision thereof shall operate notwithstanding a provision included in section 2 or sections 7 to 15 of this Charter. *Exception where express declaration*

(2) An Act or a provision of an Act in respect of which a declaration made under this section is in effect shall have such operation as it would have but for the provision of this Charter referred to in the declaration. *Operation of exception*

(3) A declaration made under subsection (1) shall cease to have effect five years after it comes into force or on such earlier date as may be specified in the declaration. *Five year limitation*

(4) Parliament or the legislature of a province may re-enact a declaration made under subsection (1). *Re-enactment*

(5) Subsection (3) applies in respect of a re-enactment made under subsection (4). *Five year limitation*

Citation

34. This Part may be cited as the *Canadian Charter of Rights and Freedoms.* *Citation*

PART II

RIGHTS OF THE ABORIGINAL PEOPLES OF CANADA

35. (1) The existing aboriginal and treaty rights of the aboriginal peoples of Canada are hereby recognized and affirmed. *Recognition of existing aboriginal and treaty rights*

(2) In this Act, "aboriginal peoples of Canada" includes the Indian, Inuit and Métis peoples of Canada. *Definition of "aboriginal peoples of Canada"*

PART III

EQUALIZATION AND REGIONAL DISPARITIES

Commitment to promote equal opportunities

36. (1) Without altering the legislative authority of Parliament or of the provincial legislatures, or the rights of any of them with respect to the exercise of their legislative authority, Parliament and the legislatures, together with the government of Canada and the provincial governments, are committed to

(*a*) promoting equal opportunities for the well-being of Canadians;

(*b*) furthering economic development to reduce disparity in opportunities; and

(*c*) providing essential public services of reasonable quality to all Canadians.

Commitment respecting public services

(2) Parliament and the government of Canada are committed to the principle of making equalization payments to ensure that provincial governments have sufficient revenues to provide reasonably comparable levels of public services at reasonably comparable levels of taxation. (92)

PART IV

CONSTITUTIONAL CONFERENCE

Constitutional conference

37. (1) A constitutional conference composed of the Prime Minister of Canada and the first ministers of the provinces shall be convened by the Prime Minister of Canada within one year after this Part comes into force.

Participation of aboriginal peoples

(2) The conference convened under subsection (1) shall have included in its agenda an item respecting constitutional matters that directly affect the aboriginal peoples of Canada, including the identification and definition of the rights of those peoples to be included in the Constitution of Canada, and the Prime Minister of Canada shall invite representatives of those peoples to participate in the discussions on that item.

Participation of territories

(3) The Prime Minister of Canada shall invite elected representatives of the governments of the Yukon Territory and the Northwest Territories to participate in the discus-

(92) See the footnotes to sections 114 and 118 of the *Constitution Act, 1867.*

sions on any item on the agenda of the conference convened under subsection (1) that, in the opinion of the Prime Minister, directly affects the Yukon Territory and the Northwest Territories.

PART V

PROCEDURE FOR AMENDING CONSTITUTION OF CANADA

(93)

38. (1) An amendment to the Constitution of Canada may be made by proclamation issued by the Governor General under the Great Seal of Canada where so authorized by

General procedure for amending Constitution of Canada

    (*a*) resolutions of the Senate and House of Commons; and
    (*b*) resolutions of the legislative assemblies of at least two-thirds of the provinces that have, in the aggregate, according to the then latest general census, at least fifty per cent of the population of all the provinces.

(2) An amendment made under subsection (1) that derogates from the legislative powers, the proprietary rights or any other rights or privileges of the legislature or government of a province shall require a resolution supported by a majority of the members of each of the Senate, the House of Commons and the legislative assemblies required under subsection (1).

Majority of members

(3) An amendment referred to in subsection (2) shall not have effect in a province the legislative assembly of which has expressed its dissent thereto by resolution supported by a majority of its members prior to the issue of the proclamation to which the amendment relates unless that legislative assembly, subsequently, by resolution supported by a majority of its members, revokes its dissent and authorizes the amendment.

Expression of dissent

(4) A resolution of dissent made for the purposes of subsection (3) may be revoked at any time before or after the issue of the proclamation to which it relates.

Revocation of dissent

39. (1) A proclamation shall not be issued under subsection 38(1) before the expiration of one year from the adoption

Restriction on proclamation

(93) Prior to the enactment of Part V certain provisions of the Constitution of Canada and the provincial constitutions could be amended pursuant to the *Constitution Act, 1867*. See the footnotes to section 91, Class 1 and section 92, Class 1 thereof, *supra*. Other amendments to the Constitution could only be made by enactment of the Parliament of the United Kingdom.

of the resolution initiating the amendment procedure there-under, unless the legislative assembly of each province has previously adopted a resolution of assent or dissent.

Idem

(2) A proclamation shall not be issued under subsection 38(1) after the expiration of three years from the adoption of the resolution initiating the amendment procedure there-under.

Compensation

40. Where an amendment is made under subsection 38(1) that transfers provincial legislative powers relating to educa-tion or other cultural matters from provincial legislatures to Parliament, Canada shall provide reasonable compensation to any province to which the amendment does not apply.

Amendment by unanimous consent

41. An amendment to the Constitution of Canada in relation to the following matters may be made by proclama-tion issued by the Governor General under the Great Seal of Canada only where authorized by resolutions of the Senate and House of Commons and of the legislative assembly of each province:

(*a*) the office of the Queen, the Governor General and the Lieutenant Governor of a province;

(*b*) the right of a province to a number of members in the House of Commons not less than the number of Senators by which the province is entitled to be represented at the time this Part comes into force;

(*c*) subject to section 43, the use of the English or the French language;

(*d*) the composition of the Supreme Court of Canada; and

(*e*) an amendment to this Part.

Amendment by general procedure

42. (1) An amendment to the Constitution of Canada in relation to the following matters may be made only in accordance with subsection 38(1):

(*a*) the principle of proportionate representation of the provinces in the House of Commons prescribed by the Constitution of Canada;

(*b*) the powers of the Senate and the method of selecting Senators;

(c) the number of members by which a province is entitled to be represented in the Senate and the residence qualifications of Senators;

(d) subject to paragraph 41(d), the Supreme Court of Canada;

(e) the extension of existing provinces into the territories; and

(f) notwithstanding any other law or practice, the establishment of new provinces.

(2) Subsections 38(2) to (4) do not apply in respect of amendments in relation to matters referred to in subsection (1). *Exception*

43. An amendment to the Constitution of Canada in relation to any provision that applies to one or more, but not all, provinces, including *Amendment of provisions relating to some but not all provinces*

(a) any alteration to boundaries between provinces, and

(b) any amendment to any provision that relates to the use of the English or the French language within a province,

may be made by proclamation issued by the Governor General under the Great Seal of Canada only where so authorized by resolutions of the Senate and House of Commons and of the legislative assembly of each province to which the amendment applies.

44. Subject to sections 41 and 42, Parliament may exclusively make laws amending the Constitution of Canada in relation to the executive government of Canada or the Senate and House of Commons. *Amendments by Parliament*

45. Subject to section 41, the legislature of each province may exclusively make laws amending the constitution of the province. *Amendments by provincial legislatures*

46. (1) The procedures for amendment under sections 38, 41, 42 and 43 may be initiated either by the Senate or the House of Commons or by the legislative assembly of a province. *Initiation of amendment procedures*

(2) A resolution of assent made for the purposes of this Part may be revoked at any time before the issue of a proclamation authorized by it. *Revocation of authorization*

Amendments
without Senate
resolution

47. (1) An amendment to the Constitution of Canada made by proclamation under section 38, 41, 42 or 43 may be made without a resolution of the Senate authorizing the issue of the proclamation if, within one hundred and eighty days after the adoption by the House of Commons of a resolution authorizing its issue, the Senate has not adopted such a resolution and if, at any time after the expiration of that period, the House of Commons again adopts the resolution.

Computation of
period

(2) Any period when Parliament is prorogued or dissolved shall not be counted in computing the one hundred and eighty day period referred to in subsection (1).

Advice to issue
proclamation

48. The Queen's Privy Council for Canada shall advise the Governor General to issue a proclamation under this Part forthwith on the adoption of the resolutions required for an amendment made by proclamation under this Part.

Constitutional
conference

49. A constitutional conference composed of the Prime Minister of Canada and the first ministers of the provinces shall be convened by the Prime Minister of Canada within fifteen years after this Part comes into force to review the provisions of this Part.

PART VI

AMENDMENT TO THE CONSTITUTION ACT, 1867

50. (94)

51. (95)

PART VII

GENERAL

Primacy of
Constitution of
Canada

52. (1) The Constitution of Canada is the supreme law of Canada, and any law that is inconsistent with the provisions of the Constitution is, to the extent of the inconsistency, of no force or effect.

Constitution of
Canada

(2) The Constitution of Canada includes

---

(94) The amendment is set out in the Consolidation of the *Constitution Act, 1867*, as section 92A thereof.

(95) The amendment is set out in the Consolidation of the *Constitution Act, 1867*, as the Sixth Schedule thereof.

(*a*) the *Canada Act 1982*, including this Act;

(*b*) the Acts and orders referred to in the schedule; and

(*c*) any amendment to any Act or order referred to in paragraph (*a*) or (*b*).

(3) Amendments to the Constitution of Canada shall be made only in accordance with the authority contained in the Constitution of Canada.

Amendments to Constitution of Canada

53. (1) The enactments referred to in Column I of the schedule are hereby repealed or amended to the extent indicated in Column II thereof and, unless repealed, shall continue as law in Canada under the names set out in Column III thereof.

Repeals and new names

(2) Every enactment, except the *Canada Act 1982*, that refers to an enactment referred to in the schedule by the name in Column I thereof is hereby amended by substituting for that name the corresponding name in Column III thereof, and any British North America Act not referred to in the schedule may be cited as the *Constitution Act* followed by the year and number, if any, of its enactment.

Consequential amendments

54. Part IV is repealed on the day that is one year after this Part comes into force and this section may be repealed and this Act renumbered, consequentially upon the repeal of Part IV and this section, by proclamation issued by the Governor General under the Great Seal of Canada. (96)

Repeal and consequential amendments

55. A French version of the portions of the Constitution of Canada referred to in the schedule shall be prepared by the Minister of Justice of Canada as expeditiously as possible and, when any portion thereof sufficient to warrant action being taken has been so prepared, it shall be put forward for enactment by proclamation issued by the Governor General under the Great Seal of Canada pursuant to the procedure then applicable to an amendment of the same provisions of the Constitution of Canada.

French version of Constitution of Canada

56. Where any portion of the Constitution of Canada has been or is enacted in English and French or where a French version of any portion of the Constitution is enacted pursuant

English and French versions of certain constitutional texts

(96) Part VII came into force on April 17, 1982. *See* SI/82-97.

to section 55, the English and French versions of that portion of the Constitution are equally authoritative.

English and
French versions
of this Act

57. The English and French versions of this Act are equally authoritative.

Commence-
ment

58. Subject to section 59, this Act shall come into force on a day to be fixed by proclamation issued by the Queen or the Governor General under the Great Seal of Canada. (97)

Commence-
ment of
paragraph
23(1)(a) in
respect of
Quebec

59. (1) Paragraph 23(1)(a) shall come into force in respect of Quebec on a day to be fixed by proclamation issued by the Queen or the Governor General under the Great Seal of Canada.

Authorization
of Quebec

(2) A proclamation under subsection (1) shall be issued only where authorized by the legislative assembly or government of Quebec. (98)

Repeal of this
section

(3) This section may be repealed on the day paragraph 23(1)(a) comes into force in respect of Quebec and this Act amended and renumbered, consequentially upon the repeal of this section, by proclamation issued by the Queen or the Governor General under the Great Seal of Canada.

Short title and
citations

60. This Act may be cited as the *Constitution Act, 1982*, and the Constitution Acts 1867 to 1975 (No. 2) and this Act may be cited together as the *Constitution Acts, 1867 to 1982*.

---

(97) The Act, with the exception of paragraph 23(1)(a) in respect of Quebec, came into force on April 17, 1982 by proclamation issued by the Queen. *See* SI/82-97.

(98) No proclamation has been issued under section 59.

SCHEDULE

to the

CONSTITUTION ACT, 1982

MODERNIZATION OF THE CONSTITUTION

Item	Column I Act Affected	Column II Amendment	Column III New Name
1.	British North America Act, 1867, 30-31 Vict., c. 3 (U.K.)	(1) Section 1 is repealed and the following substituted therefor: "1. This Act may be cited as the *Constitution Act, 1867.*" (2) Section 20 is repealed. (3) Class 1 of section 91 is repealed. (4) Class 1 of section 92 is repealed.	Constitution Act, 1867
2.	An Act to amend and continue the Act 32-33 Victoria chapter 3; and to establish and provide for the Government of the Province of Manitoba, 1870, 33 Vict., c. 3 (Can.)	(1) The long title is repealed and the following substituted therefor: "*Manitoba Act, 1870.*" (2) Section 20 is repealed.	Manitoba Act, 1870
3.	Order of Her Majesty in Council admitting Rupert's Land and the North-Western Territory into the union, dated the 23rd day of June, 1870		Rupert's Land and North-Western Territory Order

SCHEDULE

to the

CONSTITUTION ACT, 1982—*Continued*

Item	Column I Act Affected	Column II Amendment	Column III New Name
4.	Order of Her Majesty in Council admitting British Columbia into the Union, dated the 16th day of May, 1871.		British Columbia Terms of Union
5.	British North America Act, 1871, 34-35 Vict., c. 28 (U.K.)	Section 1 is repealed and the following substituted therefor: "1. This Act may be cited as the *Constitution Act, 1871*."	Constitution Act, 1871
6.	Order of Her Majesty in Council admitting Prince Edward Island into the Union, dated the 26th day of June, 1873.		Prince Edward Island Terms of Union
7.	Parliament of Canada Act, 1875, 38-39 Vict., c. 38 (U.K.)		Parliament of Canada Act, 1875
8.	Order of Her Majesty in Council admitting all British possessions and Territories in North America and islands adjacent thereto into the Union, dated the 31st day of July, 1880.		Adjacent Territories Order

SCHEDULE

to the

CONSTITUTION ACT, 1982—*Continued*

Item	Column I Act Affected	Column II Amendment	Column III New Name
9.	British North America Act, 1886, 49-50 Vict., c. 35 (U.K.)	Section 3 is repealed and the following substituted therefor: "3. This Act may be cited as the *Constitution Act, 1886*."	Constitution Act, 1886
10.	Canada (Ontario Boundary) Act, 1889, 52-53 Vict., c. 28 (U.K.)		Canada (Ontario Boundary) Act, 1889
11.	Canadian Speaker (Appointment of Deputy) Act, 1895, 2nd Sess., 59 Vict., c. 3 (U.K.)	The Act is repealed.	
12.	The Alberta Act, 1905, 4-5 Edw. VII, c. 3 (Can.)		Alberta Act
13.	The Saskatchewan Act, 1905, 4-5 Edw. VII, c. 42 (Can.)		Saskatchewan Act
14.	British North America Act, 1907, 7 Edw. VII, c. 11 (U.K.)	Section 2 is repealed and the following substituted therefor: "2. This Act may be cited as the *Constitution Act, 1907*."	Constitution Act, 1907

SCHEDULE

to the

CONSTITUTION ACT, 1982—*Continued*

Item	Column I Act Affected	Column II Amendment	Column III New Name
15.	British North America Act, 1915, 5-6 Geo. V, c. 45 (U.K.)	Section 3 is repealed and the following substituted therefor: "3. This Act may be cited as the *Constitution Act, 1915*."	Constitution Act, 1915
16.	British North America Act, 1930, 20-21 Geo. V, c. 26 (U.K.)	Section 3 is repealed and the following substituted therefor: "3. This Act may be cited as the *Constitution Act, 1930*."	Constitution Act, 1930
17.	Statute of Westminster, 1931, 22 Geo. V, c. 4 (U.K.)	In so far as they apply to Canada, (*a*) section 4 is repealed; and (*b*) subsection 7(1) is repealed.	Statute of Westminster, 1931
18.	British North America Act, 1940, 3-4 Geo. VI, c. 36 (U.K.)	Section 2 is repealed and the following substituted therefor: "2. This Act may be cited as the *Constitution Act, 1940*."	Constitution Act, 1940
19.	British North America Act, 1943, 6-7 Geo. VI, c. 30 (U.K.)	The Act is repealed.	

SCHEDULE

to the

CONSTITUTION ACT, 1982—*Continued*

Item	Column I Act Affected	Column II Amendment	Column III New Name
20.	British North America Act, 1946, 9-10 Geo. VI, c. 63 (U.K.)	The Act is repealed.	
21.	British North America Act, 1949, 12-13 Geo. VI, c. 22 (U.K.)	Section 3 is repealed and the following substituted therefor: "3. This Act may be cited as the *Newfoundland Act*."	Newfoundland Act
22.	British North America (No. 2) Act, 1949, 13 Geo. VI, c. 81 (U.K.)	The Act is repealed.	
23.	British North America Act, 1951, 14-15 Geo. VI, c. 32 (U.K.)	The Act is repealed.	
24.	British North America Act, 1952, 1 Eliz. II, c. 15 (Can.)	The Act is repealed.	
25.	British North America Act, 1960, 9 Eliz. II, c. 2 (U.K.)	Section 2 is repealed and the following substituted therefor: "2. This Act may be cited as the *Constitution Act, 1960*."	Constitution Act, 1960

SCHEDULE

to the

CONSTITUTION ACT, 1982—*Continued*

Item	Column I Act Affected	Column II Amendment	Column III New Name
26.	British North America Act, 1964, 12-13 Eliz. II, c. 73 (U.K.)	Section 2 is repealed and the following substituted therefor: "2. This Act may be cited as the *Constitution Act, 1964.*"	Constitution Act, 1964
27.	British North America Act, 1965, 14 Eliz. II, c. 4, Part I (Can.)	Section 2 is repealed and the following substituted therefor: "2. This Part may be cited as the *Constitution Act, 1965.*"	Constitution Act, 1965
28.	British North America Act, 1974, 23 Eliz. II, c. 13, Part I (Can.)	Section 3, as amended by 25-26 Eliz. II, c. 28, s. 38(1) (Can.), is repealed and the following substituted therefor: "3. This Part may be cited as the *Constitution Act, 1974.*"	Constitution Act, 1974
29.	British North America Act, 1975, 23-24 Eliz. II, c. 28, Part I (Can.)	Section 3, as amended by 25-26 Eliz. II, c. 28, s. 31 (Can.), is repealed and the following substituted therefor: "3. This Part may be cited as the *Constitution Act (No. 1), 1975.*"	Constitution Act (No. 1), 1975

SCHEDULE

to the

CONSTITUTION ACT, 1982—*Concluded*

Item	Column I Act Affected	Column II Amendment	Column III New Name
30.	British North America Act (No. 2), 1975, 23-24 Eliz. II, c. 53 (Can.)	Section 3 is repealed and the following substituted therefor: "3. This Act may be cited as the *Constitution Act (No. 2), 1975*."	Constitution Act (No. 2), 1975

INDEX